W9-CEV-602

Hope for Today

AL-ANON FAMILY GROUPS
hope for families and friends of alcoholics

For information and catalog of literature write:

Al-Anon Family Group Headquarters, Inc.
1600 Corporate Landing Parkway
Virginia Beach, VA 23454-5617
Phone: (757) 563-1600 Fax: (757) 563-1655
Web site: www.al-anon.alateen.org
E-mail: wso@al-anon.org

This book is also available in French, German, Japanese, and Spanish.
© Al-Anon Family Group Headquarters, Inc. 2002

Al-Anon/Alateen is supported by members' voluntary contributions and from the sale of our Conference Approved Literature.

Library of Congress Control No. 2002100375
ISBN- 978-0-910034-39-5

Publisher's Cataloging In Publication

Al-Anon Family Group Headquarters, Inc.
Hope for Today / Al-Anon Family Groups, Inc.
    Includes index.
    ISBN 978-0-910034-39-5
    LCCN 2002100375
    1. Alcoholics—Family Relationships. 2. Adult children of alcoholics. 3. Al-Anon Family Group Headquarters, Inc.

Approved by
World Service Conference
Al-Anon Family Groups

The Al-Anon Family Groups are a fellowship of relatives and friends of alcoholics who share their experience, strength, and hope in order to solve their common problems. We believe alcoholism is a family illness and that changed attitudes can aid recovery.

Al-Anon is not allied with any sect, denomination, political entity, organization, or institution; does not engage in any controversy; neither endorses nor opposes any cause. There are no dues for membership. Al-Anon is self-supporting through its own voluntary contributions.

Al-Anon has but one purpose: to help families of alcoholics. We do this by practicing the Twelve Steps, by welcoming and giving comfort to families of alcoholics, and by giving understanding and encouragement to the alcoholic.

Suggested Al-Anon Preamble to the Twelve Steps

The Serenity Prayer

God grant me the serenity

To accept the things I cannot change,

Courage to change the things I can,

And wisdom to know the difference.

Preface

Hope for Today is a collection of daily thoughts and meditations based on the sharings of Al-Anon members who grew up with the family disease of alcoholism. While the Al-Anon Family Groups are a fellowship of equals, ours is an incredibly diverse membership. Alcoholism does not discriminate. Its devastation affects everyone close to the drinker. However, for those who grew up in an alcoholic home, one of the primary differences is that as children we lived with alcoholism through no choice of our own. With parents and siblings also trapped in this family disease, we had no frame of reference for healthy behavior.

To meet the expressed need of our fellowship, the 1997 World Service Conference, Al-Anon's largest group conscience, passed a motion "to give conceptual approval to develop a daily reader for Al-Anon adult children." A call for sharings was issued throughout the fellowship and the Conference Approval process began.

As this book developed, however, something amazing happened. Though it definitely meets the Conference charge that it is "for Al-Anon adult children," it is much more than that. The powerful examples of recovery, use of Al-Anon tools, and love of our fellowship included in these pages are universal. They transcend boundaries and limitations. The topics cover a range of issues for *all* Al-Anon members, as well as anyone seeking insight into, or recovery from, the family disease of alcoholism.

Al-Anon's first daily reader, *One Day at a Time in Al-Anon*, states "The more varied the experience, the greater the strength and hope." *Courage to Change: One Day at a Time in Al-Anon II* continues this thought with, "Although we have our unique qualities, all hearts beat the same under the skin." Please join us, one day at a time, as we continue this tradition and open our hearts to share with you the hope, the help, and the friendship we have been privileged to enjoy.

In the past I developed many uncomfortable emotional connections with the word "home." I never knew what to expect at home and I was too ashamed to let friends visit. I wanted to escape *from* instead of *to* home. While I agreed on the outside with the adage "There's no place like home," there was a smirk on my face and pain in my heart whenever it was spoken.

With the help of Al-Anon, I have begun to create a new life with new attitudes and new definitions. The word "family" takes on the meaning of "Al-Anon Family Groups," where I have a new family of choice that helps me in a way my family of origin could not. My new family suggested I find a "home" group. This is where I feel I truly belong. Barring severe illness, I always attend my home group meetings and participate in business meetings, group conscience decisions and service. No one forces me to do these things. I do them because I have chosen to commit myself to that group, that family.

In turn I receive from my home group elements not abundant during my childhood: consistency, intimacy, emotional depth, and acceptance. Because I share with my home group members week after week, they know my innermost secrets and flaws. They see themselves in me, I see myself in them, and we learn to love and accept each other and ourselves. Without reservation in my mind or heart, I can truly say there is no place like my home-sweet-home group.

Thought for the Day

The world is much larger than my family of origin.

> "When a loved one's alcoholism brought me to Al-Anon, I found a new, second family, a family that helped me discover the me that had been hidden for so long, a family that will always be there for me."

Courage to Change, p. 11

The first tool I used in my recovery was the Serenity Prayer. "God, grant me the serenity to accept the things I cannot change . . ." taught me I can't alter the past, neither what was done to me nor what I did to others. ". . . Courage to change the things I can..." instructed me to change my attitudes and resentments, my self-pity, and my fears. ". . . Wisdom to know the difference" gave me hope that I could change for the better.

For a while it was necessary to look back and come to terms with what happened to me as a child. In my family there was a lot of emotional abuse and neglect shrouded in denial and minimizing. I still needed to face the truth and climb out of my own denial, which convinced me I would get a chance to relive my childhood and make a better past.

A wise person said in *Courage to Change* that it's necessary to "look back without staring." As long as I kept staring at my past without experiencing my feelings about it, I stayed mired in fear, resentment, and self-pity. So I continued to root out those defects that kept me from being serene. I couldn't let go of something I didn't possess. Only after I stopped long enough to feel my anguish, bitterness, and emptiness could I let them go and move ahead.

The Serenity Prayer helped me believe that serenity, courage, and wisdom were attainable. It strengthened my belief in God and gave me hope for a brighter future.

Thought for the Day

The Serenity Prayer can bring light to the parts of myself still clouded by my past.

> "And if a crisis arises, or any problem baffles me, I hold it up to the light of the Serenity Prayer and extract its sting before it can hurt me."
>
> *One Day at a Time in Al-Anon*, p. 65

It's not my fault my parents and loved ones are alcoholics. It's not their fault, either. Alcoholism isn't a fault; it's a disease. I can recover from the effects of this family disease in Al-Anon.

I may never completely eliminate the effects of alcoholism on my life, but I can stop allowing them to affect me. Al-Anon offers me the tools and guidance I needed as a child but never got because my parents were suffering from a devastating illness. The Steps, Traditions, slogans, sponsorship, and service offer me a new road map to guide me into myself and the nature of my relationship with my Higher Power. Each minute, each hour, each day, I smile a little more, let go of yesterday a little more, and live in today a little more. Each moment becomes the one I have always been waiting for. Each day becomes a precious collection of the many instances when I see myself as I truly am, a child of a loving Higher Power.

I can become the person I always dreamed of being with the hope and help found in Al-Anon. I have the freedom to start all over today. I do this with baby steps, "One Day at a Time." I can "Let It Begin with Me" and "Keep It Simple." All I need to do is begin somewhere by applying a slogan, reading Conference Approved Literature on a Step, or praying and meditating my way to a deeper relationship with my Higher Power.

Thought for the Day

Al-Anon is helping me to navigate life with ease, dignity, and hope. Today I will share my hope with others.

> "Working a program for me means taking one of the tools—a slogan, a Step, the Serenity Prayer, the phone list, my sponsor—and using it in my life."
>
> From Survival to Recovery, p. 107

Step One: "We admitted we were powerless over alcohol—that our lives had become unmanageable."

What I do *not* admit in Step One is as important as what I *do* admit. I do not admit that I am a failure. I may *feel* like a failure, but I've learned in this program that feelings aren't facts. If I stop to reflect, I realize that I'm not diminished when I admit my powerlessness over alcohol. In fact, in some important way, I join the rest of the human race because we are all powerless over something at one time or another.

When I admit my life is unmanageable, I don't admit that I am a bad person. In my attempts to maintain the delusion of exercising power where I am powerless, my life has become disorderly. Although I may have temporarily lost control of my life, I have not committed a crime. I need only apply Step One to begin to regain my serenity.

Thought for the Day

Step One encourages me to build my life in a balanced perspective.

> "With the understanding that alcoholism is a disease, and with the realization that we are powerless over it, as well as over other people, we are ready to do something useful and constructive with our own lives."
>
> *Alcoholism, the Family Disease*, p. 3

During each Al-Anon meeting when our Suggested Welcome is read, I hear, ". . . in Al-Anon we discover that no situation is really hopeless." At first I had a hard time comprehending that idea in my mind and heart. I felt anchored in a place so dark and full of despair that it seemed nothing would ever change. Even if Al-Anon folks *could* stop my mother from drinking, they certainly couldn't go back in time and give me a happy childhood. I felt doomed. Yet as I looked around me at meetings, I saw many smiling faces. Maybe there was hope after all.

I had to attend many meetings and begin using the slogans and Steps before I began smiling. Then this simple realization traveled the long journey from my head to my heart—no *situation* is *ever* hopeless. Situations don't lose hope; people do. What is lost can often be found, restored, replaced, or recovered. Even though the members of Al-Anon didn't change my mother or my childhood, they did help me change my attitude. Once I changed my perspective, my all-encompassing perception of doom and gloom began to evaporate. Today I am grateful and appreciative of all that has happened in my life, including my childhood and my mother's drinking. They brought me to where I am today, and I like being here.

Thought for the Day

Situations can change. I've noticed that they change much faster when I change my attitude.

> "As we watch those around us in our meetings begin to find greater freedom and greater joy in their lives, most of us realize that, no matter what situation we face or how desperate we feel, there is good reason for hope."
>
> *How Al-Anon Works for Families & Friends of Alcoholics,* p. 12

I see more clearly how I have grown in the Al-Anon program as I recall my past behavior and my misunderstanding of the nature of alcoholism.

I did not know or believe that alcoholism is a disease. I truly believed that the alcoholic in my life could control or stop the drinking. Therefore I had difficulty in communicating with the alcoholic. Frequently we had serious disagreements resulting in physical injury to one or both of us.

Fortunately a professional recommended Al-Anon to me. Sharing at meetings, as well as studying and applying the Al-Anon tools, has given me a firm understanding of alcoholism as a disease. I can see now that my attitude toward the alcoholic was seriously flawed. Understanding and accepting alcoholism as a disease helps me separate the disease from the person, thus allowing me to have compassion for the alcoholic while setting loving boundaries regarding unacceptable behavior.

Thought for the Day

Understanding alcoholism as a disease helps me have compassion for the alcoholic and take care of myself at the same time.

> "Specialists in the field of alcoholism regard it not as a moral weakness or sin, but as a complex disease, perhaps part physical and part emotional."

> *Freedom from Despair*, p. 1

One of the first Al-Anon sayings I remember hearing, known as the three Cs, embodies the concept of powerlessness over alcoholism: "I didn't cause it, I can't control it, and I can't cure it."

I like the message of the three Cs. "I didn't cause it" relieves me of any lingering guilt I may feel: If only I had been a better son—worked harder at school, done more chores around the house, or not fought so much with my siblings—my parents may not have become alcoholics. In reality their suffering from the disease has nothing to do with me.

"I can't control it" gives me permission to live my life and to take care of myself. No longer do I have to spend my energy trying to manipulate people and situations so that the alcoholics will drink less. Nothing I say or do, or don't say or do, will have any effect on the alcoholics' choice to drink. That choice is completely out of my hands.

"I can't cure it" reminds me that I don't have to repeat my insane behavior over and over again, hoping for different results. I don't have to keep giving one last exhausted effort to stop the drinking, hoping that "this time it will work." I don't have to search for the magic cure that isn't there. Instead I can use my energy for my recovery.

Thought for the Day

When I get confused about what being powerless over alcohol really means, the three Cs give me a clarifying touchstone.

> "Active alcoholics are people who drink. They don't drink because of you or me, but because they are alcoholics. No matter what I do, I will not change this fact . . ."
>
> *Courage to Change*, p. 74

I truly believed talking to God continuously about my problems was a form of both prayer and meditation. However, I didn't find the sense of tranquility I sought. It wasn't a matter of tuning out distractions; I had been doing that most of my life. When I was young, I'd cover my head so that I wouldn't hear my parents fight. I could go numb and not feel the belt when my mother beat me. I was so good at tuning out, it scared me. Once, while pleading with God to help me, I ran a stop sign. I didn't even hear the siren or see the flashing lights of the police car behind me.

I once heard an Al-Anon member share that he deliberated so much about his troubles, he often didn't hear the solutions offered at meetings. He said if he couldn't even focus on recovery at the meeting, he surely couldn't do it at home. I didn't see how this insight applied to me, but I found he had a point. The chairperson hadn't finished the first sentence of the meeting welcome when my mind went right to one of my problems. After seeing this pattern, I began to concentrate on the experience, strength, and hope shared at the meeting.

Now, instead of dwelling on my troubles, I meditate on my Higher Power's strength, power, and love for me. In doing this, I gain a feeling of peace that carries me through the day. I still have problems, but they just don't seem so big anymore.

Thought for the Day

Prayer and meditation allow me to focus on the solution, not the problem.

> "During my daily quiet time, I try to focus all my attention on God. When I take my problems to Him, I try to leave them there and keep my focus of attention on Him."
>
> *As We Understood . . .*, p. 196

Before Al-Anon I allowed the behaviors of the alcoholics in my life to cause me great unhappiness. While it was true I was suffering, was my pain really their fault? Al-Anon has taught me to take responsibility for my own happiness.

Early in my recovery, I called my sponsor because I was once again suffering in reaction to an alcoholic's behavior. During that phone call, my sponsor used an expression that changed the way I respond to relationship difficulties. She explained that once is a fluke, twice is a coincidence, and three times is a pattern.

What does this mean for me? If I'm still suffering in reaction to a specific behavior that has occurred three or more times, I need to stop hoping the behavior will cease and instead detach and start changing my attitudes, expectations, and responses.

Once I was able see my suffering as my own reaction to others, I could begin to identify my contribution to the problem. Sometimes my part is bringing up something that was better left unsaid, or starting a serious conversation at an inappropriate time. Other times my part is harboring unrealistic expectations. When I see my part in the pattern, I can choose a response other than suffering.

There is no need for me to suffer because of the behavior of others. I can only change my responses. This sets me free to enjoy my own life.

Thought for the Day

The next time I react to another's behavior, I'll ask myself how many times I've reacted the same way before.

"If I am always reacting, then I am never free."

Al-Anon Is for Adult Children of Alcoholics, p. 17

Like many children of alcoholics, I vowed I'd never drink like my father. Nevertheless, I do get drunk; only I get drunk on feelings. If not checked, my hurt, anger, and fear can trigger a downward spiral that leaves me feeling completely unmanageable. I'm often unable to function as I allow my bad moods to drag me into a pit of depression. It's as if I'm an emotional drunk. I can't hold my feelings any more than an alcoholic can hold his or her liquor.

I use the First Step to accept that, just for today, I'm powerless by myself to stop these emotional binges once they gain momentum. I do have the power, however, to make small choices that reunite me with my Higher Power and the sanity spoken of in Step Two. Sometimes these choices are so small, all I need to do is to change the position of my hand. I remove it from my tearful face and pick up the phone to call my sponsor, read an issue of *The Forum*, or turn the ignition in my car and go to a meeting.

When I do one of these things, peace, and serenity begin to seep back into my mind and heart. Now I'm working on having my feelings while not allowing them to control me. I pray daily for the ability to feel and to express my emotions in ways that honor me, and those people who touch my life.

Thought for the Day

If I make myself available, my Higher Power can do for me what I cannot do for myself.

> "... In Al-Anon we found a Twelve Step program of spiritual help and human caring that has brought us the priceless gift of serenity and has shown us a path toward emotional maturity that was lacking in our families."
>
> *From Survival to Recovery*, p. 19

I had few friends when I was young. I was too embarrassed to invite anyone over, and I didn't want to visit anyone else for fear of what I might find when I returned home. I thought being around would somehow keep my mother from drinking. Time passed; I got married, created a family, and focused on my spouse's alcoholism. My life soon felt unmanageable. I heard about Al-Anon and started attending meetings. Since then I've connected with the important staples of recovery, including friendship.

In my home group, I became friends with someone who is supportive, positive, and serious about recovery. I recently learned that this friend is moving to another state. I'll miss my friend. It has always been difficult for me to let go of people in my life. I tend to hold, clutch, and grab as if the relationship is my last opportunity for intimacy. However, Al-Anon taught me that I have choices. Relationships don't have to end because of distance.

I've learned how to better deal with my friend's relocation by accepting it and focusing on gratitude for the gifts of our relationship. I appreciate the time my friend and I spent together. I am grateful I was healed enough through Al-Anon to experience intimacy. I'll always value the many things she taught me. Although she's moving, we can chat on the phone, write letters, and maybe visit one another occasionally. If we lose touch, that's okay, too. I can focus on the positive and be happy for her in her new place. I can let go and let God determine the future of our friendship.

Thought for the Day

Now that I'm more confident in my recovery, I can let my friendships follow God's will rather than mine.

> "My challenge is to work on myself and let God take care of my friends."

Living Today in Alateen, p. 8

Alcoholism is a thief. It robs us of our loved ones. It pickpockets job opportunities, close relationships, and physical safety. In my mother's case, it eventually stole her life. Alcoholism robbed my childhood of trust and security. I grew up feeling like a counterfeit adult—well-adjusted on the outside, but lost and frightened on the inside.

In Al-Anon I've learned that even without ever taking a drink, I struggle with the effects of the disease of alcoholism. They can rob my life of the joy each day holds. Denial steals from me the ability to see my situation clearly and honestly. Stubborn self-reliance wipes out the guidance and comfort available from my Higher Power. Resentment erodes love and goodwill in my relationships with others. Obsessive worrying raids my willingness to accept and enjoy life as it is.

Hope comes in the words of the Second Step. My Higher Power can restore to me what I once believed to be irrevocably lost—my sanity and serenity. I am not promised that my loved ones will find sobriety. What I *am* offered, however, is the gift waiting for me in the form of the Al-Anon program, which fills the void carved into my mind and heart by the disease of alcoholism. I have a program to practice with the help of my Higher Power, Who restores me to mental, emotional, and spiritual health one day at a time.

Thought for the Day

What has alcoholism stolen from my life? What can my Higher Power help me regain?

"Doesn't letting your Higher Power run your life make more sense than letting somebody else's illness run it?"

Forum Favorites, Volume 4, p. 102

At first I really disliked it when my home group took a group inventory. I sat gritting my teeth and feeling impatient to get back to the "real" meeting. I figured at least if *I* didn't participate, the inventory would end that much faster. But since I wanted to get better, I examined my behavior and found a pattern. Not only did I refuse to take part in the group inventories, I barely participated in the group at all. I just kept to myself, isolated even when surrounded by fellow members.

When I started feeling victimized by the group's decisions, I looked into my pattern more deeply. My efforts revealed the memory of how I felt as a teenager growing up in an alcoholic home—ignored, invisible, and insignificant. Decisions were often made without taking my thoughts and feelings into account. Eventually I chose not to bother making myself heard. I told myself I didn't matter.

It was a real shock to realize I was acting the same in my Al-Anon groups. When I allowed the group to make decisions without my input, and chose once more not to speak up, I perpetuated the victim role that had plagued me.

I finally decided it was better to risk sharing than to become resentful. As I started participating in group matters, I noticed fellow members listening to what I had to say. They spoke with me after meetings to express gratitude for sharing what had also been on their minds. Slowly my self-esteem increased. I *do* matter, but I had to take the risk to find that out.

Thought for the Day

The answer my group is seeking just might come from the Higher Power through my voice.

> "The comfortable feeling that we are all equals encourages us to take an active part in the work of our fellowship. . ."
> *Al-Anon's Twelve Steps & Twelve Traditions*, p. 95

January 14

One of the most valuable skills I've learned in Al-Anon is to discern acceptable behavior and to set limits with others. Setting boundaries helps me take care of myself in relationships and keeps me from being a victim. Responses to boundaries help me evaluate the quality of my relationships.

Nevertheless, I still feel some trepidation when I set limits. I fear that the other person may become angry and end the relationship. I experienced different forms of abandonment during my alcoholic upbringing, and it's not a feeling I relish re-experiencing. Sometimes dread prevents me from setting limits. Other times I state my boundaries in overly rigid terms, hoping I'll never have to deal with the problem again. My best success comes when I set my limits one day at a time.

For example, my spouse watches television late at night and often unintentionally wakes me when he comes to bed. Depending on how my day went, sometimes this bothers me and sometimes it doesn't. I no longer set a global, black-and-white boundary with my spouse. Instead of saying, "From now on when you watch television after 11:00 pm, I'm going to sleep in the guest room," I ask him, "Are you going to watch any more of that show?" If he responds affirmatively, I tell him I'm going to sleep in the guest room and bid him a pleasant evening. In this way I care for myself, and I don't set myself up for resentment. I leave options for both of us, which makes our relationship run more smoothly.

Thought for the Day

Boundaries don't help me when they're too loose or too rigid. If I set them flexibly—one instance at a time—they can help improve my relationships.

"Al-Anon taught me the difference between walls and boundaries."

Courage to Change, p. 201

I came to Al-Anon because of my husband's drinking. I embraced the literature, the slogans, the Twelve Steps, and the people of this wonderful fellowship, and gradually I got better. However, one thing continued to puzzle me. Since I had not grown up in an alcoholic home, why did I answer yes to almost all of the questions in the Al-Anon leaflet "Did You Grow Up with a Problem Drinker?" I didn't receive a quick answer, but by working my program diligently I was able to change my answers to many of those questions. In time I overcame my dependency on others' approval, my fear of failure, and my excessive sense of responsibility for people, places, and things beyond my control.

After several years, my Higher Power finally chose to reveal to me the reason for my identification with that leaflet. My parents were adult children of alcoholics. Those alcoholics were my grandparents. Being raised by adult children can be just as damaging as being raised by alcoholics. Although both of my parents had chosen not to drink, they had not chosen recovery, either. Unknowingly they had passed on unhealthy attitudes and behavior to another generation.

Now I have a choice to make, and this is where I stand: "Let It Begin with Me." Today, with the help of the program and a loving Higher Power, I choose recovery. I choose to do my part to stop the wide-ranging, tragic effects of the progressive, multi-generational disease called alcoholism. I am willing to do what I must to stop this disease. With Al-Anon's help, my family can experience a better way of life.

Thought for the Day

Before Al-Anon I was a carrier of this disease. Living the Al-Anon program immunizes me from its effects and helps prevent me from spreading the devastation.

> "Sometimes alcoholism seemed to skip a generation . . ."
>
> *From Survival to Recovery*, p. 15

During my early Al-Anon days, I had trouble understanding humility and how to develop it. I related to the concept of being teachable, however, and began to look at what I could change about myself to become more open and willing to learn.

When I begin to think that I know it all or that perhaps it's all right to skip some meetings, I'm in dangerous territory. Being teachable means I go to meetings and really listen to everyone, newcomers and long-time members alike. It also means I listen when I talk with my sponsor or another program friend. Sometimes I'll hear suggestions and think, "No, that doesn't apply to me." When this happens, I need to open my mind and remain receptive to what I hear. The Al-Anon program works to the extent that I am open, honest, and willing, each of which is an important component for a humble state of learning. Being teachable means I admit that I don't know it all. Walking the path of self-improvement is a lifelong journey.

Thought for the Day

The more available I am to listen and learn, the more available I am to be healed by my Higher Power.

> "Humility frees me from outside pressures and allows me
> to learn at any time from anyone or any experience."
>
> *Courage to Be Me*, p. 137

I meditate frequently on the meaning of letting go. Now and then I think I comprehend it until yet another situation challenges me to broaden my understanding. Again I ask myself, "What does it mean to let go?"

Recently I reflected on a beautiful bouquet of flowers. While inhaling the exquisite fragrance of the open blossoms, I found myself wishing the closed buds might open, too. Then I recalled occasionally seeing flowers whose buds never opened or unfolded.

Sometimes I have trouble opening up and unfolding—letting go—into my true magnificence. I often restrain myself for fear that others will misunderstand and criticize me. Applying this idea in the context of flowers, holding back might mean I'm trying to hide my yellow, thick, round bloom behind the façade of one that appears red, slender, and elongated. When I look at it this way, holding back seems a sad misuse of energy.

In any spray of flowers, all appeal to me—each one as an individual bloom, and all of them together as a beautiful symphony of color and fragrance. They remind me to relinquish false reserve and to allow my own particular bloom to develop to its brightest and most fragrant so that I can joyfully claim my rightful place in the bouquet of people around me.

Thought for the Day

Am I hiding or holding back some part of myself? What beauty can I release or embrace today?

> "By learning how to lovingly 'let go'... I have been given a wonderful gift: a life of my own."
>
> *Homeward Bound*, p. 4

This was the only thought I remembered from my first Al-Anon meeting: We can learn to live at peace with ourselves and others. "Live at peace with ourselves and others?" I wondered. "How do people do this?" From my alcoholic upbringing to my own family and workplace, I had never experienced a peaceful way of life. With myself, I was constantly fighting against the guilt, fear, and anger that ruled my life. With others, I was always fighting for some cause or belief, trying to make them see that my position was the right one. Of course I never won, and the wars never ceased.

When I came to Al-Anon, I finally found the peace I desired so much. Al-Anon taught me that the path to peace is accepting the people, places, things, and situations I cannot change. Accepting myself as I am, by working Steps Four through Nine, freed me from my self-inflicted inner judge and jury. Accepting others with the use of the Serenity Prayer allowed me to stop fighting. Acceptance allows God to do what I cannot. Acceptance opens the door for my growth and leads me on my spiritual journey, one day at a time.

Accepting the things I cannot change is not always easy; sometimes I really fight it. Because my life is always changing, there is always some new person or situation to accept. Fortunately I don't have to go through the acceptance process alone. My Higher Power provides the power, Al-Anon provides the path, and the people in the program provide the support. All I need to experience peace is to keep coming back.

Thought for the Day

Peace is a natural outgrowth of acceptance.

> "Acceptance comes through the comfort we receive from members at meetings when we slowly begin to understand and care about ourselves and others ..."

Alateen Talks Back on Acceptance, p. 3

The opportunity to share what is in my mind and heart has been key to my recovery. When I came to Al-Anon, I was ready to receive help but unsure how to get it. I knew something was very wrong, and I assumed it was me.

My first year in Al-Anon was difficult. I listened to others courageously share their feelings and childhood experiences; I could only sit and pay heed in shame-filled silence. Surely everyone could see my shameful childhood secrets as I sat silently. As if that weren't enough, I felt shame for being so quiet in the meetings.

Despite this sometimes-overwhelming sense of mortification, I kept coming back to Al-Anon. In time I understood that though I wasn't alone in my suffering, I would continue to feel isolated as long as I chose to remain silent. So I began to open up and trust people. I started sharing my "worst" secrets with the group. To my relief, telling my experiences was met with love and compassion.

These days you wouldn't know I had been the man sitting quietly in the back of the Al-Anon meeting. Today I say what is in my mind and heart. I know that in doing so, I not only help myself but others as well. If during my first year of Al-Anon meetings no one had been willing to share, I never would have known there were others like me. I never would have received the gifts of this wonderful program.

Thought for the Day

In Al-Anon I can say what is in my heart and know that my words will be received with understanding and compassion.

> "I used to live in my own little prison, locked in by my feelings of hatred and shame. Now I'm free. The key is using the program to do something for me."
>
> Alateen—a day at a time, p. 175

I think taking Step Three, "Made a decision to turn our will and our lives over to the care of God *as we understood Him*," is as much an attitude as it is an action. My attitude can influence my progress with the rest of the Steps. A student-and-classroom analogy helps explain my perspective. I believe God has put me here to learn certain spiritual lessons. I have choices. I can skip my homework, stay out all night, sleep through the alarm, miss breakfast, get to school late, and doze through class—in which case I will miss out on many of my lessons and have to keep repeating them.

On the other hand, I can do my homework, get a full night's sleep, wake up on time, eat breakfast, get to school early, and apply myself in my classes. If I do this, I will make progress, even during those occasional setbacks, which are bound to happen.

I've learned that I become teachable when I surrender. In surrendering I am emboldened to act on my Step Three decision by taking Steps Four through Twelve. I'm heartened to know I will take with me a loving God to guide me through the spiritual lessons I need to learn.

Thought for the Day

My attitudes influence my recovery choices. What kind of recovery do I choose today?

> "The time has come for me to realize that my attitude, toward the life I am living and the people in it, can have a tangible, measurable effect on what happens to me day by day."
>
> *One Day at a Time in Al-Anon*, p. 246

Becoming an Alateen sponsor allowed me to open my heart and reclaim all the lost sorrows and joys of my past. Sitting in a room full of young people every week—seeing parts of myself in each of them and hearing aspects of my story retold in their words—finally turned me around to face the mirror. My Higher Power spoke through the teens' vivid, personal sharings, allowing me to remember and to heal my dark, buried memories.

Alateen sponsorship brought me face-to-face with my younger self. The experience, strength, and hope shared by the teens, who were using the program to cope with the devastating effects of their parents' alcoholism, gave me the courage I needed to look at my own youth. My recovery accelerated rapidly as I used the Al-Anon tools to examine the attitudes, perceptions, and behaviors I had cultivated to survive the alcoholism in my family. I finally surrendered completely to the fact that I am powerless over my past.

The Alateens have helped me bring back to life all the beauty and joy buried underneath the abuse that came with the alcoholism in my family and to find a new clarity and definition of who I am today. Learning to love these amazing children, and learning to accept their love for me, broke down the walls that imprisoned my heart and allowed me at long last to love the remarkable child I found inside myself.

Thought for the Day

Alateens have much to offer Al-Anon members. Today I'll consider how we can help one another.

> "My reward for the time I spend as a sponsor is seeing the members dealing so well with the same problems I found so difficult to handle. This gives me the confidence and faith that I, too, can change myself."
>
> *A Guide to Alateen Sponsorship*, p. 20

Seeking progress rather than perfection and minding my own business are the two Al-Anon recovery suggestions that mean the most to me. I grew up with problem drinking. I carried the notion into adulthood that I *must* be perfect and that I was responsible for everyone. Of course I never achieved this goal of perfection, which left me feeling less than, not smart enough, not attractive enough, simply not good enough. To cope with my failure to achieve my goal of perfection, I focused on the character defects of those around me. My need to be perfect fed into my preoccupation with others.

In Al-Anon I found out that I didn't have to be perfect; I couldn't be, no matter how hard I tried. Instead, I learned to be happy with forward motion, no matter how small. I practiced minding my own business and shifting my focus from others to myself so that I could change what I was capable of changing. I discovered that I wasn't alone with the insanity of striving to be something I would never become. I learned how to identify and let go of unreasonable expectations and that other people, especially fellow Al-Anon members, did not have those same expectations of me. I am still learning to treat myself with gentleness, kindness, and love. I'm still learning that I cannot change those around me, but I can change how I treat them—with dignity and respect.

Thought for the Day

Today relaxing with my imperfection and enjoying my own business are enough for me. For this I am grateful.

> "I have learned in meetings that tiny steps are perfectly acceptable and that they add up."
>
> *How Al-Anon Works for Families & Friends of Alcoholics*, p. 323

One of the gifts I have received from Al-Anon is learning how to maintain an attitude of gratitude. Before the program I didn't really understand the true nature of gratitude. I thought it was the happiness I felt when life happened according to my needs and wants. I thought it was the high I felt when my desire for instant gratification was fulfilled.

Today—thanks to countless meetings, phone calls, talks with sponsors, inventories, and readings—I know better. Gratitude is an integral part of my serenity. In fact, it is usually the means of restoring my serenity whenever I notice I'm straying from it.

Gratitude opens the doors of my heart to the healing touch of my Higher Power. It isn't always easy to feel grateful when the strident voice of my disease demands unhealthy behavior. However, when I work my program harder, it is possible.

The Steps remind me to seek God's will, and I believe it is God's will for me to attend meetings, read literature, call my sponsor, and be grateful. Grateful? Yes. For what? For all of it! I'm grateful for the disease that brought me to Al-Anon, for a Higher Power that loves me just as I am, and for my sponsor, phone lists, and telephones. I'm thankful for meetings and all I learn there, and for knowing that gratitude leads to growth. I'm also grateful for my beloved family members who suffer from the disease of alcoholism, and for AA, Al-Anon, Alateen, serenity—all of it!

Thought for the Day

This moment gives birth to the next. If I fill this moment with gratitude, the next moment can't help but bring blessings.

"Just for today I will smile . . . I will be grateful for what I have instead of concentrating on what I don't have."

Alateen's Just for Today

Someone once explained the maintenance of serenity to me like this: Suppose someone asked me to pass him the salt at the dining table. "Sure," I'd say while handing it over. Now suppose someone asked me to pass him my serenity—would I give it up so willingly? I doubt it.

However, when I react to alcoholic behavior, that's exactly what I'm doing. I lose myself and thereby lose my serenity. I give it up as automatically as I pass the salt and pepper.

To maintain my serenity, I need to work my program. In particular I need to practice the principles that prevent me from losing myself as well as those that steer me back if I do get lost. For example, detachment helps me focus on my program. So does the slogan "Think," to which I add "Stop." I remind myself to stop and think—to determine what the person is really requesting—before I respond.

If I do lose my serenity, ideas that bring me back include "Live and Let Live" and placing principles above personalities. When I find myself in the midst of reacting, thinking of these ideas is often enough to make me stop and consider my response, which usually restores me to sanity.

Even if I don't know exactly which principle to apply to regain my serenity, all I need to do is ask myself if I'm truly applying these principles in all my affairs. It might seem that the loss of my serenity is a theft by someone else, but it usually has more to do with how well I'm working my program. They say in Al-Anon you have to give it away to keep it. However, this doesn't apply to my serenity!

Thought for the Day

Wouldn't I rather share my serenity than give it up?

"Today, maintaining my serenity is my first priority."

Courage to Change, p. 318

Part of my recovery today from the family disease of alcoholism includes learning to have fun and to play. Play? What's that?-As a child of parents who each grew up with alcoholism, I was raised to be industrious and goal-oriented. Today I am discovering what play means. My newly-adopted dog is helping me. Every evening without fail, she brings me one of her many toys so that we can play.- We sit in the middle of the living room floor and play tug, chase, and hide and seek.

Years ago I challenged myself to learn to play once a week. I really didn't have any idea how to do this, but I was willing. I started by discussing the subject with my sponsor. We looked for program tools that could help put me in the mood for play, such as "Let Go and Let God," "Easy Does It," and turning myself and my problems over to my Higher Power in Step Three. I also observed my friends at play. Eventually, I found my personal toys of choice and learned to laugh openly and hard.-

What fun I have today! I may not have played much as a child, but as an adult I'm making up for those lost moments. I wonder if, with this new furry member of my family, my Higher Power is saying I need to play more often than once a week. Now I get the message. My dog expects me to play nightly, and this expectation is not negotiable. My dog is an aid to my recovery process.

Thought for the Day

Having fun is a part of my recovery one day at a time.

> "With a decreased sense of always having to do something useful to justify my existence, I now allow recreation, enthusiasm, and delight into my life."

From Survival to Recovery, p. 185

I glanced toward the glass coffee-table top and saw in it the reflection of the ceiling and the hanging lamp in my living room. My mind wandered as I thought of the story I had been reading. I looked at the glass once more and was startled to perceive that the ceiling now looked like a floor, and the hanging lamp resembled a standing floor lamp! I wondered if my Higher Power was trying to tell me something. Could my frequent feelings of hurt and anger toward my alcoholic husband be caused by my perceptions?

As these thoughts coursed through me, I started talking to God. I told Him I was sorry for dwelling angrily on what I lack in my relationship with the alcoholic rather than expressing gratitude for what I do receive, such as insights like these to help me with the realities of my life. I asked Him to remind me that there is a spiritual reason for everything and to help me regard my alcoholic as a blessing rather than a curse, which is often how I view him.

After praying, I relaxed. I heard the message God was trying to convey through the reflections in the glass: My perceptions were distorted. My husband possesses so many lovely qualities that are obscured by my view of his disease. Then I thought of all my good qualities that are obscured by *my* disease. At that moment I knew in my heart that God had created my husband as His beautiful child, as He did me, and I was flooded with compassion for us both.

Thought for the Day

Everything about my recovery—my perceptions, attitudes, and choices—begins and ends with me.

"And gratitude, a cornerstone of my Al-Anon recovery, brings hidden loveliness clearly into view."

Courage to Change, p. 67

Living one day at a time as an adult child of an alcoholic can seem insurmountable when faced with the myriad feelings and memories that surface during recovery. This is when Al-Anon meetings and phone calls remind me that I am *not* alone. Contact with others can help me stay in today. Just as my Higher Power guided me to Al-Anon in the first place, I know I will be guided to where I need to go today. I may not always notice my Higher Power's help, but I have faith that it exists. It's up to me to accept help in whatever form it is available to me today

How do I stay in the present when faced with horrifying memories of the past? Sometimes I pray one moment at a time, calling on my Higher Power's help through the Serenity Prayer. Other times I talk it out, yell it out, or cry it out to God or to a trusted friend. Sometimes I listen at meetings or read my literature. Yet other times I write it out, walk it out, or do something else safe and comforting.

Facing the past as it may surface in my life today doesn't mean I have to stay stuck in it. I can let the healing power of the program help me feel my old, buried emotions and then put them where they belong—in the past. Coming to terms with my history and letting go of it does not deny what happened. Instead, it allows me to enjoy today and to move into the future, unencumbered by the weight of ancient emotions.

Thought for the Day

Every time I use the Al-Anon tools to work through old feelings, I give myself the chance to have a better today.

"The Steps show me how to release the past and not fear the future."

From Survival to Recovery, p. 25

As stated in Tradition Five, Al-Anon has but one purpose—to help families and friends of alcoholics. We can't be all things to all people. At Al-Anon meetings we devote our time and energy to doing what we do best—helping others touched by alcoholism—rather than diverting our focus to other causes. As individuals we may have a variety of other interests, but as an Al-Anon group we voluntarily limit ourselves in order to maximize the successful outcome of our primary purpose.

I, too, need to know my focus. I cannot be all things to all people. Yet, I believe God put each of us here to love and serve one another. So how do I know what is mine to do out of all the possible things I can do? Tradition Five spells it out for me. My primary concern is, and must be, my personal recovery. I cannot give to anyone else something I don't have. I learn to love myself enough to seek my own healing. When I can love myself as I am, I'm better able to accept the human limitations of all God's other children. Finally, because God loves me, I express gratitude for this love through service, which keeps the program alive for me. I do what is in my power to do. I am given the opportunity, desire, ability, and time to do whatever God assigns me, one day at a time. If I lack any of these four things, then I need to humbly let go and accept my limitations.

Thought for the Day

Part of recovery is sorting out the primary focus from competing ones, whether I'm acting alone or as part of an Al-Anon group.

> "If Al-Anon's singleness of purpose were diluted, we would no longer be able to identify and our own recovery would suffer."
>
> *Al-Anon's Twelve Traditions Illustrated,* p. 12

Concept One, "The ultimate responsibility and authority for Al-Anon world services belongs to the Al-Anon groups," lays out clearly the source of accountability for Al-Anon. Other legacies describe how the groups can best exercise this accountability. In this way there is a match between what is expected of the groups and their capacity to meet these expectations. Al-Anon as a whole can move forward with confidence.

Such a match between expectation and ability was missing in my alcoholic family. Authority and responsibility were often misplaced. I can remember as an adolescent often mediating my parents' drunken fights. Thanks to Al-Anon I know ending their fights was not my responsibility. As a child I simply didn't have the authority to do so. I also remember my alcoholic father once suggesting I had caused the breakup of his second marriage. I didn't know better at the time, so I took on the guilt of that allegation. It took me a while in the program before I understood that the success or failure of a relationship depends on the particular parties involved.

Concept One teaches me that I am an individual person separate from other human beings, and as such I have no responsibility for or authority over them. I still have people in my life who want me to take on their responsibilities. However, Al-Anon helps to make clear delineations between what does and doesn't belong to me. It also gives me tools—such as detachment, "Live and Let Live," Step Ten, and keeping the focus on me—to help me keep those demarcations clear.

Thought for the Day

Just because someone tries to throw his or her responsibilities my way doesn't mean I have to catch them. My program helps me detach from what doesn't belong to me.

"Concept One shows me where my responsibility is."

Paths to Recovery, p. 252

January 30

The alcoholic was obsessed with alcohol, and I was obsessed with the alcoholic. I watched, monitored, controlled, and exercised my need to feel hurt. I felt self-pity, embarrassment, superiority, resentment, and anger. All of these took obsessive turns filling my mind and heart. I wondered why I indulged in these draining behaviors and emotions, which only resulted in further misery for me.

In Al-Anon I began to realize that wretchedness and gloom, although familiar and comfortable to an extent, were optional. Serenity is possible with changes in my attitude, expectations, and responses. Today I want to exercise my option to be happy, to feel calm and good.

One of my favorite ways to turn my attitude around is to apply the slogan "How Important Is It?" I close my eyes and begin to look at my situation in a larger, maybe even universal context. First, I imagine my little apartment and then my town. I visualize my state and then my country as if on a map. Then the whole world comes into view. If I need to, I even extend my imagination into the planetary universe and the Milky Way. I think of all the living beings in this great big world and I ask myself, "How Important Is It?" The larger my world becomes, the more my problem and I shrink. In the grand scheme of things, what I'm dealing with usually is not earth-shattering. This visualization enables me to realize how important it really is, so I can relax and enjoy the pleasant things in my life.

Thought for the Day

Sometimes happiness and serenity are a matter of perspective.

"Saying 'How Important Is It?' can help us to be cool under stress. That way we can save energy for the things that really matter."

Alateen—Hope for Children of Alcoholics, p. 52

Tradition One took on new meaning for me when another member shared her interpretation that unity included coming to meetings even when life was going well for her. Her insight helped me look at meeting attendance as both an act of unity with other members and a commitment to my own growth and well-being.

In the beginning unity of purpose meant I could come to a room full of people who accepted my irrational thinking. They offered me an encouraging hug rather than telling me to shape up. Instead of rejecting me for being different, they showed me how alike we all are by sharing their experience, strength, and hope. Through these types of healthy encounters, I began to feel a bond with other members. I felt united with them through common experience. As I worked my program, I became more unified in my own mind, body, and spirit.

Now unity of purpose means it's time for me to attend meetings not just for what I need, but for what I can offer. How else will newcomers know there's an end to their suffering if I and other members in recovery don't show up when things are going well? How will they learn that they, too, can smile again if they don't see our smiles? What about the long-time members who slip and forget the help available to them until we offer it? I might need this type of prompting sometime myself. When I come to meetings during my good times, others are reminded that whatever their problems, there is help and hope in Al-Anon.

Thought for the Day

As Al-Anon leads me to peace and serenity, I increasingly become an example to struggling members that such a life is possible.

"Reaching out . . . gave me a new perspective on our common welfare."

When I Got Busy, I Got Better, p. 38

My best thinking and my best efforts proved insufficient to the task of restoring me to sanity. My life had become completely unmanageable. In Al-Anon I heard that a Power greater than myself could bring order into my life. I began opening my mind to the possibility.

To me Step Two is all about hope. It's the process by which I become free from whatever problem is bothering me. It gives me something else to do, somewhere else to go when my life becomes unmanageable. I learn to look beyond myself for answers.

Coming to believe is a process for me. First, I come to believe that others have faith and that their belief in a Higher Power somehow makes a difference in their lives. I can see peace, love, and happiness in many of the people at meetings, and I yearn to possess those qualities myself. Gradually my mind opens to the possibility that I, too, can experience serenity. Eventually I become *willing* to believe, but even that comes in stages. Plenty of times I need to ask my Higher Power for the willingness to be willing. Finally I believe.

Exhilaration flows through me. The door to a new reality opens wide. I realize this revelation is just the beginning. I am not restored to sanity in an instant. However, Step Two gives me hope I can be healed because I now know—and believe in—the Source of all healing. My Higher Power is there for me once I choose faith, sanity, and healing for my life.

Thought for the Day

The phrase "came to believe" reminds me that faith is a process, not an event, from which sanity arises.

> "The basic spiritual principle introduced in Step Two
> suggests that there is a Power greater than we are that
> provides hope for sanity, whether we are living with active
> alcoholism or not."
>
> *Paths to Recovery*, p. 18

I remember awakening one night when I was a teenager to hear my drunken mother gossip with a friend about intimate details of my life. Nothing was sacred when she was drunk. The pain was intense, and I tried to hide my sobs in the pillow.

For many years I hid my feelings and the details of my life, just as I had hidden my sobs. Gossip and my fear of it propelled me deeper into perfectionism. After all, if I were perfect, no one would have anything to talk about. Gossip created a judgmental atmosphere in which I did not feel free to be myself. So I continued to hide and did not accept who I really was. Gossip was just as harmful to me when I was the one doing it. When I gossiped about another, I avoided feeling and looking at my own life.

Then I came to Al-Anon, where gossip is considered detrimental to recovery. For this reason it is listed as one of the "Three Obstacles to Success in Al-Anon" in our Conference Approved Literature. I felt such relief when I heard the following in our Suggested Al-Anon/Alateen Closing: "Talk to each other, reason things out with someone else, but let there be no gossip or criticism of one another. Instead, let the understanding, love, and peace of the program grow in you one day at a time." What peace that statement brings. Today I avoid gossip, and in doing so I keep from being controlling and judgmental. I put the focus on myself, one day at a time.

Thought for the Day

"Whom you see here, what you hear here, when you leave here, let it stay here" is a lesson not only in maintaining anonymity but also in avoiding gossip.

> "Gossip never enriched anyone's character. It was only an excuse to avoid focusing on myself."

> *Courage to Change*, p. 300

When I was a baby, my grandfather gave me a plush toy chimpanzee. As I grew up, my parents often told me my grandfather had given me the chimpanzee because he thought it looked just like me. I became self-conscious about my looks, especially my long upper lip and big ears. I believed myself to be as ugly as that stuffed chimp.

Years later as I worked on my Fourth Step using Al-Anon's *Blueprint for Progress*, I faced this question: "Can I accept my physical appearance?" Even after years of recovery in the program, my answer was still, "No." At first I was embarrassed by my lack of self-acceptance. Then I became angry and resentful of my alcoholic family members for their cruel remarks.

My sponsor suggested what I considered an odd route to self-love. She asked me to embrace my toy chimp, which like me had miraculously survived my childhood. She told me to surround it with love. I thought it was a crazy idea, but I did it anyway. I set it on my dresser where I could see it during the day, and I slept with it at night.

In due time that "ugly" chimp started to look beautiful to me. I began to treasure the worn but still smiling face that is always happy to see me. The features I once thought hideously distorted now seem in perfect proportion.

Today I love myself as I love that toy. I now believe the only real ugliness that exists in me lies in my attitudes. Acceptance changes everything.

Thought for the Day

How ready and willing am I today to invite the transforming power of acceptance into my will and my life?

> "Al-Anon offers us a new beginning. ...We can learn to accept ourselves and become willing to change our attitudes for the better."
>
> *Blueprint for Progress*, p. 21

When I came into Al-Anon, I didn't understand the meaning of serenity. I grew up as an older child of a large family and consequently had very little quiet time. After high school, I left home and moved into a small apartment with three roommates; no privacy there. Shortly after, I married and became the perfect wife who cooked, cleaned, gardened, and raised a family. Alcohol and the chaos that comes with it were ever present, so I took it upon myself to create a picture-perfect front for my friends, neighbors, and acquaintances. Obviously there was no time for me to relax under these circumstances.

Thank God for Al-Anon. In the program I've learned I can experience serenity any time I want it simply by making small choices. I can wake up an hour earlier and read, or watch the sunrise and listen to the sounds of early morning. I can turn off the car radio and drive to work in prayerful silence. While doing my housework, I can choose to listen to tapes I've accumulated from Al-Anon conventions, rather than to the chatter of the television. If I'm struggling with a stressful family situation, I can excuse myself, duck into a quiet room, take deep breaths, and say the Serenity Prayer over and over. Sometimes before bed I just sit quietly in the dark not thinking about anything, imagining myself wrapped in my Higher Power's beautiful cloak of moon and stars.

Thought for the Day

Serenity isn't a matter of chance; it's a matter of choice.

"This best of all possible gifts is a tranquil mind. You can't go out and buy it. You have to earn it for yourself . . ."

Forum Favorites, Volume 1, p. 47

Our shortest slogan, "Think," can be very helpful. However, as with most tools, I need to use it with care and reason. As I've heard it said around the Al-Anon rooms, my best thinking is what got me here. For me, thinking too much or in a negative way is almost as dangerous as not thinking at all. Obsessive thinking can be my symptom of this family disease as much as obsessive drinking is the alcoholic's. It has even occurred to me that I might be better off if I could get licensed to think safely! Al-Anon meetings are the closest place I've found to safe-thinking training grounds.

This slogan is intended to help me "Think" before I act, making sure my actions are well thought out, not impulsive, compulsive, or reactive. I need to remember, though, that the slogan is *not* "Think, think, think, think!" Along the lines of "Easy Does It" (but do it), I sometimes need to expand the scope of this slogan: "Think" (in moderation), "Think" (and pray), "Think" (out loud with a sponsor), or "Think" (and feel).

Thought for the Day

"Think" is an invitation for clarity, not endless rumination. God, help me to think, but not too much!

> "I have a program that helps me to make sense of my mixed-up thinking and feeling."
>
> *Alateen—a day at a time*, p. 14

I have realized since coming into Al-Anon that to have a peaceful existence, I need to be in relationship with the God of my understanding. For me there is a big difference between simply acknowledging the presence of God in my life and truly finding a spiritual connection. Step Eleven suggests I seek this deeper connection through prayer and meditation. When I discipline myself to observe some type of prayer and meditation, my day goes more smoothly and feels richer, more meaningful. No longer half-asleep to the wonders around me, I become aware that each moment fairly vibrates with the possibility of healing and wonderment.

I like to take Step Eleven even further by engaging in a daily running dialogue with my Higher Power, much as I would with my best friend. Sometimes this conversation is silent; sometimes I talk out loud or write in my journal. In any case I bring all of me, uncensored, to the relationship. Rather than being formal, my communication with Him is spontaneous and authentic. I'm just as likely to curse God out of anger, believing He understands my anguish just as an accepting parent would, as to praise Him out of awe and gratitude. I can tell Him that although I don't always like His will, I will defer to it; it just might take me a little while. I can cry my heart out to God, knowing my wordless sobbing somehow creates a prayer of its own. I can also celebrate with Him in joy and playful laughter as I rediscover parts of myself I thought were gone forever.

Thought for the Day

When I invite God into my life through prayer, meditation, and conversation, I open myself to infinite possibilities.

"I have an unlimited source of strength and comfort at my disposal. Today I will take the time to cultivate that spiritual connection."

Courage to Change, p. 327

Before Al-Anon, I always compared myself to others, particularly my family members, and vowed to be better than them. I sought the elation of winning and wanted to be praised. My constant comparing and competing gradually edged most people out of my life. Ultimately I was not even good enough for myself, an attitude that led me to harsh self-abuse.

As I attended Al-Anon meetings, I gradually learned about the concepts of balance and perspective. I listened as other members shared about their mistakes and character defects. Their reactions to them—self-acceptance, making amends, and patience—showed me that there are different ways to behave in the world. I started to apply the slogans "Keep It Simple", "Easy Does It," and "How Important Is It?" to my daily goals, choices, and actions.

In studying the Steps with my sponsor, especially the Fourth and Fifth, I realized that beneath my extreme competitiveness lurks the true nature of the problem—pride and fear along with a sense of inadequacy. I'm afraid of not being liked, of making mistakes in front of others, of being vulnerable. In short I'm afraid of being human.

Today I know that in trying to be "better than," I'm actually diminishing my opportunities for fun and spontaneity. I'm isolating myself from those very people I wish to invite closer to my heart. I'm putting myself in competition with my Higher Power. In battling God's will for me, I risk losing the thing I *really* want to win—personal recovery.

Thought for the Day

I need not always win, succeed, or be right to be worthy of acceptance and love. In fact, trying to do so may actually prevent me from receiving those very things I seek.

"If I compare, I lose."

Courage to Change, p. 140

In the past I focused on anyone but myself—my husband, my children, my friends. I scurried around trying to meet what I perceived to be their needs, trying to make their lives orderly, comfortable, safe, and secure. I didn't see that I was still trying to control the disorder, discomfort, and lack of safety and security of my own childhood.

Al-Anon teaches me that I cannot make life a fluffy bed for others. When I keep the focus on myself, I can make my life better. First, I need to stop running away from my own fears and feelings; it is important to face them. Then I can concentrate on myself and learn how to discern what my responsibility is and what it is not. I've learned that when I take responsibility for my own side of the bed and accept that the mattress may have a few lumps in it, I can rest comfortably.

Thought for the Day

When I keep my focus on myself, I can make my own bed as comfortable as possible. I just might give others the opportunity to do the same.

> "Focusing on ourselves actually allows us to release other people to solve their own problems and frees us to find contentment and even happiness for ourselves."

> *From Survival to Recovery*, p. 75

Until recently I never paid much attention to the Twelve Concepts of Service. They didn't seem relevant to anything in my recovery other than performing service at the World Service Office, a scenario in which, just for today, I don't see myself. However, I was so impressed with some of the Conference Approved Literature I read on Concept Nine, which speaks of good personal leadership at all service levels, that I decided to give this particular Concept some attention.

In a world of leaders and followers, I am decidedly a follower, which is just fine with me. Concept Nine tells me that I can demonstrate leadership by following program suggestions, thus inspiring others to follow as well. I asked myself some questions to determine if I model healthy leadership behavior: Have I made a commitment to attend specific meetings unless I'm sick or out of town? Do I listen attentively when others share? Do I take complex problems to my sponsor instead of to the meeting? Do I volunteer for service? Am I informed, and do I take part in group conscience meetings?

I found that I do well with some of these points and that I have room for progress with others. I'm thankful that Al-Anon raised my awareness about leadership. Concept Nine taught me that I could be a leader in the program, even if I don't feel comfortable standing for an elected position. Following my heart and conscience, performing service work, and cooperating with others are all forms of good leadership.

Thought for the Day

The power of example works through me, even if I prefer to follow rather than lead.

> "Each and every member of Al-Anon has the potential to become a leader."
>
> *Paths to Recovery*, p. 301

The roles I played for a long time in my family were those of caretaker and fixer. I was the nurturing mother my mom never had. It was my responsibility to care for her emotionally and often physically. I was an over-vigilant child, constantly on guard lest something awful should happen.

As I grew in Al-Anon, it became clear that my true responsibility was to care for myself. I began to see how my caretaking and controlling actually hurt others, possibly cheating them out of an opportunity to learn and grow. I decided to attempt detaching with love. For me detachment doesn't mean abandoning others. It means that I mind my own business and that I don't have all the answers or solutions.

It hasn't been easy for my family to accept the changes I've made. My new ways often are met with opposition and attempts at manipulation, even tears, to get me to resume my old role. In some cases my changes have inspired a new respect in my family relationships, a respect which allows more acceptance of each other, more freedom for each of us to be the individual that God intended.

Thought for the Day

It's not easy to change my role in my family. Some may want me to revert to the old me, but some will appreciate the new me. Today I'll do what I can to feel good about myself and let others take what they like and leave the rest.

> "I can't be all things to all people, but I can be someone special to some people."
>
> *From Survival to Recovery*, p. 284

I really struggled with the process of finding a sponsor. I felt as if I were asking someone to be my friend. If I had to ask then I didn't really need that kind of friend. However, what I yearned for was someone with whom I could talk deeply and who would receive my confidences with respect and trustworthiness. I finally asked a long-time member from my home group whose sharing often touched me. She told me she would be my sponsor as long as I worked the program.

As we moved through the relationship-building process, my sponsor demonstrated acceptance and love toward me. At that point, I didn't love and accept myself, and here she was giving me the very gifts I was so sure I didn't deserve. I grew to trust my sponsor without hesitation by gauging her reactions as I shared increasingly intimate thoughts and feelings. Each time I revealed a fact I was certain would fill her with disgust, she surprised me by sharing something similar from her past or by asking me a question that framed my behavior in a self-loving light. She never judged or berated me.

I fought her very hard. Sometimes I would pick fights so that maybe she would go away, but she never did. So I kept hanging on because I liked the good feelings that came from being cherished. Eventually, I came to realize that I did deserve to be treated with love and respect, and I started to act accordingly.

Thought for the Day

Asking for help can be hard, but what I miss out on if I don't ask can be even harder.

> "In fact, for many of us, the respect and caring we shared with our sponsor grew so great that we hardly recognized the moment when we were *saying*, 'my sponsor' and *thinking*, 'my friend'."

> *Sponsorship, What It's All About*, p. 2

If I were to draw a coat-of-arms representing my experience growing up in an alcoholic home, I might draw a fire-breathing dragon hovering menacingly over a tablet bearing the message "Divide and Conquer." The dividing came in many forms. I saw my parents divide on important parenting issues during drunken arguments. Their words divided my siblings and me by pitting us against each other in unfair comparison: "Why can't you be more like your brother (or your sister)?" I felt divided within myself when I tried to share my nagging fear of my father's escalating drinking and was told there was no problem. Which was I to trust—my instincts and experience, or the words of others? In the end I learned to trust neither.

To remedy this particular effect of alcoholism, Tradition One states, "Our common welfare should come first; personal progress for the greatest number depends upon unity." The word "common" tells me I am bonding with people who understand and have gone through variations of my own experience. "Welfare" tells me the nature of this bond is about well-being and safety. "Unity" tells me that in order to get well, we need to work *together* to do what is best for the whole.

Unity feels uncomfortable simply because it's unfamiliar, but I know there is nothing to fear. We join not to divide and conquer but to face our common adversary—the effects of the disease of alcoholism. We turn to each other with the common hope and growing understanding that we can help each other heal.

Thought for the Day

The disease of alcoholism is our common problem, and Al-Anon is our common solution.

" . . . The unity of our group . . . provides us with a core of stability we can depend on."

Twelve Steps and Twelve Traditions for Alateen, p. 28

When I first came to Al-Anon, I conceived of God as punitive. I thought He was like my alcoholic father who always
seemed to be looking for someone to punish or blame. I thought
that the awful happenings in my life were God's way of hurting
me because I had messed something up. At that time my prayers
usually consisted of something like this: "Please don't punish me
today because I can't take it."

As I spent more time in Al-Anon, applied the first three
Steps, got a sponsor, and came to know many people whose
outlook on life was very different from my father's, I became less
fearful of God. I began to trust Him more and considered the
possibility that He might actually help me. During this period
my prayers were other-directed, such as "Please make my father
stop drinking" or "Please make my mother stop yelling at me." I
didn't understand the process encouraged in Step Eleven to pray
"only for knowledge of His will for us and the power to carry that
out."

Now after consistent attendance at meetings and working
the Steps, I can honestly say I trust God to take care of me. I
don't pray anymore for my father's sobriety. Instead, my prayers
might say this: "God, I haven't a clue as to what's going on with
him, but I know You do," or "I'm glad You're in charge because
there's nothing I can do." Sometimes I just say, "Thank God I
don't have Your job!" I pray for God to do His work and for the
willingness and ability to do mine.

Thought for the Day

I tried to get God to listen to me through my prayers. He did,
once I stopped telling Him what to do.

> "How greatly my prayers have changed since I came into
> Al-Anon!"

As We Understood . . ., p. 202

My wife and I were taking our morning walk when the conversation turned to her mother's drunken abuse of her as a child and a teen. I've heard the story before, but this time it got me thinking about my own mom, who was not a drinker but who was abusive and tried to control me with angry, degrading words. I told my wife that at least she could explain her mother's abuse because of the alcohol; my mom abused me while sober. My wife then tried to share, and I said, "Yes, but . . . " Again she tried to share, and again I said, "Yes, but . . . " We walked on in silence; I had "won" this little verbal exchange.

Suddenly I remembered my wife once explaining that sometimes she just needs someone to listen to her. She doesn't want to be fixed or made to feel better; she just needs to be heard. I recalled the many times I had shared in Al-Anon meetings and how good it felt, and how healing it was, to be heard and validated. Gently I reminded myself to listen, not compare. How did I make amends at the end of our walk? I embraced my wife and acknowledged her need to be heard. I let her talk as long as she needed to, and I listened as long as she needed me.

Thought for the Day

Al-Anon meetings teach me and allow me to experience and to practice first hand the tools that transform communication barriers into bridges.

> "Really listening meant being open to others, being free of my own attitudes."
>
> *Having Had a Spiritual Awakening . . .*, p. 21

Certainly I have periods of tremendous enthusiasm for the Al-Anon program. During those times I feel alive, eager, and receptive to growth. However, I also experience periods of complacency during which I am close-minded, self-satisfied, and lacking in progress. I tell myself that to some extent this is probably normal; life is composed of mountains, valleys, and plateaus. However, when my complacency gets out of hand, it interferes with the quality of my recovery.

I can't achieve the degree of health I want by using yesterday's program. I've found that if I'm not moving forward, I don't just stand still; I go backwards. I forget that the tools of the program have worked for me before and start to think I can manage my life on my own. That's when my will and my life become insane.

I once heard a speaker say if we don't grow, we get so uncomfortable that we stop going to meetings. The verbs "continued", "sought", "tried," and "practice" in Steps Ten through Twelve sound suspiciously like work to me. These words indicate that I need to persist in going to meetings, even when I don't feel like it. However, they also offer reward for the effort—a renewal of my enthusiasm for life and a regeneration of my spirit.

Thought for the Day

The best way for me to stay moving and growing is to keep attending Al-Anon meetings.

"Complacency . . . is rarely listed among the major human faults, yet it can hinder us in every form of personal growth."

One Day at a Time in Al-Anon, p.197

"When you have to go into your head," says an Al-Anon friend, "don't go alone. It's not a safe neighborhood." My experience certainly corroborates the truth of this statement. Now when I have to go inside my mind for some serious thinking and I can't travel with a program person, I take my Higher Power. When I have trouble contacting that Power, I follow a simple, three-point plan my sponsor taught me.

- First, I remind myself that I've been in this neighborhood before.
- Second, I make a gratitude list, usually beginning with food, clothing, and shelter.
- Third, I meditate and pray that my Higher Power will give me a sign that I'm going in the right direction. Much as I might like to see a lightning bolt hurled from the sky, I make myself receptive to less dramatic moments of insight.

With the glint of light this process provides, the neighborhood may not look like an amusement park, yet it still feels passable. It is, after all, my neighborhood.

Thought for the Day

When I think myself into a troubled state, I will remember this: Don't look around, look up.

> "It can help to replace obsessive thoughts with something positive, such as an Al-Anon slogan, the Serenity Prayer, or another comforting topic that has nothing to do with my problem."

Courage to Change, p. 306

I developed some fairly negative attitudes about life while growing up in an alcoholic family. If nine people complimented me and one person insulted me, I focused all of my attention on the one insult. However, as I recover in Al-Anon, I'm beginning to see the glass half-full instead of half-empty. Our slogans and sayings are taking on a richer, fuller meaning for me. To me the slogan "How Important Is It?" used to mean there are things in life not worth putting much energy into, such as obsessing about the one insult I might receive along with a whole bunch of compliments. Now I see that it can also mean there *are* important things worthy of my time, energy, and love, such as my self-esteem and my recovery. If it is truly important to me, then it's worthy of my time and effort.

Similarly I used to apply the expression "This Too Shall Pass" only when I was facing a painful and difficult situation. I used it to remind myself that no matter how much anguish I felt or how unbearable my situation seemed, nothing lasts forever. Then my sponsor told me that this saying applies to all circumstances, not just the rough ones. Applying "This Too Shall Pass" to pleasant experiences was something I had never thought of doing. Yet the same truth applies. Nothing lasts forever—the beautiful or the horrid. So I might just as well patiently ride out the bad times, knowing they will end, and joyously embrace the good ones while they last.

Thought for the Day

There are more facets to our simple slogans than I may realize.

> "You may have heard some of these slogans hundreds of times before without ever taking them seriously or trying to put them to work."
>
> *How Al-Anon Works for Families & Friends of Alcoholics*, p.66

As I began writing my Eighth Step list—the persons I had harmed—many wise Al-Anon members suggested I put my own name on it. The coping behaviors I had developed as a child had helped me survive the chaos in my alcoholic home. However, those behaviors were no longer necessary. By continuing them, I not only hurt other people but I also hurt myself. I needed to make amends to myself, too.

Some of my actions that harmed me were saying yes when I wanted to say no; stuffing my feelings when I was angry; avoiding the people I resented; allowing others to take advantage of the fact that I was often afraid to speak up for myself; and in general allowing other people to run my life either by direct manipulation or by controlling me.

It seemed that to make amends to myself, I had to immediately change all these behaviors. However, I realized I couldn't change them all at once. Taking small steps in the right direction would work better than attempting a major overhaul. Gradually I started saying no when I meant it, speaking up for myself when I needed to, and allowing other people their anger without reacting to it.

I also needed to learn to forgive myself for the times I felt unable to carry out these healthier behaviors. Today I accept myself as imperfect and allow myself to make mistakes. When I do, I use the Tenth Step to help me forgive and amend my own behavior. I find that the more I learn in Al-Anon, the less frequently I act against my own best interests, and the easier it is to forgive myself when I do.

Thought for the Day

Am I including myself among the persons I have harmed?

> "I didn't realize that I had harmed myself more than anyone else."

Paths to Recovery, p. 86

My parents drank and were oblivious to the activities in our home. As a child I never told anyone my secret: a babysitter sexually abused me. Life went on as usual, but emotionally I was empty, as if I truly had a hole in my heart. As an adult I thought other people, such as my alcoholic husband, could fill my emptiness, but it never went away.

When my husband got sober, I came to Al-Anon. I was 28 before I told anyone about the abuse. I told my sponsor. At first I didn't feel any better; I felt worse. However, as I worked the Steps, particularly the Fifth, I began to heal. I came to realize that no human being could relieve my suffering; only God could take it away.

Today I know there is no anguish so great that my Higher Power cannot remove it. By not talking with someone, I was prolonging my pain. Once I told someone trustworthy, I could go on with the Steps and ask God to heal my hurt.

Thought for the Day

It takes courage to change. Now that I have a Higher Power and program friends to help me, I know there are no limits to my recovery in Al-Anon.

> "...The only way to release ourselves from the hold of these dark demons is to break the isolation and bring them into the light by sharing with others who understand."
>
> ... *In All Our Affairs*, p.32

Slips? I experience them most when I'm caught off-guard by someone with whom I have a complicated history—such as my dad. For example, no matter what adult thoughts or feelings I'm having beforehand, I almost always revert to acting like a little girl when my dad and I interact. These are peculiar encounters, as if the person I was many years ago suddenly inhabits my mind and body. It takes me several hours, sometimes days, to come back to my adult self. Inevitably, when I recall my behavior, I feel as if I've lost my program.

Thanks to Al-Anon—particularly "Progress Not Perfection" and "Easy Does It"—I'm getting much better at accepting my slips. I strive to give myself credit for how far I've come and to learn something from my mistakes. I remind myself that I have all the time I need to improve. Recovery is not a contest.

I once shared at a meeting how I felt when I discovered my husband was having an affair. I told how I had been in so much pain that I wanted only to die and cried for hours, even days, at a time. A fairly new member told me after the meeting she couldn't imagine I had ever been in such a spot. Since she had known me, I always sounded so happy and serene. I thought about her words for a moment, and I realized that she was right. I *had* become much happier and had gained much from working my program. Although only a few months separated our entry into Al-Anon, I needed this woman's eyes to help me see my growth.

Thought for the Day

If I can't see my growth, perhaps the perspective of a fellow member will give me a better view.

"... 'Progress Not Perfection' encourages me to give myself credit ..."

How Al-Anon Works for Families & Friends of Alcoholics, p. 323

It took me a long time to admit that I had experienced some horrible things as a child growing up in a family affected by alcoholism. In Al-Anon I found a safe place to remember the pain and to face it. As I began to accept the truth about my past by writing in my journal and talking about my memories, some members of my family suggested I stop what they considered excessive reflection and let bygones be bygones. Even a few well-intentioned members of Al-Anon asked whether I couldn't live just one day at a time. Yet as long as I hid from the emotional realities of my history, its unresolved poisons seeped into each new day. To live fully in today, I had to come to terms with yesterday's circumstances as well as my reactions to them.

Facing the feelings I had stored since childhood didn't change the facts of what happened, but it *did* change my emotional climate. Because my good memories didn't have to compete so hard with the bad ones, they began to unfold in my consciousness. Now I'm free to move forward and to take responsibility for the attitudinal and emotional responses I choose today. As I make new and better choices and allow my Higher Power to guide me in making them, those awful events of the past become a much smaller part of who I am.

Thought for the Day

Facing the worst of my past opens the door to remembering the best of it, too, creating room for serenity, wonder, and joy in my life.

> "Denial is broken when we quit hoping for a better past, accept the reality of that past, and set about creating a different present."
>
> *From Survival to Recovery,* p. 68

I found a carrot and two lumps of coal on my sidewalk and wondered what they were doing there. I thought it odd. Suddenly remembering that a snowman once stood on that place, I chuckled at my own suspicious thoughts. Even so, I had an eerie feeling of something strangely familiar. I kept staring at the coal and the carrot as I unloaded groceries from my car. A snowman—cold, frozen, hard. I hadn't noticed his melting; I only noticed what was left, which wasn't much.

I thought of how I had built frozen layers around myself to cope with the terror and chaos of alcoholism. I had grown up encased in the iciness of the disease. Then the warm and loving members of Al-Anon encouraged me to let my Higher Power thaw the icy layers until, like the snowman, there was but a speck of me left. It was a genuine speck, however, and I trusted God to employ the Al-Anon program to build upon it until I became the healthy person I was meant to be.

I've learned that becoming healthy means tolerating a melting away of my old self. If I feel empty during this process, I shall not permit myself to want the disease back. Instead, I will trust my Higher Power to help me bring forth the genuine me. I'll trust that the emptiness I feel is because God has left some room for my true self to develop.

Thought for the Day

The empty spaces I feel during recovery will become filled as I allow my Higher Power to heal me through Al-Anon.

> "The desire to grow and to heal has brought me to this uncomfortable point . . . I need only trust that, when the time comes to move forward, I will know it."
>
> *Courage to Change*, p. 221

I work as a seamstress. During a recent sewing project, I thought about how similar my sewing is to my progress in recovery. Before Al-Anon my sewing had to be perfect. Many a time I ended up not wearing my creation because I was sick and tired of going over it again and again. I'd leave it hanging in the closet and eventually give it away. If I ever did wear anything I made, I was quick to point out its imperfections when anyone gave me a compliment.

Since using the tools of Al-Anon, my sewing is much simpler. Using the thread of willingness and asking my Higher Power to guide my hands, I now enjoy experimenting with fabrics and techniques and even reworking my stitches. I go about this knowing that my garment will not be perfect and that the imperfections make it uniquely mine. I enjoy wearing it knowing that I learned much in its creation.

My material garment and my recovery garment are so very much alike. No longer do I expect to be perfect, and I don't hide away in isolation for fear of having my imperfections discovered. Neither do I so easily give away the precious, vulnerable parts of myself; I wait until I deem the other person trustworthy enough to receive me with love. I don't pre-criticize myself, thinking that it won't hurt so much if I beat somebody else to it. Today I wear my self and my hand-sewn apparel proudly, knowing that each was created with the willingness, the abilities, and the help with which my Higher Power blesses me daily.

Thought for the Day

My imperfections reflect my humanness and my oneness with others.

> "In partnership with my Higher Power . . . I can always be me."

From Survival to Recovery, p. 284

How many times have I stopped my car at a red light, late at night and with no other vehicles in view, and considered not waiting for the green light in order to proceed? What about the times I've flirted with the idea of going the wrong way down a one-way street because it would make my trip shorter? There are so many traffic rules to adhere to, whether or not the police are around. However, if I disregard those rules, I put my life and those of others at risk.

I think it's the same thing with the suggested Traditions, guidelines, and policies in Al-Anon. When I don't follow the program's suggestions, I seem to hurt myself as well as others. I obsess and react as I did before I had a program. I have slips. I put my recovery at risk.

In Al-Anon this process of following guidelines is called "obedience to the unenforceable." I know deep down in my heart and mind what is right and wrong for my recovery. From experience I've learned to respectfully fear the outcome if I ignore the Traditions. The price I pay in terms of my integrity and self-esteem, as well as possible damage to the groups that make my recovery possible, just isn't worth it.

I came to this beautiful fellowship to change the alcoholic. Soon I learned that I could change only myself. The best way to accomplish this is to follow the suggested guidelines that have worked for so long for so many. All I need to do is practice "Keep It Simple" and work the program.

Thought for the Day

What can I share from my experience, strength, and hope to help others?

> "Al-Anon's Twelve Traditions help me maintain not only a discipline in my program, but also in life. They help me be a safe person for others."

The Forum, October 1998, p. 4

One of the Al-Anon slogans often heard in meetings is "Let It Begin with Me." I interpret "It" as carrying the message of Al-Anon to others in need, as suggested by Step Twelve. Given my particular character defect of thinking I know what's best for other people, I especially like what this phrase *doesn't* say. It doesn't say I need to convert anyone to my way of thinking. It's a modest declaration that suggests I need only contribute what I can in the way of experience, strength, and hope. How that information is received is out of my control.

If I am asked about Al-Anon directly, I can respond. If people confide in me about problems with an alcoholic friend or relative, I can inform them of Al-Anon's existence. If I choose, I can go so far as to share how much the program has helped me. If the other person expresses no interest or waves away my suggestion, I can rise above the reaction and do my best to embody the principles of the program by letting go and letting God and detaching with love. It *is* true that when the student is ready, the teacher appears. I just need to remember that I am not the teacher. I am just the vehicle my Higher Power uses to carry this message of hope and recovery. Who hears this message is up to God.

Thought for the Day

How I respond to someone's lack of interest in Al-Anon may convey the message of recovery better than any detailed personal testimony.

> "The problem is that those who need it don't always want it. We can share our experience, strength, and hope with them and be a good example of Al-Anon recovery by practicing its principles in all our affairs."
>
> *Paths to Recovery*, p. 227

When I came into Al-Anon, I felt it was not in my capacity to forgive. As much as forgiving others seemed to be the right thing to do, my good intentions didn't take away the pain or allow me to forget what certain people had said or done. I equated forgiveness with accepting unacceptable behavior.

In Al-Anon I learned new ways to protect myself around abusive people, including the alcoholics in my life. Now I know how to walk away from a verbally offensive situation. I can tell someone I feel angry or uncomfortable with their behavior and say what I mean without being mean when I say it. I find that the more I stand up for myself, the more willing I am to forgive. Once I discuss my anger or hurt with the other person, it often becomes clear that my resentment is about a one-time mishap I blew out of proportion. Then we discuss ways to avoid repeating the calamity, often becoming closer in the process.

In other cases my resentment is based on a persistent pattern of behavior I'm not willing to accept. I forgive the other person because that's what I need to do for me. I don't continue accepting unacceptable behavior. Sometimes forgiving includes letting go of a harmful relationship and moving on. When I forgive before I leave, I can walk away feeling clean, with no negative ties to prevent me from continuing my journey toward health and wholeness.

Thought for the Day

Sometimes the forgiveness process fosters deeper unity and connection between people. Sometimes it points to an exit sign.

> "Through the Al Anon program I have learned that forgiveness ... does not call for going back to an abusive or destructive relationship and saying, 'Oh well, I forgive you one more time.' For me, forgiveness is the natural outcome of working the Twelve Steps."

The Forum, November 1999, p. 9

Before I came to Al-Anon, fear was my biggest obstacle. My reactions to fear included withdrawing, hiding, procrastinating, running, or berating myself. None of these behaviors helped me to face my fears. In fact, they only made situations worse. Fear still sneaks up on me, but I have found tools in this program to help me overcome it. I now realize that fear in and of itself is neither good nor bad. It's not a sign of weakness or cowardice, as I once thought. It's just a signal that some decision or action is needed on my part.

The first thing I try to do now is recognize when I am acting out of fear. Reacting rather than acting out of conscious decision-making is a clear sign. Often I react by putting off something beneficial to my spiritual growth. I may fear telling my ex-spouse my needs concerning visitation with our children, chairing a meeting, or talking to a newcomer.

Next, I use the Serenity Prayer and ask my Higher Power for the courage to do the thing I'm scared to do. Just because I pray for courage doesn't necessarily mean I will immediately receive it. Rather, as I practice the Steps and continue praying, I am able to act more courageously when confronted by situations that usually generate fear in me.

Finally I remind myself when I make a decision and take action that the outcome is in my Higher Power's hands. I pray, "Thy will, not mine, be done," trusting my Higher Power to provide what is best for my growth.

Thought for the Day

With the help of the program and my Higher Power, I can handle almost anything life brings—sometimes hurls—my way. Today I no longer fear my fear.

> "Now I know I can take care of my problems without being so crazy with fear."

Courage to Be Me, p. 292

I had been in Al-Anon for two years before I took Step One. How could I admit I was powerless over alcohol when I was 27 years old, single, living independently, and my alcoholic father had been sober for 10 years? I was no longer living with alcohol, so I couldn't figure out how to admit I was powerless over it.

I listened to others speak at Step meetings, read the literature on Step One, and even tried to share when Step One was the subject of the meeting. However, I still didn't know how to make it apply to me. How could I be powerless over something that was no longer an issue in my life?

One night, God sent me a beautiful spiritual awakening. When I was the young daughter of an alcoholic father, I was powerless. I was powerless over every criticism that came from his mouth, and I was powerless over every blow he struck against me. To survive such an upbringing, I developed many defenses. When no longer needed, these defenses became character defects. As an adult, I was still powerless over the effects of my father's abuse. It was the *effects* of alcoholism over which I was powerless! That awareness helped me to take my First Step.

My understanding didn't end there, though. I realized that my father had been just as powerless over his alcoholic father as I had been over him. When my father was a little boy, he didn't say, "When I grow up, I want to be an alcoholic." The insight my Higher Power gave me into Step One also brought me understanding, compassion, and forgiveness for my father.

Thought for the Day

Alcoholism doesn't have to be active in my life for me to be affected by it.

> "Our pressures and anxieties don't disappear just because we are living with sobriety."

Living with Sobriety, p. 18

One of my earliest revelations in Al-Anon could be called a lesson in the algebra of recovery. One day I was feeling totally frustrated by the alcoholic's behavior. When I sought clarity by turning to my Higher Power in prayer and meditation, I received a swift and clear but seemingly strange answer: $a + b = c$.

Thinking of this classic algebra equation long after my high school days fairly shocked me into wondering how it might apply to my situation. So "a" was me, "b" was my alcoholic loved one, and "c" was the total of our relationship. Our relationship was the total outcome of all the interactions between us—our words, emotions, and choices.

In algebra, altering one variable, even if the other variable remains constant, will change the entire equation. In applying this algebraic truth to my present and hypothetical future problems, I realized that I could transform "a" (myself) and get a different "c" (relationship), even if "b" (the alcoholic) never changed.

As I practice changing the things I can—such as my attitudes and actions—the outcomes of my interactions with my alcoholic family member also shift, often for the better. Making different choices for myself brings the total equation of the relationship to a sum of serenity that I never dreamed possible.

Thought for the Day

What choices do I want to figure into my relationship equations today?

"She realized that if a . . . relationship were to change, *the one who first saw the kind of attitudes required* had the obligation to hold these attitudes and behave accordingly."

The Dilemma of the Alcoholic Marriage, p. 65

Having witnessed the miracle of sobriety in my alcoholic father's life, I prayed for the same gift for a man I loved. His unsuccessful battle with alcoholism had torn our relationship apart. When he joined AA, got a sponsor, and remained sober, I thought my Higher Power had answered my prayers. When he chose to reconcile with his former girlfriend and made plans to marry her, I was crestfallen. I continued to work my program, got a sponsor, and earnestly tried to practice "Let Go and Let God," but it still hurt.

Could this really be what my Higher Power had in mind? How could I possibly detach from someone I still loved so much? At a meeting someone shared that we detach with love not because it's the nice thing to do but because it really is the only way we can let go. Disappointment, bitterness, and resentment are ties that bind, and until we release these feelings to our Higher Power, we remain bound to the past.

Suddenly it became clear that I am free to feel immeasurable love for the alcoholic as I pray for the strength to detach from my longing and disappointment. Even when someone's choices do not include me, I can still choose to love both of us by letting go and letting God loosen the ties that bind me to sadness and frustration.

Thought for the Day

Detaching from the pain of losing an important relationship is difficult. It helps to remember that I have a constant, consistent life partner who will never leave me—my Higher Power.

> "I accepted the problems I was faced with, and handled them with understanding and courage with the help of Al-Anon and a Higher Power."
>
> *To the Mother and Father of an Alcoholic*, p. 14

When I first came to Al-Anon, I struggled daily with never-ending negative emotional responses to life—anger, resentment, and self-pity. I felt trapped by these feelings. I couldn't detach from them to get perspective because I thought they were part of me, embedded in my nature.

My Fourth Step helped me realize that I had many of the same shortcomings as my alcoholic father. I shared my awareness with my sponsor, and she pointed out several pieces of Al-Anon literature suggesting that emotional responses and shortcomings are learned rather than innate. For the first time, I realized that I may have embraced some of my father's alcoholic attitudes. I could almost feel a slight breeze pass between my character defects and me. Maybe my shortcomings were not as bound to me as I had thought. Perhaps there was hope I could be free of my self-defeating attitudes.

I continued working the Steps, and finally came to Step Seven. I humbly asked God to take away my negative outlook. Now when I feel angry or resentful, I stop and "Think." I examine the thoughts that led to the feeling. Are they based on reality or on old patterns of reacting? When I'm honest with myself, I begin to see anger, resentment, and self-pity as choices I've made, not emotions someone made me feel. With the help of my Higher Power, I am learning to give careful consideration to choices that affect my emotional quality of life.

Thought for the Day

Whatever difficulties I have in recovery, I need to remember that I am not an inherently flawed person. Whatever has been learned can be unlearned.

> "Someone said, 'I wasn't born this way; I learned.' When I heard that, I felt more hope than I had ever experienced."
>
> *From Survival to Recovery,* p. 281

My mother, who was stressed by trying to cope with my alcoholic father, often loudly accused me of being irresponsible. Many times she screamed at me, "Why can't you be more responsible!?" Responsibility seemed like an unattainable goal because I thought I had to be responsible for everything and everyone. Then a fellow Al-Anon member taught me a new way to define responsibility: "respond-ability"—the ability to respond.

This definition opened a completely new world for me. My ability to respond in early recovery was not very strong, but the program and the people in it taught me to honor what skills I did possess and could use. So my earliest expression of my "respond-ability" was to answer the call of recovery. The most I could do at the beginning was just show up at meetings. I was too afraid to share, so I let listening become another way I could respond. After a lot of showing up and listening, the teachings of the program began to sink in. Little by little I grew to really acknowledge and respond to my pain, my needs, myself. To encourage my recovery, I took some risks—I shared, got a sponsor, and volunteered for service. The longer I kept coming back, the more whole I became.

Today my "respondability" is not always the same; sometimes I can respond more than at other times. One aspect of this new skill is realizing when I can't handle something alone and need help from my friends and from my Higher Power. Today meetings, Conference Approved Literature, and my Higher Power help me discern the responses that are right and healthy for me.

Thought for the Day

Keeping the focus on me is a good way to start responding to myself.

> "What's important in my life? What do I want? What do I need?"

Alateen—a day at a time, p. 13

I had been a member of the program for several years when I was invited to attend an Al-Anon adult child meeting that was struggling to get started. I told the members I was a friend of an alcoholic, not a child of one. They told me I was welcome.

I was amazed at what I learned that night. I wondered how they found out my secret characteristics so quickly. How could I have so many traits of an adult child when neither of my parents ever drank? I continued to attend the meetings in spite of my confusion because I got something there I couldn't get anywhere else.

More than a year later, I mentioned to my mother that I was attending the adult child meetings although there was no direct alcoholism in our family. At that time she revealed the family secret that had been kept from me for more than 40 years. Her father—my grandfather—had been an oilfield worker and a fighting drunk who was jailed at every town where he worked.

My grandmother had been the wife of an alcoholic, and Mom was the child of an alcoholic. Suddenly everything made sense. I finally understood why I acted as I did. I was the grandchild of an alcoholic and the daughter of an adult child! The effects of the disease of alcoholism had been handed down in my family from generation to generation, but no one before me had received the loving help of Al-Anon. Thanks to my Higher Power, I found the program. Now I can start passing down recovery instead of disease.

Thought for the Day

In recovery sometimes I get answers even before my heart knows it has a question.

> "When we go to enough meetings, we will hear someone tell a story that sounds amazingly like our own—our comfort level increases."

Al-Anon Is for Men, p. 4

I sometimes worry that I'm not doing something truly important with my life. Caught up in day-to-day trivialities, it doesn't seem that I accomplish much. Yet I forget that through all of my daily routine, I am working my Al-Anon program.

Working my program is about learning how to love myself, my Higher Power, and those around me. To be loving is to be fully alive. To be fully alive is to use all the splendid faculties of my personality in every area of my life.

As I grow in love, I worry less about doing something important. Instead, I stretch my abilities as far as they can take me. My action is now the spontaneous expression of a loving heart. I have done more in the past year as a result of working my program than in the previous ten without it. To me there is nothing more important I can do with my life than becoming more loving and spiritual.

Thought for the Day

When I start feeling unaccomplished, I will remember that loving myself is the greatest accomplishment of all.

"I used to believe *thinking* was the highest function of human beings . . . I now realize *loving* is our supreme function. The heart precedes the mind."

Lois Remembers, p. 196

One of the reasons this program works so well is that we don't all experience our insane times at once. The alcoholic isn't sick in all areas of life at all times, and neither are we. We come together to tell a story of healing by sharing our experience, strength, and hope.

We share: We join our stories together to paint a deeper, truer picture of the family disease of alcoholism. When we share our true thoughts and feelings, we let each other know that no one takes the recovery journey alone.

Experience: We each have survived the effects of alcoholism. By sharing what we have lived through ourselves, we provide opportunities for others to identify with our experiences and to dispel their feelings of uniqueness. When we relate how we've applied the Al-Anon program to our problems, we give each other concrete ideas to take home and use.

Strength: By allowing others time to tell their stories, we forge a mutual, unified support stronger than any one of us is alone. We learn to let the collective support of the group sustain us.

Hope: At times when we feel the insanity of the disease, we hear those who are saner. Even during our darkest times, there is usually a member whose path is even darker. As we reach out to those members, we rediscover the hope we thought we had lost.

Thought for the Day

Recovery cannot occur in isolation. Together we can accomplish what we cannot do alone.

> "By sharing what I have to say and listening to what others have to say, I learn how to deal with some of my problems."
>
> *Living Today in Alateen*, p. 28

When I heard at my first Al-Anon meeting that I could "find contentment and even happiness whether the alcoholic is still drinking or not," I thought to myself, "Hardly."

I thought my wife's drinking was the source of our problems. Here's an example of a typical evening. My wife bathes, feeds, and puts the children to bed before she starts drinking for the evening. Then I provoke her by saying she should know better than to give the children such a poor role model. I repeat this until she explodes in anger. Then the kids wake up and all of us argue. Soon I point out, "Look at what you are doing to the kids." Later, my bed pillow cradles an angry mind as I berate myself for not keeping my mouth shut.

I've learned that my wife has a disease. I've also learned how to keep the focus on myself and to detach from potentially explosive situations without feeding into them. Now I'm playing with the children. My wife has a drink in her hand and comments how nice it is to be together as a family. Suddenly I think, "None of this would be happening if it weren't for Al-Anon." In a flash I realize what a wonderful treasure my wife really is, alcohol and all. She is good to me in so many ways. I consider myself fortunate to have her in my life.

Thank you, Al-Anon, for helping me change my attitudes, and so my life. I've had a beautiful spouse by my side all along, and my Higher Power gave me a beautiful program to help me realize it. What more could I want?

Thought for the Day

Changed attitudes do aid recovery.

> "It was a gift knowing that we desire to be together . . .
> with both our defects and virtues."
>
> *Having Had a Spiritual Awakening . . .*, p. 105

One of my favorite Al-Anon pamphlets is *A Guide for the Family of the Alcoholic*. It discusses the "weapons" the alcoholic might use to relieve his or her anxiety or to create additional reasons to drink. These include the ability to provoke anger and to arouse anxiety.

The alcoholic in my life used to arouse my anger and anxiety by criticizing me and breaking plans and promises. He often created scenes in public and was generally inconsistent and unreliable. Before Al-Anon I allowed these behaviors—these weapons—to dictate how I felt and behaved. I took offense and had my feelings hurt. I reacted with angry self-defense or silent withdrawal into depression and self-contempt.

I learned that the word "take" in the phrase "to take offense" meant I had a choice. Why would I want to take offense and feel hurt and sad? Wouldn't I rather take joy and serenity from the tools of the program?

Eventually I stopped acting on my hurt feelings. Rather than displaying them to the alcoholic, I discussed them with my sponsor. I opted out of playing games, displaying defensive behavior, and feeling miserable. As long as I gave the alcoholic the power to hurt my feelings, he had control over my serenity. If I didn't give him permission to relieve his misery by attacking me, I didn't play into his illness. I performed an exercise in detachment, which led to serenity and greater self-esteem.

Thought for the Day

Detaching myself from a person with the flu protects me from catching the illness. Emotionally detaching from alcoholism increases the likelihood that I won't catch an overabundance of anger and anxiety.

> "The only way love can be retained is by family members learning not to suffer when drinking is in progress and refusing to undo the consequences of drinking."
>
> *A Guide for the Family of the Alcoholic*, p. 7

Al-Anon tells me I don't have to accept unacceptable behavior. It has taken me a long time to learn what acceptable, even desirable, behavior looks like so that I can determine what is unacceptable. I believe strongly that these difficulties have a lot to do with my growing up with alcoholism. Because I seldom experienced acceptable behavior, I thought unacceptable behavior was normal. It wasn't until I came to Al-Anon that I discovered a better way to live.

One particular area I struggle with is sorting out hurtful criticism from constructive comments. One suggestion that helps me is to consider the source. This helps me to stop assigning equal importance to everything everybody says about me. If constructive comments come from my sponsor, whom I know is grounded in the program, I listen and give careful consideration to her words. If the active alcoholic in my life criticizes me in an abusive manner, I consider the source. In other words, I remind myself it's the alcohol speaking, not my loved one. Therefore there's no point in my assigning the same weight to the alcoholic's words as I do to my sponsor's.

When I consider the source I am reminded to detach and place principles above personalities. I don't have to spend so much energy resenting those who speak to me through the fog of this insidious disease. Once I've done this, I can ask myself, "How important is it?" Considering the source also reminds me to have compassion for the person struggling under the thick layers of the disease of alcoholism. For me considering the source is a large portion of the program in action.

Thought for the Day

Among the people in my life, whose words are worth taking to heart?

> "When cruel words fly from the mouth of another person, drunk or sober, Al-Anon helps me remember that I have choices."

Courage to Change, p. 297

The slogan "Live and Let Live" makes me feel nervous, like the proverbial circus animal unwilling to leave its cage when the door is left open. It has taken me some time to believe that I can trust in the hope and possibility of this slogan.

A speaker at an Al-Anon meeting presented a metaphor that helps me better understand and practice "Live and Let Live." He said that he has an emotional acre to tend. While it is important for him to tend that entire acre, it is also important for him *not* to tend beyond those limits. This reminded me of how often I spend more time focusing on others' feelings—trying to fix them or protect them—than on my own.

The limits of my emotional acre are not always as clear as those of my physical acre. However, if I pay close attention to the inner signals I receive from my Higher Power, I can sense when I am trespassing as plainly as if I had climbed my neighbor's fence.

Thought for the Day

"Live and Let Live" helps me stay on my own plot of recovery where I can do the most good, rather than wasting my time on someone else's.

> "Our only concern should be our own conduct, our own improvement, our own lives. We are entitled to our own view of things, and we have no right to inflict it on anyone else."
>
> *Alcoholism, the Family Disease,* p. 20

"Take care of yourself" is a common phrase, but I didn't always pay attention to its deeper meaning. When I came to Al-Anon, the idea of caring for myself was foreign. I usually tried to take care of others and expected them to take care of me. In Al-Anon I learned to care for myself physically, emotionally, and spiritually.

Learning financial responsibility, however, was an unexpected part of my recovery. I had hit fiscal bottom, and I couldn't see how healing from alcoholism could restore my credit. I often borrowed money from one family member because I had loaned my own money to another. Tradition Seven states, "Every group ought to be fully self-supporting, declining outside contributions." Studying this principle showed me that I was trapped in a fruitless pattern of behavior which ate away at my self-esteem. I learned to let my family members be responsible for their finances so that I could manage mine.

Warranty One of Concept Twelve states, "that only sufficient operating funds, including an ample reserve, be its prudent financial principle." This introduced me to the idea of practical, responsible living. I began making a budget and sticking to it. I also started putting money away little by little, saving for my future needs without neglecting my present ones.

Al-Anon has helped me become fully self-supporting by becoming financially responsible and living within my means. My monetary situation gradually improved, as did other aspects of my life. Today I live in a saner manner on many levels.

Thought for the Day

Al-Anon teaches me to take thought for the future based on the lessons of the past.

> "For Al-Anon, prudence is a middle ground, a channel between fear on the one hand and recklessness on the other."

Al-Anon/Alateen Service Manual, p. 191

Negative thinking is a destructive force, but for me it's a way of life. When I feel tired, sick, bored, or stressed, I tend to focus on what's wrong. Sometimes I'm unhappy with myself or with others. Sometimes I don't like my circumstances. Whether I complain aloud or suffer in silence, a negative attitude invites self-pity and discontent. With the help of Al-Anon, I've learned that I can overcome this dreadful force. Regardless of how discouraged I may feel, I can always find *something* for which to be thankful today.

I have a calendar displaying a nature photograph on the left and the days of the week on the right. For each day there's just enough space to write a sentence or a few short phrases. After reading my daily Al-Anon meditation, I write something I'm grateful for on the calendar. If the sun is shining, I appreciate its light and warmth. If it's raining, I remember how much moisture the dry land needs. Sometimes a new bird graces the backyard feeder, or I see a deer on the way home from work. Other days I appreciate a good meeting or the ability to work my program during a potentially tense moment at home.

Invariably I discover that I've been focusing on my problems while forgetting about the good things that have happened. Through the process of writing my good fortune on my calendar one day at a time, I've compiled a list of inspiring blessings. Now when I feel down, I read a few pages of my gratitude calendar. It reminds me that despite pain and problems, life is good.

Thought for the Day

I can start my day over at any time. Finding a reason to feel grateful is a great way to do it.

> "Today I am grateful for everything—even things that surprise me ..."

The Forum, June 1998, p. 7

Growing up in an alcoholic home, I was exposed to many unhealthy ways of dealing with life. Although I vowed that I would live differently as an adult, I found myself repeating numerous childhood behaviors. After listening to many Al-Anon stories, I came to see how, as a child, I had played a role in creating the dynamics of my family. Not knowing how to manage uncomfortable feelings, I tried to stuff them deep down inside, but they didn't go away. Instead, they led me to behave in ways that perpetuated the feelings.

My life began to change as I attended meetings and applied the first three Steps. I still felt perplexed, however, about how to find the roots of these destructive behaviors. Therefore I decided to practice "First Things First" with my Fourth Step. I did a thorough written inventory of my *childhood* guilt, shame, resentments, and fears as well as the behaviors that went with them. Then, as I released the burden of these repressed feelings through working Steps Five through Nine, I was better able to do a similar inventory of my adult years. Now I more clearly understand the origins of the behavior that I need to change.

Thought for the Day

How can I apply "First Things First" to clarify a confounding task today?

"'First Things First' helps us make more workable choices and to live with the choices we make."

How Al-Anon Works for Families & Friends of Alcoholics, p. 69

At one of my Al-Anon meetings, I heard an interesting way to categorize the Twelve Steps into four groups—giving up, owning up, making up, and keeping up. Steps One through Three are about giving up. I give up the illusion that I can control the alcoholic, that I am sane, and that I can manage my life alone.

Steps Four through Six are about owning up. In these Steps I seek the truth about my strengths and my weaknesses. I admit those truths to God, to myself, and to another human being and then I become entirely ready for God to remove my shortcomings.

Steps Seven through Nine are about making up. I look at my broken relationships with God, with myself, and with others, and I strive to see my part in how these unions became damaged. I ask my Higher Power what I can do to make amends, and to make up for what harm I've done in the past.

Steps Ten through Twelve are about keeping up. I don't try to keep up with others; I keep up with myself and my growth in the program. Continuing to take personal inventory helps keep my slate clean. Through prayer and meditation, I keep in line with God's will for me. Carrying the message keeps me grateful and focused, and practicing the Al-Anon principles in all my affairs keeps me coming back.

If I feel overwhelmed by the hard work, I remind myself I really need to do four things to continue recovering—give up, own up, make up, and keep up. This way I can "Keep It Simple."

Thought for the Day

Sometimes the "It" in "Keep It Simple" can be the program itself.

> "To get a good, firm hold on the Al-Anon idea . . . 'keep it simple!'"

One Day at a Time in Al-Anon, p. 143

I was about one year into my Al-Anon recovery and still feeling overwhelmed with life when I had the following dream . . .

I was on a beautiful beach getting ready to go surfing on some of the most ferocious waves I'd ever seen. I swam into the rolling waves. My surfboard caught and crested a large wave, and I rode it into the shallow surf at the edge of the beach. My Higher Power was waiting there and waded out into the water to meet me. Together we laughed, splashed, and played among the shallow breakers. He didn't say anything, but looked intently at me with loving eyes. His penetrating gaze knew my heart and my struggles.

This dream revealed to me the following analogy to use when I felt overwhelmed by life . . .

The ocean is life. The waves are situations happening in my life. The surfboard is all the Al-Anon slogans, on which I can ride to overcome times of despair, mistrust, fear, and anxiety. The slogans are supplied by my Higher Power to help me break the cycle of the negative attitudes I learned in my alcoholic family. With them I can "surf" over the high waves of destructive attitudes onto the beach of healthier thinking.

Now it seems to me that whenever I repeat an Al-Anon slogan, the simple act of saying it out loud breaks the enslaving grip of damaging thoughts. The waves of life no longer overwhelm me so easily. Thanks to Al-Anon, my feelings no longer claim such strong ownership over my being.

Thought for the Day

What slogans could I use today to glide over the "waves" in my life?

> ". . . I'll stick to the slogans…when they're put into action,
> they have the power to change my life."
>
> *Alateen—a day at a time*, p. 7

The slogan "Let Go and Let God," has been a great aid to me in finding the peace and serenity of detachment. When I first came to Al-Anon, I cared too much and in the wrong way. I obsessed about my alcoholic mother's drinking and tried to find ways to make her stop. As I kept attending meetings, I learned that when I obsessed, I hurt myself. I drove myself to madness— insane thoughts and ideas—by trying to fix or control that over which I had no power.

Later I went in the other direction, the direction of not caring at all. However, when I became careless and indifferent, I left myself open to allow the cunning and baffling disease of alcoholism to outsmart me. I reacted to and played into the alcoholic's manipulation. My emotions became a tangled web over which the alcoholic had control. Again I ended up hurting myself.

To truly detach with love, I practice "Let Go and Let God." I give up trying to control the alcoholic and instead increase my efforts to keep my focus on myself without falling prey to alcoholic games. When I let go and let God, I'm more apt to find a place of compassion between obsession and indifference, where the serenity of ordered thoughts and emotions lies. With God's help, the hope of a happy medium can become reality.

Thought for the Day
When I let go and let God work in my life, the pendulum that swings between the black-and-white of obsession and indifference finds balance in the peaceful colors of serenity.

> "This slogan gives us permission to replace stress, worry, and suffering with serenity and faith."
> *How Al-Anon Works for Families & Friends of Alcoholics*, p. 76

I developed a distorted sense of responsibility while growing up. Al-Anon helped me see that I am responsible only for myself. This lesson became clear when I became group representative for my home meeting.

I thought that as group representative I always had to open the meeting place and set up the chairs, coffee, and literature. As controlling as I was, taking on responsibility came naturally.

It was rare for anyone else to take the key and open the meeting place. Soon I developed resentment about all the work I was doing. After listening to my complaints, someone suggested I have my own key made and leave the group key for someone else. This way I could close up, but I wasn't obligated to open up for the next meeting.

I decided to test this idea. I asked for and received permission to copy the key. One night when no one had taken the extra key, the group sat outside in the blustery January wind. The next week they blamed me. I calmly told this isn't *my* group, it's *our* group. According to Tradition Two, no one person should be the group authority. I wanted everyone to have the opportunity to grow.

Today our group is much healthier, and so am I. I now trust that a Higher Power is the ultimate group authority and that some groups may have to "hit bottom" before they can flourish. It's not my job to rescue my group any more than it is to save the alcoholic. I need only do my part.

Thought for the Day

Before anyone else can pick up the ball, I need to be willing to drop it.

> "Part of extending a hand is eventually letting go and noticing that, when my job is done, there are more hands willing and able to carry on."

When I Got Busy, I Got Better, p. 6

I'm not accountable for being born into an alcoholic environment where I couldn't clearly see my choices. As an adult, however, it is now my responsibility to deal with the consequences of past decisions.

Many of the amends I need to make center around letting go of the past. It's time to give myself and others a second chance. The people I grew up with have changed, and so have I. Our relationships can be different if I allow them to be. This means I need to alter my attitudes and my actions. In Al-Anon I learned to take care of myself even around people with whom I have a long and painful history. I can lower my expectations of others and myself, and choose to be happy with progress rather than perfection. I can assert my needs and respect others whose desires differ from my own. If disagreement occurs, I can use my program to help me make decisions I won't regret. My eyes are open now to my choices, and I choose to act in ways that allow me to respect myself.

I know I can ask my Higher Power for help with this letting go process. I have had experiences of getting what I needed instead of what I wanted. Through these occurrences, I have felt nourished in ways I have never felt before. Gradually I've learned to trust my Higher Power. Today I choose to be gentle with myself and to love unconditionally while detaching from the past. Taking this risk is a giant step, which I know will benefit me immeasurably.

Thought for the Day

What behavior could I change today to give myself and others a second chance?

> "Through working the Al-Anon program, children of alcoholics begin to change attitudes and behaviors that no longer work into rewarding and productive ways of living."
>
> *Al-Anon Sharings from Adult Children*, p. 3

My father died of alcoholism when I was in my 20s. I knew others who had lost parents to more respectable diseases, and their grief was evident. Where was mine? Instead I felt relief, pity, a vague sense of sadness, and a great deal of anger. I also felt guilty because my emotions seemed cold and inappropriate.

I hadn't found Al-Anon yet, so I continued my old destructive patterns. I married an alcoholic. As her disease progressed, I wondered why I was reliving the same old nightmare, unaware of my self-destructive choices. A crisis finally drove me to Al-Anon, and I began learning the basics—detachment; the three Cs, which told me I couldn't cause, control, or cure alcoholism; and taking responsibility for my own serenity. I relied on my Higher Power while turning my wife over to hers. Day by day I stopped controlling, and bit by bit I mourned the loss of yet another charming human being to the ravages of alcoholism.

My wife rejected recovery, and we divorced. Eight years later the phone call came that said she had been found dead, another victim of the disease. This time I recognized my feelings and allowed them to be. I had grieved for my wife long before she died physically—just as I had done for my father during my childhood and adolescence. This time I felt neither anger nor pity. Al-Anon helped me let go and acknowledge the cleansing power of the tears I had already shed along the way. What seemed like the absence of feeling was actually a final step in a grieving process that had been going on for many years.

Thought for the Day

Many of us grieve frequent, small losses. Like recovery, death and mourning are processes.

> "In Al-Anon I found a safe place to experience grief from all the losses of my childhood."
>
> From Survival to Recovery, p. 25

One of my family's methods for coping with the insanity of alcoholism has been to declare certain members outcasts. The decision is never overt, and explanations are never made openly. The outcasts simply find themselves excluded from the family for a period of time. An important part of my Fourth Step has been to uncover my own shifting roles in this process. Over the years I sometimes have been judge, sacrificial lamb, or member of the lynch mob.

My Eighth and Ninth Step work has been a powerful force allowing me to view my family members as creatures of God whose shortcomings are beyond my power to change but whose charm and strengths are links in a chain of love. My work to view them in this light has included writing a letter to each one, expressing the gifts I see in him or her as well as some connection the two of us share. It is my hope that seeking and expressing these connections will begin to amend the damage done by participating in my family's habit of casting members out.

Thanks to these Steps, I'm finding friendships within my family based on who we are rather than on how closely we fit some artificial family code. I'm also finding ways to detach with love and respect from those who are traveling down paths I prefer to avoid. Whichever is the case, I am learning to live my relationships in the present rather than spending my energy hoping for a better past.

Thought for the Day

A statue looks different depending on the angle from which I view it. If I change the angle from which I view my family members, they might look different, too.

> "Leaving the door open to allow a relationship to redevelop slowly was a helpful approach . . ."
>
> *Paths to Recovery*, p. 98

I've heard that we don't necessarily gravitate toward what is good for us; we gravitate toward what feels like home. Negative thinking, so predominant in my alcoholic family, is so familiar to me it often feels safe, comfortable, and natural. I know my thinking can get me into trouble faster than anything else. If I'm not careful, problems become exaggerated and I end up projecting my current circumstances and trying to live in the future.

Today my attitude is everything. I can be negative, as when I lived with the alcoholic, or I can be positive. I'm not always good at making choices, but now I know they are mine to make. Choices that are always good for me include getting to a meeting, reading Conference Approved Literature, and calling someone in the program. Doing these things helps me adjust my attitude.

I want to think positively about myself, my community, and the world around me. Today I know I don't have to be anywhere but in the present moment. I also know that my Higher Power is always there for me and that nothing is bad unless I make it so. I don't always know the answers to my dilemmas, and that's all right. All I need to do is decide whether I want to feel good and loving or just plain miserable. Thanks to what I am learning in the program, day by day, one day at a time, I more often choose the positive instead of the negative.

Thought for the Day

Life is as good as I think it to be.

> "The program can open up some new doors in my mind
> if I let it."

Alateen—a day at a time, p. 221

When I came into Al-Anon, I didn't know how to meditate. I thought meditation and prayer were crutches for people who couldn't stand on their own two feet. My sponsor, bless her heart, has since asked me what is wrong with crutches. Sometimes we need assistance.

Well, I decided to open my mind. Now when I think about meditation, I think about my dog. My husband and I take her along on our bike ride almost every night. She runs in front of us in the park, and every so often—especially when she gets to a fork in the path—she stops and looks back at us. She seems to be checking to see if we are still with her and asking in which direction we want her to head.

That's what meditation is for me today—little moments in my day when I can check to make sure that my Higher Power is still with me and ask for direction as I bound off down the road on my journey through life.

Thought for the Day

Even if it seems trite or foolish at first, today I will practice one program tool that I may have previously disregarded and keep an open mind to the results.

> "Prayer is asking our Higher Power for guidance and direction in our lives. Meditation is listening for a reply."
>
> *Alateen—a day at a time*, p. 102

I was around a lot of anger this weekend. Some of it belonged to the alcoholics in my life, and some of it belonged to me as I came to grips with my powerlessness over people, places, and things.

By applying the Serenity Prayer to the various situations that occurred, I was reminded that my anger can be an attempt to change someone or something because *I* don't want to change. Being willing to change—to acknowledge my anger, identify its source, look at my part of it, and express it lovingly—is a big part of my Fourth and Tenth Steps. I gain self-worth when I change the things I can and accept responsibility for my reactions rather than blaming or shaming another.

I have choices. I can stay in my anger, or I can use it as a signal that I need to change. I trust my Higher Power to show me what I need to do so I can experience the self-esteem that comes from accepting my emotional responsibilities.

Thought for the Day

The how, what, when, and why of expressing my feelings is one major part of life over which I *do* have control.

"The Al-Anon program encourages me to acknowledge my feelings and to be responsible for how I express them."

Courage to Change, p. 193

I put my Fourth Step off for years because I couldn't seem to find a method that worked for me. I didn't want to bring to the process the attitude of getting rid of or cutting out a part of myself. After all, I was striving for wholeness, and I couldn't get there by throwing parts of myself in the trash. Then at my home meeting, someone shared that his character defects had actually been protective at some point in his life. I liked this idea and tried looking at a few of my flaws through the lens of gratitude.

First, I chose a character defect particularly bothersome to me. As I began to grasp the degree of its presence in my life, I looked for specific behavioral examples of that defect. Then I searched my past to see how this character defect had helped me survive the pain and chaos of growing up in an alcoholic home. Listing the benefits of the defect made it easier to see why it had become such a big part of me. It also helped me see how the flaw was just a positive attribute run amok.

By looking at my shortcomings in this way, I saw how damaging they had become now that they were no longer necessary for self-protection. Now every time I take another inventory, I discover a previously unknown survival tactic. As I examine the role this unneeded characteristic plays in my life, it loses its power to dominate me. Then I am free to choose from a veritable treasure-trove of Al-Anon principles with which to heal and replace the old defect.

Thought for the Day

All of my personality traits are valuable, even if some of them have worn out their welcome.

"I am *already* okay—defects and all."

The Forum, June 1999, p. 30

Al-Anon tells me today I have choices. Sometimes that fact makes my life a little more confusing, even at my precious meetings. For instance, when I see the Traditions being ignored at our group, I often hesitate to say anything, especially if no one else brings attention to it. After all, I am working very hard to give up control, and no one ever appointed me to the "Al-Anon Police Squad."

At the same time, I also work hard at speaking up. In the alcoholic family of my youth, I didn't dare express myself for realistic fear of the consequences. Haven't I finally found a new, safe family where I am free to share what's in my mind and heart?

In Al-Anon I've heard that if I am aware, I am responsible. My understanding of our Twelve Traditions requires me to take responsibility by speaking up when I see them being ignored or misused. Then I trust the group to find an answer to the problem. We have but one authority, a loving Higher Power as expressed through our group conscience, of which mine is only one voice.

Thought for the Day

If I am willing to call attention to a problem and equally willing to trust the group conscience with a solution, then it is not control that guides my words but rather my Higher Power's will.

> "The inclusion and consideration of every member's opinion in our fellowship of democracy fosters our unity."

Paths to Recovery, p. 280

When I first came to Al-Anon, the meetings seemed strange; they were so orderly and peaceful. I was more accustomed to being in chaotic environments where everyone shouted, talked at the same time, and criticized everything they heard. Hence I didn't speak up at meetings for fear of being ridiculed, shunned, or criticized. After coming for a while, I became more comfortable because many aspects of Al-Anon's meeting structure seem designed to encourage and support self-expression.

Some aspects are about the right to be heard. For example, when members limit their sharing to the topic, everyone gets a chance to speak. Refraining from advice-giving or criticizing creates an accepting and respectful environment in which each member is truly heard and valued. Concept Five assures that differing opinions are welcomed and considered useful.

Other aspects are about the responsibility to speak up. Tradition Two says a Higher Power, as expressed through the group conscience, governs the group. Concept One says that the ultimate responsibility for Al-Anon's welfare belongs to the groups. Concept Four suggests participation as the key to harmony.

Accordingly as a group member, I am part of the group conscience. Because the welfare of Al-Anon lies in the voice of each member and participation is the key to harmony, I'm responsible for sharing my informed opinion to ensure that welfare. Since minority opinion is guarded carefully, I don't have to fear the consequences of expressing a different viewpoint. In Al-Anon my thoughts and feelings are both invited and protected.

Thought for the Day

Do I exercise my right to be heard and my responsibility to speak as part of my group's conscience? Am I comfortable stating my views?

"In Al-Anon I'm learning that it is safe to be myself."

Courage to Change, p. 111

To me compassion requires patience. Compassion is what I can choose to feel toward myself and others after my patience has been tested to the limits and I'm exhausted. It takes a great deal of effort for me to extend compassion to certain people. To do so sometimes requires me to look beyond my anger and exchange my fits of rage for acts of kindness. It means letting go of resentments resulting from unrealistic expectations. It requires setting aside minor annoyances by asking myself, "How important is it?" Compassion is about accepting people, including myself, as they are and loving them still.

A recent event underscored the importance of compassion in my life. A former colleague died as the result of a car accident. One moment she was full of life; the next moment she was gone. This helped me realize that each and every moment is precious. Life is both priceless and unpredictable; I don't know how long it will last. I don't want to waste a minute of it on self-pity, worry, guilt, resentment, anger, or any character defect that may stand in the way of becoming the kind of person I want to be. I don't want to leave, or be left with, a long trail of regrets. I want to have as many good memories as possible. Compassion can help me create those memories. Patience can help me create compassion.

Thought for the Day

Patience in my recovery will lead me to compassion. How can I practice patience in my life today?

> "Compassion and understanding on my part can have the power to heal . . ."
>
> *One Day at a Time in Al-Anon*, p. 24

The greatest gift I've received from Al-Anon is the experience of feeling safe. So many elements provide me with the sense of protection I craved but never received from my alcoholic family.

Growing up with alcoholic parents, I felt as if we were *all* kids. When I came home from school, my mom would often be passed out on the couch. My dad would come home drunk, wake my mom up, and start fighting. I usually took care of the house and made sure my younger brothers did their homework. In a tiny corner of my heart always lurked the fear that something bad would happen.

Al-Anon has been such a different experience. Although I don't have "parents" in Al-Anon, I receive so much one associates with them—consistency, structure, and steadfastness. No matter where I attend a meeting, the comforting structure of the opening, sharing, and closing is the same. When I feel afraid of making a wrong choice, I know Steps Eight and Nine will help me make amends and clean my slate. The Steps provide me with guidance, and the Traditions and Concepts of Service ensure that those Steps, as well as the other elements of the program, will not sway easily. These Three Legacies stand strong for me to lean upon and count on. Then there are the hugs and encouragement I get from other members. They shower me with the acceptance and affection for which I've always yearned. Finally there's that special connection between my sponsor and me, which provides me with the intimacy that feeds my soul.

Thought for the Day

Indeed, there is safety in numbers, especially when those numbers are at an Al-Anon meeting!

> "After having suffered alone with the effects of this brutal disease, the Al-Anon fellowship is an unexpectedly rich and nourishing source of compassion and support."
> *How Al-Anon Works for Families & Friends of Alcoholics*, p. 11

I love the slogans, particularly the ones that come in two parts, such as "Let Go and Let God." However, I struggle with working the second half of that one. It is easy for me to concentrate only on the first part. When the alcoholic in my life left our home, I found it simple to let go. I let go of meetings, literature, and many of my Al-Anon contacts. I also let go of my mental, physical, and spiritual health. The part of me still harboring resentment toward the alcoholic gave way to guilt for enjoying the fact that he was gone from my house. I thought if I were free of the alcoholic, then I would be free of the disease. In the process I lost my conscious contact with my Higher Power. I gained weight, stopped exercising, and lost interest in my home and family. I started isolating, and I sank into a depression.

Finally things got so bad I went back to Al-Anon. I realized that I didn't suffer only from symptoms of the alcoholic's disease; I had my own disease, too! Just because he was gone didn't mean I was going to miraculously get better. Now I know the second part of the slogan, too. "Let God" balances the first part and keeps me from proceeding with my own will. For the letting go part to work, I keep God in my life by attending meetings, reading literature, calling other members, and doing service. My Higher Power helps me when I help myself.

Thought for the Day

If I'm going to let it go, then I need to give it to a Power greater than myself.

> "Those who simply turn their backs on their problems are not 'letting go and letting God'—they are abandoning their commitment to act on God's inspiration and guidance."
>
> *One Day at a Time in Al-Anon*, p. 163

I developed a lot of confusion about relationships and intimacy while growing up in my alcoholic family. I yearned for closeness yet was terrified when I was in any sort of relationship.

My father wasn't able to give me the experience of love and intimacy I needed. I used to resent this until I came to Al-Anon. Through working the Steps and letting them work on me, I came to understand that my father didn't give me the love I needed because he didn't have it to give. He, too, struggled with intimacy.

Today I am learning how to have the ultimate close relationship—with myself. Until I am intimate with myself and treat myself with compassion, kindness, trust, acceptance, and love, I can't be the spouse, friend, son, or father I want to be.

Intimacy involves sharing my deepest fears and secrets while trusting the other person will accept them. This behavior feels risky to me. I grew up trusting no one, but I know if I keep doing what I've always done, I'll get what I've always gotten. I want to change.

Thought for the Day

Sharing my intimate self in a safe Al-Anon environment is a risk I'm willing to take.

> ". . . I learned to be intimate with, and accepting of, myself."
> *How Al-Anon Works for Families & Friends of Alcoholics*, p. 295

Before Al-Anon I despised and feared God. I detested organized religion. I believed if I didn't give generously, I would pay horribly for not doing so. I was convinced I was bad. I magnified every reprimand and diminished every compliment. I used to feel angry with God for making me so wrong, so misshapen, so shy, so sexually charged, and so fearful of the objects of my cravings.

Then I came to Al-Anon. I attended meetings, got a sponsor, read Conference Approved Literature, applied the Steps and Traditions, and volunteered for service positions. I took risks. I shared my thoughts and feelings at meetings and in between. I found a Higher Power like nothing I had ever encountered in any organized religion despite everything promised by them.

I found I could express my anger to my Higher Power. I know I cannot hurt Him or Her or It, and it's a relief to scream my anger and pain into a sunset or at the stars. Trusting my Higher Power helps me not to obsess about outcomes and not to be bitterly disappointed when things don't turn out my way. By turning things over to my Higher Power, I can let go of my attachments and feel more at peace with myself, my life, and my world.

Thought for the Day

Whenever I go to an Al-Anon meeting, I place myself in an environment conducive to changing my attitudes. In this way, my world is transformed.

"In the group we meet people like us who are coping with many of the same problems and finding creative solutions we had not considered or attitudes that make the similar situations in their lives more tolerable."

Paths to Recovery, p. 19

Growing up in an alcoholic home gave me ample preparation to become a perfectionist. Almost nothing I did as a youth was ever right. Inside I felt rage at never meeting my parents' impossible expectations. I promised myself I would do things differently. By the time I reached my thirties, however, I could hear my parents' critical voices speaking through me. I knew I was using the same words spoken to me.

When I finally came into Al-Anon and heard "Live and Let Live," it all began to make sense. If I worked at it, I could change what I had learned in childhood and become a more pleasant person. This slogan sounds easy, but working it was a different matter. I started backwards with ". . . Let Live," which was exceedingly difficult. I had to keep out of other people's business and let them make their own decisions. I couldn't judge whether what they had decided was right, by my standards.

Finally I caught up with "Live . . ." How do I just live? What is life if I am not constantly involved in others' affairs? I felt lost. Then I remembered a suggestion from my meetings, "take care of yourself," and I had a glimmer of understanding.

I already have the individual components of a life—a body, a mind, and a soul. All I need to do to make them work is to nourish them and take care of them. What a simple concept. If I keep my focus on myself and take care of the things I need to be serene and happy, I can have a real life of my own!

Thought for the Day

Whose body, mind, and soul am I nourishing today?

> "If I stay out of others' affairs and become more aware of my own, I have a good chance of finding some serenity."
>
> *Courage to Change,* p. 234

I've heard some people condense the activities of spiritual life into these words: quiet the mind; open the heart. In encouraging myself to expand my understanding of prayer and meditation, I like to recall those suggestions. I think of anything that quiets the mind as meditation and anything that opens the heart as prayer.

My sense of the conscious contact with a Higher Power described in Step Eleven has changed over time. Sometimes my contact seems to come from a place many call intuition, with which I make choices based on a strong feeling or hunch. Sometimes my contact comes from a source that doesn't necessarily feel rational, explainable, or contained by thoughts and words. Many times the seemingly random suggestions and answers that come to me from my Higher Power don't have an obvious source at all. As I grow in Al-Anon, my need to isolate and categorize my experiences of conscious contact with the God of my understanding begins to fall away. I don't need to worry where our contact will come from or in what form it will arrive. I only need to open my mind and heart through meditation and prayer and then "Let Go and Let God."

Thought for the Day

The possibility of conscious contact with a Higher Power is always present, even if the form in which it comes doesn't seem to make sense.

"I think I've developed an understanding of God that I don't fully understand."

As We Understood . . ., p. 227

I always prided myself on being in control of my faculties. So it came as quite a shock when I realized that I used the buzz of busyness the same way my alcoholic relatives used the buzz of alcohol—to anesthetize myself and to isolate. I was always filling every minute with the noise of "important" activity. My life was one big, busy evasion.

I wasn't exactly a workaholic, but at various times I was a learn-aholic and an achieve-aholic, all the while never focusing on my relationships with my Higher Power, with others, and with myself. Fortunately an Al-Anon friend reminded me that who I am, not what I do, makes me worthwhile. Now I'm keeping the focus on me—my thoughts, feelings, motives, and attitudes. When I keep these parts of myself on track, my activity becomes a reflection of, rather than a running away from, a healthy self. Today I can quiet myself to listen for God's whispers and hear my heart's own spontaneous response.

Thought for the Day

Today I will be available to my Higher Power. Through prayer and meditation I will no longer choose obsessive activity.

> "God was calling. The only problem was, he was getting a busy signal."
>
> Having Had a Spiritual Awakening . . ., p. 35

Before I came to Al-Anon, I felt angry and resentful toward my alcoholic mother. I resented her for being unable to give me the things I needed, such as unconditional love and financial support. I forgot about the good things she instilled in me, such as open-mindedness and respect for my fellow human beings.

In Al-Anon I learned that forgiveness is for me. I realized how much of my energy was drained by maintaining my resentment and by reminding myself that I was angry. Fortunately the people in Al-Anon didn't just *talk* about the importance of forgiveness. They offered me an actual plan for forgiveness called the Twelve Steps so that I could experience its value for myself. First, I had to forgive myself, which I accomplished mainly through Steps Four and Five. The disease of alcoholism had filled me with such shame and self-hatred that I perceived myself in a distorted fashion. A searching and fearless moral inventory helped me see myself in a balanced way. This humble and realistic view of my gifts and shortcomings helped me forgive myself and in turn forgive others, especially my mother. I've come to believe that we all do the best we can at any given moment. If my mom had known better back then, she would have done better.

Since then I've been amazed at how my mental and physical energies have been freed. Now I feel more available to develop new friendships, cultivate a new hobby, or even go back to school. No longer frozen in the icy grip of resentment, my spirit can follow wherever my Higher Power leads.

Thought for the Day

Have I ever tried to tally the time I take every day to feed resentful thoughts and feelings? What else could I be doing with that energy?

"I will not allow old resentments to drag me down any longer."

Courage to Change, p. 178

HALT. Don't get too hungry, angry, lonely, or tired. I use this reminder to help me set healthy limits for myself, which I never learned as a child of an alcoholic. In the past, I often believed I should be able to go for days without food or sleep. I also tested the limits of my ability to handle enormous doses of stress and isolation without tending to my own emotional needs.

Al-Anon has taught me a gentler, simpler way of caring for myself. I find it of great benefit to have a brief list of the most basic areas in which I neglect my own well-being: nourishment, emotional wellness, fellowship, and physical rest. First, is my stomach rumbling? Then I need to stop what I'm doing and eat some food. Am I too angry about the trivial details of my life? If so I can take a break and punch a pillow or engage in some physical exercise. Am I lonely? I could go to a meeting or call my sponsor. Finally, am I so tired that I can't keep my eyes open? Then it's time to lie down for a nap or a good night's sleep.

Thought for the Day

When I feel stressed, I'll stop to check whether my basic needs are being met.

> "We can watch for the need to HALT and give ourselves special attention when we are feeling **H**ungry or **A**ngry or **L**onely or **T**ired."

> *Courage to Be Me*, p. 139

I always used sarcastic humor to protect myself from the inevitable alcoholic attacks in my home. I became a master at the art of bludgeoning people with bitter words and shredding them with scorn. I thought this hid my pain and showed people they couldn't hurt me. I also used humor as a manipulative tool to get people to like me. My witty comments were carefully timed. My sense of humor wasn't spontaneous or appropriate. I used it to please people. When no one was around to please, however, I was miserable and self-loathing.

In Al-Anon I learned that if I wanted serenity, I had to examine certain aspects of myself and undertake certain actions. To do this I used the three A's—awareness, acceptance, and action. First, I became aware that my humor, when used as a defense weapon, is a character defect that contributes to the unmanageability of my life. Next, I accepted that my sarcastic nature wasn't my true nature after all; it was a defense I developed to survive my alcoholic environment. Lastly, I took action by asking God to remove this shortcoming and to reveal my part in allowing that to happen.

Today my sense of humor is a natural reflection of who I am. I experience the world through smiles and laughter rather than through bitter smirks. I share joy with others rather than seek company for my misery. I help others heal rather than attack them. I allow my sense of humor to unfold naturally, just the way it was meant, and I watch the wonderful results as my Higher Power works through me toward a higher good.

Thought for the Day

Are there motives in my humor other than expressing fun?

"I will realize that the wounds made by sarcasm are slow to heal, and may defer the longed-for improvement in my life."

One Day at a Time in Al-Anon, p. 114

For me the priceless gift of Al-Anon has been freedom from worry. I've come to believe that my Higher Power is managing my life and that everything occurs for a reason. At any given moment, I am the sum total of all that has gone before, both painful and pleasurable, so everything I've experienced has value.

When I surrendered myself to God's care in Step Three, I also surrendered the notion that things would go my way. It took me a long time to come to terms with this, but I did it by slowly turning situations over and by trusting my Higher Power with the outcomes. Now I can look back and see how everything fit together. Certain events had to occur before changes could be made. As a result my life eventually improved beyond my wildest dreams. If the situations had gone my way, I would not be enjoying the things that bring me pleasure today—improved relationships, a better job, and more self-esteem. The list continues.

Today it doesn't take me as long to "Let Go and Let God" because now I know a shortcut. I can go straight to my Higher Power in prayer and meditation and bypass the worrying. He's aware and waiting for me to ask for help. He helps me sort my worries about the past and future from the realities of today, which breaks my concerns down to manageable size. Then I apply the Serenity Prayer by changing the things I can and letting go of the rest. Today I can live serenely in the present knowing my Higher Power is solving all my problems and concerns in His perfect time.

Thought for the Day

Worry is like a rocking chair. It gives me something to do, but it gets me nowhere.

"...I can let go of a problem and let God help me with it."

Courage to Be Me, p. 66

Taking part in a group conscience decision can arouse some of my most difficult character defects. Sometimes I would rather deny that a decision needs to be made than to tolerate the discomfort that comes with participating in the decision-making processes. I'd prefer to shut down and say nothing. For example, when my home group had to move because the church where we met expanded their day care services, I felt anxious. I don't like change, so I really had to work the first three Steps and practice "Let Go and Let God."

While I was growing up, my alcoholic father acted like a dictator, making decisions for everyone in the family without consulting anyone. On the other hand, my mother was subservient and rarely contested my father. I grew up seeing the extremes of decision-making—dominance and lack of participation. Before Al-Anon I had never experienced being part of a group working in unity to make collective decisions in a respectful manner, as suggested by Tradition One and Concept Four. Because I hadn't learned how to find my own balance between domination and deference, I usually kept quiet.

As a result, when I state my position, it's hard to determine if I'm being meek or overbearing. My sponsor taught me that I could achieve balance by doing three things: make sure my audience can hear me, state my position, and then let go and let God. If I speak up again about the same thing, I am probably trying to impose my will on the group.

Thought for the Day

Being part of a unified group feels strange if I'm not used to it. Working my program in such situations helps me feel more comfortable and confident.

> "A fight always started when I expressed my opinion at home. I always gave in to keep the peace. In Al-Anon I learned a different way."
>
> *Paths to Recovery,* p. 140

My father, who was a violent drunk, died of alcoholism when I was 18 years old. For many years I thought of him as bad, evil, and weak. I judged him and felt confident I was correct in my harsh assessment of his behavior. I said in meetings that I understood alcoholism as a disease, yet I continued to condemn my father for willfully mistreating his family.

Recently I gained a new understanding. I found out his father, who died before I was born, had also been a violent alcoholic. I am now flooded with new feelings for my father—compassion, understanding, and kinship. Before this awareness I always perceived my father as one of "Them," the Perpetrator, the Problem. It was hard to think of him as one of us. I can never know what shaped him into the person he became, yet I am grateful to Al-Anon, where I learned to replace condemnation with compassion.

Thought for the Day

I feel compassion when I realize that my parents may have endured an upbringing similar to mine.

> "I take into account how affected I am by my past when I meet people who seem difficult, and I try to give them a break."
>
> *From Survival to Recovery*, p. 171

Miracles happen in Al-Anon, but they don't happen by magic. Individual participation, "the key to harmony" according to Concept Four, is the behavior that makes the miracles happen. The God of my understanding wants me for my availability as well as for my abilities. When I become willing to act on faith, God helps me create miracles for myself and assist others in creating their own.

I was in Al-Anon for a while before I started to think of doing service. I knew it would help me, as so many other members had attested, but my biggest fear was that I wouldn't do my job perfectly. "Easy Does It," my sponsor told me, "Keep It Simple." With her support, I began slowly. I chaired meetings, greeted newcomers, and answered the district telephone line. These simple acts connected me with the Al-Anon program and the recovery to be found there.

After a few months, I was ready for more. I began attending district and area meetings with my sponsor. We would have lunch afterwards, and these Saturdays have become our special time together. When my home meeting needed a group representative, I volunteered. Recently I was asked to serve as the area literature coordinator.

Along this path I discovered that the secret to successful service is to perform it according to the suggestions set forth in our Twelve Traditions and Twelve Concepts of Service. There's no guesswork when I read the *Al-Anon/Alateen Service Manual*. The biggest gift of service is that it helps me, too. Giving the program away is an affirmation that I have some program to give.

Thought for the Day

God doesn't call the qualified. God qualifies those who are called. Am I listening?

> "Al-Anon believes that our benefits are measured by our willingness to share them with others. For we know we can never give as much as we receive."
>
> *Al-Anon/Alateen Service Manual,* p. 19

I didn't feel particularly safe drawing attention to myself in my family. Sometimes I didn't think I even had permission to exist. As a result most of my energy was directed toward staying out of the way. The "elephant in the living room," my father's alcoholism, took a lot of care and feeding. This left me feeling leery of spontaneous expression. It was best for me to behave in a predictable and controlled way.

My version of a Higher Power does not insist on my being happy all the time. It enjoys whatever expression I send Its way. That includes joy as well as sorrow, delight as well as frustration, excitement as well as boredom. A fully-developed relationship with my Higher Power is one in which I share all of me, not just the parts that feel troubled or in need.

Thanks to Al-Anon, while I may appear to be quite solemn, my emotional life now bubbles with enthusiasm, excitement, and joy. By focusing on myself and placing my life in the protection and guidance of my Higher Power, I've made progress toward a life in which I can feel playfulness and delight.

Thought for the Day

I welcome the help of a Higher Power in meeting the challenge of experiencing the entire gamut of human emotions.

> "I am profoundly grateful for laughter and light spirits—and also for anger and fear, because all of these feelings are part of what makes me whole."
>
> *Courage to Change*, p. 238

One of the greatest gifts I have received in Al-Anon has been
the privilege of being a sponsor. I originally came into the program because of my wife's alcoholism. Most of my recovery work
at that time involved learning how to live with her drinking and
eventually with her sobriety. Although I had also grown up with
drinking and all the difficulties that come with it, it wasn't until
I started sponsoring a couple of men who were adult children of
alcoholic parents that I started to realize the insidious effects of
my past alcoholic environment on my present life.

These men didn't currently live with alcoholics, but their
entire perception of life had been distorted by the actions and
reactions of alcoholic parents and their non-drinking spouses.
As I worked the Steps with my sponsees, I saw more clearly the
effects of the disease on my own behavior. As I showed these
grown men how to do simple things like taking care of themselves by eating right, resting well, and establishing clear and
appropriate boundaries, I began to acknowledge where I had
been and how far I had come. I felt inspired to deepen my commitment to recovery.

By working the Twelve Steps with these men, I have developed a deeper trust in the program's power to help me and others
recover from the profound effects of alcoholism. It is often easier
for me to see the program working in others than in myself, yet I
know that when I apply the tools of Al-Anon, I feel my life has
meaning and purpose. Sponsoring others has been a wonderful
and valuable part of my healing process.

Thought for the Day

The process of sponsoring others serves as a powerful affirmation
of how much I've grown.

"How can I even begin to explain the miracle of sponsorship in my life?"

Courage to Be Me, p. 270

Before I came into Al-Anon, my attitudes were based on fear. I cast all my doubts and feelings of unworthiness onto other people. I set myself up as a victim. I always acted upon my anxiety, and I was forever reacting. Most times my reactions came in the form of blaming, running, or freezing. When I blamed others, I didn't have to feel my deep sense of shame. I ran because facing my fear and hurt seemed too difficult. I froze because frozen hearts cannot feel pain.

Al-Anon has given me a fresh way to view my life. I no longer choose to be a victim. Now I choose to take responsibility for my actions. I choose how I act, how I think, and how I feel about any situation that arises. I can choose fear, or I can choose love. Fear keeps me shut off and unhealed. Love opens me up and heals me. Today I choose love.

Choosing love means I stay away from physically, emotionally, or spiritually unhealthy situations. I no longer accept unacceptable behavior. I love myself and care about myself enough to walk away from hurtful people and relationships. I look at my part in situations, own my mistakes, and change my behavior. Choosing love means I accept and embrace my humanity and that of others. Then, with my Higher Power's help, I can see defects and weaknesses with compassion, which brings me release, joy, and serenity.

Thought for the Day

If I look for fear, I'll find fear. If I look for love, I'll find love. Which one do I choose to seek today?

> "The well of love refills itself. The more one gives of love, the more one has to give."
>
> *Lois Remembers*, p. 195

We are Al-Anon Family Groups.-The word "family" in our name is very important to me. The Al-Anon family extends far beyond the traditional family consisting of mother, father, grandparents, siblings, cousins, aunts, and uncles. I am so close to the members of my Al-Anon family that I consider their family mine, and mine theirs. This includes members of Alateen, AA, and even those who never find the gift of recovery from this family disease.

Today my Al-Anon relatives and I lost a special member of our spiritual family. Together we traveled the rough terrain of grief, sadness, empathy, and heartache. We hugged, cried, sought solitude, prayed, and reflected. We faced fear, beseeched faith, and experienced new peace. Although this extraordinary person is no longer here in physical form, the memory of his unconditional love encourages us to seek and offer each other unconditional love in coping. Even in the midst of death we grow, we stretch toward life.

No one will ever be able to replace this generous, loving, funny man, but today my memories are full, and life goes on. I will laugh again. I will fondly remember good times. I will find new people to love and will miss them, too, when they are gone. So the cycle of life and acceptance repeats itself. Today I know that no matter what happens, nothing in this world is as strong, powerful, and all encompassing as the love and friendship I receive in my Al-Anon family.

Thought for the Day

Today I will accept the things I cannot change, as well as appreciate the life my Higher Power has so abundantly given me.

> "Al-Anon has given me everything—the desire to live again, love for my fellow man, courage to face any difficult situation, the serenity it takes to accept certain realities and hope for the future."
>
> *As We Understood . . .*, p. vi

My Al-Anon sponsor once suggested I detach from my problem and attach instead to my Higher Power. Until I practiced Step Three and turned my will and life over to God's care, detaching was more like constructing a wall of protection from fear and threat of harm. Before I seriously practiced meditation and prayer with Step Eleven, asking only for knowledge of God's will for me and the power to carry that out, detaching was an exercise in futility.

Today detachment is different for me. It's an opportunity to make a choice. I can focus on the problem, or I can attach to my Higher Power and see what is before me with fresh, new eyes and thoughts. I am learning to detach from old reactions that interfere with my serenity, old fears that feed into expectations and judgments, and the part of me that diverts me from my primary spiritual aim. I am learning to attach to the loving God I found in Al-Anon, the tools and principles of the Al-Anon program, new friends, and a sponsor who shares experience, strength, and hope with me.

Thought for the Day

My belief and reliance upon a Higher Power and the Al-Anon program help me choose to be happy. Today I choose the serenity that comes from attaching to God.

"I have made some choices that help allow me to live more sanely."

. . . *In All Our Affairs*, p. 178

Growing up around drinking, I developed an overall confusion about my feelings. My father drank, cried, and raged. My mother didn't seem to feel much of anything. She rarely cried, and I don't remember her being very affectionate. Given this childhood environment, how does anyone, particularly a man, learn how to deal with emotions? I dealt with them by hiding, denying, and stuffing them down deep. Then they would come out in inappropriate ways at inappropriate times.

Fortunately I found Al-Anon. I started to work the program and found through the literature and through others' sharing that living without feelings was cheating myself of a full life. I learned that happiness was as much a part of life as sorrow and that denying pain only stunted joy. I started to let my feelings out, and did *that* ever hurt at first! It was as though I had placed a lifetime of feelings in unlabeled cans on a shelf, and I didn't know what I was going to get when I opened them. With the aid of the Al-Anon tools, my sponsor, and some professional help, I was finally able to find healthy ways to express my emotions. I now believe that my greatest recovery gift has been the healing I began when I recognized the trauma of denying my feelings.

Thought for the Day

We humans are a package deal. When I shy away from pain and sorrow, I risk shutting out joy and happiness.

> "...I recover from the inside out. I don't have to hide behind a mask anymore because everyone can see right through me anyway...After playing 'The Great Cover-up' for so long, it feels good to let the real me out."
>
> *Alateen—a day at a time*, p. 305

In Al-Anon I learned to choose wiser responses to my father's drinking. Even then my relationship with my parents was still poor. My best efforts to be noticed, listened to, appreciated, and loved were failing. Then, through a series of coincidences, I was reminded of Tradition Twelve and its suggestion to place principles above personalities. I decided to let it begin with me and to focus on what I could give instead of on what I could get. I asked my Higher Power to help me give my parents the attention, appreciation, and love I so desperately wanted them to give me. I asked God to help me place this principle above my strong-willed personality, which was bent in the opposite direction.

The next time I visited my parents' home, I listened to them. I gave them my undivided attention instead of seeking their interest in me and my life. I looked for things to appreciate about them, such as my father's great timing when telling a joke or my mother's eye for detail when relating an anecdote. I loved them.

In the light of my changed attitude, their stories seemed interesting and even funny! The results of my new behavior thrilled me. As I focused my actions on a loving principle, my character defect of craving attention from people who couldn't give it was removed. To me this is a way of working the Steps. I continue to give freely and to receive the relief of a shortcoming removed.

Thought for the Day

Placing principles above personalities guides me to be someone I'd like to have in my own life.

> "Anonymity is the spiritual foundation of all our Traditions,
> ever reminding us to place principles above personalities."
>
> Tradition Twelve

When I expressed difficulty with the word "sanity" in Step Two, my sponsor suggested I write a list of all the insane things I had done to try to control the alcoholism with which I grew up. I didn't think the results of this task would be very revealing. After I finished, however, I looked at the list and felt as though I was looking in a mirror for the very first time. I could finally see myself as I really was, and I wasn't happy with what I saw.

After I shared my list with my sponsor, she suggested I tear it up. I did, and then we went to a meeting. The topic for the evening was acceptance and the Serenity Prayer. Tearing up my list had felt good, but I recognized that I still hadn't truly let go. As I listened to others share, one thing became clear. Much of my present insanity stemmed from my inability to accept and feel compassion for myself because of my past choices and behaviors. A smidgen of Step Two entered my heart that night. I started to believe a Power greater than myself would restore me to sanity if I would let go and put trust in my Higher Power's capabilities. The Serenity Prayer helped me realize that although I can't change my past, I can increase the degree of serenity in my life by making peace with it. The way I do this is to claim a piece of my past by writing it down, sharing it, thanking my Higher Power for its purpose, releasing it, and then trusting the arrival of peaceful acceptance.

Thought for the Day

I can't turn something over until I truly own it.

"I don't regret the past, because I am turning my painful history into today's blessings and strengths."

From Survival to Recovery, p. 88

When I first stopped trying to fix other people, I turned my attention to "curing" myself. I was in a hurry to get this healing process over. I wanted immediate recovery from the effects of growing up in a family riddled with alcoholism and from being married to an alcoholic. I looked forward to the day I would graduate from Al-Anon and get on with my life. As year two and year three passed, I was still in the program. I began to despair as the character defects I had worked so long to overcome came back to haunt me, particularly during times of stress and during periods when I didn't attend meetings.

I have severe arthritis in my joints. To cope with my condition, I have to assess my body each day and patiently respond to its needs. Some days I need a warm bath to get going in the morning. On other days I apply a medicated rub to the painful areas. Yet other days some light stretching and exercise help to loosen me up. I've accepted that my arthritis will never go away. It's a condition I manage daily with consistent, on-going care.

One day I made a connection between my medical condition and my struggle with recovery. I began to look at myself as having "arthritis of the personality," requiring patient, continuous care to keep me from "stiffening" into old habits and attitudes. This care includes attending meetings, reading Al-Anon literature, calling my sponsor, and engaging in service. Now, as long as I practice patience, recovery is a manageable and adventurous process instead of an arduously sought end point.

Thought for the Day

Al-Anon is like physical therapy for my soul, aligning my principles and behavior so that I can move joyfully through life!

"... Patience would become the foundation for my recovery."

The Forum, March 1998, p. 14

Letting go of my loved one was a hard concept for me to grasp. I was confused at first about Al-Anon's suggestions to detach, to "Let Go and Let God," and to turn my problems over to God. Wasn't I expected to solve my own and everyone else's problems, have all the answers, and support the behavior patterns, no matter how destructive? How could I keep my family together?

Al-Anon has shown me that the answer lies not in letting go of people but in letting go of my outworn, painful thinking patterns. I can replace them with honesty, openness, and willingness to change into a more positive person. It is possible for me to learn about the family disease of alcoholism. I am capable of studying and applying the Twelve Steps, Traditions, and Concepts of Service to my daily life, as well as sharing and receiving experience, strength, and hope at meetings. There is also literature to read, service to offer, phone calls to make, and anniversaries and conventions to attend. All of these help me replace worry and control with the serenity that comes from letting go and letting God take care of anything where I have no power.

For me letting go is like a tree shedding its leaves in autumn. It must let go of them to grow and produce even more beauty in the following spring and summer. Letting go of what I do not truly need—whether it be old thoughts, things, or behaviors—makes room for new growth in my life.

Thought for the Day

Just for today I will let go of an old behavior or attitude and let God guide me to a new, more positive one.

> "Turn that problem over to God, as you understand Him. Then begin to do something about your own life."
> *The Al-Anon Family Groups—Classic Edition*, p. 78

One indication of maturity is the ability to consider the opinions of others. However, somewhere along the line in my alcoholic upbringing, I developed the idea that what I believed to be true was always right. My way was *the way* to think. Such black-and-white perception didn't allow me to hear, let alone consider, different viewpoints. My intolerance was rooted in two of my main character defects—fear and insecurity. My opinions were inseparable from my self-image. If my opinions were wrong, I was wrong. If my philosophy wasn't good enough, I wasn't good enough.

Thanks to particular elements of the Al-Anon program, such as allowing members to share without receiving advice and the slogans "Listen and Learn" and "Live and Let Live," I've learned a healthier way to hear and respond to views that differ from mine. Just as feelings aren't facts, opinions aren't either. They simply reflect how an individual sees a particular issue. I don't have to decide whether another's angle of vision is right or wrong. I can listen with detachment, accept the other person's right to have an opinion, and perhaps even say, "You may be right." Such behavior gives freedom to both the speaker and the listener.

Thought for the Day

Today I'll allow others to say what they think and allow myself to think about what they say.

> "... I took another step to maturity as I continue to recover from my illness of not listening."
>
> *Forum Favorites*, Vol. 4, p. 11

One beautiful spring day I was walking in the forest. A slight breeze blew through the trees. The birds sang and fluttered. I bent down, picked up a rock, which I named loneliness, and put it in my knapsack. I walked along a little further, enjoying the wildflowers as I passed. I paused again and picked up another rock, which I called hatred for my alcoholic stepfather. As I traveled further, I picked up some more rocks—suspicion of others, isolation, fear, and uncertainty. Soon the beauty of the forest ceased to capture my attention. My knapsack was so heavy I couldn't think of anything else. The rocks weighed me down so much I felt as if I had almost lost myself beneath their weight.

Eventually I walked through the doors of Al-Anon and found the tools I needed to start emptying my gunnysack (my knapsack had grown!). Surrender in Step One helped me admit how heavy my sack had become. Hope in Step Two taught me there was Someone who could help me empty the sack—a Power greater than myself. Step Four helped me determine which rocks were mine and which ones belonged to others, and "Let Go and Let God" helped me rid my sack of the rocks that weren't mine. Living one day at a time and sharing with my sponsor helped me shrink my gunnysack back into a knapsack and find new things to put in it, such as kindness, compassion, love, and humor. Instead of weighing me down, these lift me up into the light and life of recovery.

Thought for the Day

Am I carrying unnecessary burdens? With the tools of Al-Anon I can lighten my load.

> "We know we have character defects and have some idea of the pain and difficulties they have caused us; surely it would be a relief to get rid of them."
>
> *Paths to Recovery*, p. 65

My alcoholic father sexually abused me when I was young, and I never dealt with the thoughts and feelings from that trauma. When I came into Al-Anon at age 52, my resentment and anger were deep-seated. As I painfully worked the Steps and took my Fourth Step inventory, my buried pain and anger started to surface. I shared these thoughts and feelings in my Fifth Step with my sponsor. Through this process I came to feel forgiven for the many wrongs I had committed, including judgment of my father. Gradually, as I released my long-held anguish, I started to see my father and myself in a softer light.

I had a spiritual awakening in this area as I drove to work on a beautiful April morning. When I stopped at a red light, my Higher Power brought a thought into my mind. If God could forgive me for my mistakes, then I guess I could forgive my dad for his. Warmth washed over me in waves. I felt my anger and resentment begin to fall gently and easily away from me.

This spiritual awakening transformed the relationship I was privileged to have with my father for the two years before he died. We never achieved the father-daughter closeness for which I had so longed. Instead, I grew to respect him and appreciate his good qualities, previously clouded by my view of the past. I'm proud to say that my father and I were friends when he died. Although I felt much sorrow when he died, I'm grateful that the additional pain of unresolved resentment didn't add to my burden of grief.

Thought for the Day

Self-forgiveness often clears the path to forgiving others.

> "The peace that comes with forgiveness is the serenity we learn in Al-Anon."
>
> *As We Understood . . .,* p. 62

One thing I lacked while growing up was consistency. My dad was an alcoholic, and I could never tell when he was going to get drunk or how he'd react to things. There was no pattern to his moods. I learned to keep to myself and to "walk on eggshells." My mom tried a lot of things to cope with his drinking, but there was no rhyme or reason to her remedies. In short, I didn't feel I could depend on my parents for anything.

My relationship with my sponsor has been good for me in so many ways. For the longest time, I didn't think I could depend on God any more than I could depend on my parents. My sponsor tried to emphasize that despite my doubts, my Higher Power is always by my side. Finally during a talk one afternoon, I experienced a turning point in my recovery. I had listed many fears and expressed much doubt. To appear strong and get back to my program, I told her I knew God would be there for me and would take care of me. When I finished speaking, my sponsor said only one word, "always."

Today the word "always" is a symbol for my recovery and a sort of personal slogan. It reminds me that my Higher Power is consistently available to me, waiting for my conscious contact through the prayer and meditation suggested in Step Eleven. However, I need to be consistent, too. It only works if day after day I turn my will and my life over and listen long enough to hear God's will. It's up to me.

Thought for the Day

Connecting is a two-way street. God is already waiting for me, so the next step is mine.

> "My commitment to Step Eleven includes making time to work on this relationship with my Higher Power."
>
> *As We Understood . . .*, p. 196

Introspection and meditation are healing tools, but they are not recovery in and of themselves. However, used together along with courageous action, they lead me to a deeper, more solid recovery.

I am introspective when I turn my spiritual energy inward to observe my actions, character, motives, and reactions. The ensuing awareness helps me see behavior patterns that hold me back from becoming the person I want to be. However, if I become immobilized in a continuing exercise of merely thinking, my recovery stagnates. Acceptance, the process by which my understanding travels the sometimes painful path from my brain to my heart, must naturally follow. Then I must wait for guidance to some form of action.

I find that guidance through meditation. Although meditation may lead to introspection, the two are not the same. When meditating I quiet my body and mind—my personal turmoil—and turn to my spiritual energy, listening to God's message for me. Just as prayer is my way of talking to my Higher Power, meditation is my way of listening for direction. I offer God the results of my awareness and acceptance, and I ask how to translate them into new behavior.

True recovery takes place when I step out on faith and carry out that new behavior. Then I know a small portion of me has grown. When I take action based on introspection and meditation, I push my recovery boundaries further. I know if I keep on this path, I will always keep growing.

Thought for the Day

Outward action must follow inner work for recovery to truly take root in my life.

> "As our faith in a Power greater than ourselves begins to grow, we need to become willing to act on the guidance we receive."

> *From Survival to Recovery*, p. 155

I've always had a prideful, exaggerated sense of my abilities, assuming I could do anything and knew the right answers to everyone's questions. It's probable I developed this attitude while growing up with alcoholism. Thinking of myself as the smartest, most conscientious, and most responsible one in the family was easy because my parents, struggling with the disease, let even the most basic things slide.

Carrying this attitude into my adult life, I offended many people with my opinionated, know-it-all manner. Then I came into Al-Anon, where I heard the word "humility." As I grew in my knowledge and experience of the first three Steps, I came to believe in and trust a Power greater than myself. This new relationship with a Power who knows best invited me to rethink my position in life; it also invited me to consider the concept of humbleness.

Attempting to work the program has given me some humility. Although I may know some answers to many questions, they may not be the only or the best answers. I may not truly believe someone's idea is better than mine, but I'm willing to concede that it *might* be. Their answer might be as worthy of applying as my own. When I don't know the answer, that's okay, too, because I don't need to know everything. A Power greater than myself may offer a solution, which I can consider or maybe even use. This doesn't mean that I am weak, only humble.

Thought for the Day

Humility can lead to a full, open experience of life. Am I willing to be more humble?

"... Pride often makes recovery difficult ..."

One Day at a Time in Al-Anon, p. 326

A family member recently called and left a message that she wanted to talk to me. When I heard the recording, I was immediately flooded with fear and apprehension. She's an alcoholic who doesn't drink but who still overflows with the "-isms" of the disease. Based on some previous experiences, I anticipated she would attack me about something I said or did of which I was unaware.

My first reaction was to call her right back so that I could get it over with. Despite my anxiety, I decided to meditate. Before doing so I wrote down my fear and put it in my God box. I reminded myself of Steps One through Three. Then I settled down for a deep meditation followed by a restful nap. I still felt anxious when I awoke, so I applied my favorite decision-making slogans, "First Things First" and "Let Go and Let God."

When I finally returned her call, it turned out to be less confrontational than I had imagined. I thanked my Higher Power for giving me yet another opportunity to apply the program and to maintain serenity in spite of my fears.

Thought for the Day

When fear tempts me to abandon my responsibilities to myself, practicing my program will help me resist the trap.

> "I pray that I may not fall into the error of anticipating trouble. If it should come, let me meet it with equanimity and love."
>
> *One Day at a Time in Al-Anon*, p. 73

I resisted the suggestion in Step Eleven to pray "only for knowledge of His will for us and the power to carry that out." Surely I wasn't meant to take this idea literally. I had what I thought were legitimate needs, desires, and concerns. Hadn't I every right to take them to my Higher Power? I continued to do just that and slowly, over time, a pattern emerged: Praying for my will to be done often led me to pain, trouble, and confusion.

I finally understood one day as I was playing with my little dog. He was begging persistently to go outside. He really, really wanted to go outdoors just like I plead for my Higher Power to grant me something I really, really want. However, some construction was going on near my house, and I knew my dog could easily get hurt. My answer to his begging was no. There was no way in his limited understanding for him to comprehend the reason behind my decision.

So it is with my Higher Power and me. God sees the whole picture, whereas my knowledge of what is best for me is based on my fluctuating perceptions of my tiny world. My Higher Power created me with human limitations, so I need to depend on Him. If I follow His guidance willingly, my life will be easier, saner, and safer. Today I am experiencing the true meaning of trust.

Thought for the Day

How many times do I have to be hurt by self-will before I'm willing to seek another way?

"God whispers softly to me all the time. When I don't listen, I'm headed for trouble or pain."

From Survival to Recovery, p. 226

When I came to the Eighth and Ninth Steps, I still felt some confusion and anger. I felt harmed by both the alcoholic and the non-drinking parent. Shouldn't they make amends to me? Wasn't I the one who deserved an apology? Then an Al-Anon friend asked me to consider the definition of the word "amends." "A change for the better" is how my dictionary defined it. I realized that I could make amends by changing my relationships for the better.

Doing this with members of my alcoholic family began with honestly evaluating what was best for me in those relationships. For many years I had swallowed hurt or unwillingly attended family functions to maintain peace. Changing that behavior sometimes meant deciding not to participate in family functions at which I knew alcohol would be served. On several occasions it meant expressing to my parents the true way I felt about an action or comment that hurt me.

Making choices that support my serenity and self-respect has allowed me to mend important relationships in a way that brought some healing after nearly 40 years of denial and resentment.

Thought for the Day

With the help of Al-Anon, I gain the courage to live with honesty and integrity, even if my family remains in the grip of alcoholism.

> "Being true to myself is one of the greatest gifts I can give to those around me."
>
> *Courage to Change*, p. 356

The Serenity Prayer helps me maintain a sense of inner peace amidst the chaos present in my home and at work. At home I ask God to grant me serenity to accept the things I cannot change, such as my family's behavior. I accept that my family members act the way they do because of their diseases: My son is an alcoholic, and my husband is the adult child of an alcoholic. Neither chooses to pursue recovery. I request courage to change the things I can. Accepting alcoholism as a disease allows me to detach personally from their actions and to set limits to unacceptable behavior. Now I am brave enough to make decisions based on what is best for me. I also ask for wisdom to know the difference, and God grants me the ability to handle with humor situations that would normally keep me awake at night. How sweet my home life is now.

At work I am a substitute teacher. I need serenity, courage, and wisdom to deal with each new class, whether it's a group of rambunctious kindergartners with a reputation of taking advantage of substitutes or a troop of emotionally disturbed youngsters who have difficulty adjusting to change. If I maintain an air of quiet peace, things usually go well. My use of the Serenity Prayer at work must show because I often receive compliments on my substitute teaching. On the rare occasions I get a negative comment, I consider what I can learn and turn it over to my Higher Power as something over which I have no control. How sweet my work life is now.

Thought for the Day

When I project serenity, courage, and wisdom, they come back to me like metal to a magnet.

> "The Serenity Prayer leads me toward harmony with myself—which is what serenity means to me."

> *The Forum*, November 1998, p. 24

Today I know I was the perfect enabler. My autocratic behavior deprived my husband of responsibility. I tried in vain to control him, and to keep him "dry." Eventually I felt only hate and disgust toward my husband and alcohol. My life seemed totally worthless, and I felt deprived of a shoulder to lean against, a safe place to cry.

Then I was led to Al-Anon, where I learned to do something just for me—recover. I learned I wasn't responsible for my husband's actions, so I didn't have to feel ashamed. I learned that I couldn't save him, but I could save myself. This was my chance to jump off the merry-go-round called denial before I slipped under it and was crushed.

I especially learned that my way of helping was not really helping. I had to do something differently. At Al-Anon meetings in my country, they call detachment "letting off in love." I felt unable to let him off in love. However, I decided I could let him fall gently.

That's what I did, and slowly my life started to feel worthwhile again. I began taking care of myself. I practice thinking positively by using the Steps and slogans. Prayer and meditation help me become balanced and content. I cry on my sponsor's shoulder when I need comfort, and then we talk about which program tools can help my present situation. My husband's illness has enriched my life by leading me to Al-Anon. With the help of like-minded friends, I have been fortunate to realize my mistakes and learn from them. This, to me, is the key to real happiness.

Thought for the Day

Can I "let off" the alcoholic in love or at least let him or her fall gently?

> "Get off his back. Get out of his way. Get onto yourself.
> Get to meetings. Give him to God."

Forum Favorites, Volume 4, p. 142

Growing up in an alcoholic environment, I had no idea just how unclearly I viewed the world around me. I did what I had always done, just as my parents and their parents before them had done. There didn't seem to be any alternative way of looking at life, and quite frankly I saw no need for one. Nothing was wrong. I was "fine."

Then the cumulative effects of living around alcoholics brought me into Al-Anon. For me coming into the program has been like going to an eye doctor. Like an ophthalmologist, Al-Anon constantly tests my vision. It gives me choices about how I want to perceive my life. There is no one-prescription-fits-all view. I am free to wear the lenses that fit most comfortably right now and to switch to a different pair when I'm ready.

For a while I berated myself for having been so blind. I hated denial and considered it the worst character defect. In the interest of being gentle with myself, I gradually came to understand that denial could be a wonderful thing. It kept me alive until I was ready to face the truth, my truth. Now I believe when I'm ready to face more truths, my Higher Power and the Al-Anon program will lift the veils that cloud my vision. To see that bright light before I'm prepared for it could possibly blind me further.

Thought for the Day

Denial can be a shock absorber for the spirit. I can respect and be grateful for that survival mechanism, but I'll not hang onto it longer than necessary.

"... In Al-Anon I am encouraged to grow at my own pace. As I do, I find some of my defenses and ideas too tight, too limiting."

Courage to Change, p. 298

I often ask myself what is the insanity referred to in Step Two? For me insanity is working the Al-Anon program for some time and still thinking I can engage in certain attitudes and actions and somehow stay sane. These include resentment, jealousy, isolation, unrealistic expectation, arrogance, fear, and revenge. Are my defects my insanity? No. Hanging on to my defects when I know what the answer is and what I must do is insanity.

Step Two tells me there's a spiritual solution to my insanity. If at any particular time I don't believe I'm worthy of God's blessings, there are other program tools to which I can turn. I can go to a meeting, call my sponsor, and do the next right thing. When I do the things that are right for me to do, I feel better about myself. I begin to feel worthy. I begin to trust that God is still there for me once I again choose sanity, faith, and healing for my life.

Thought for the Day

I don't have to wait for sanity to descend on me from above. I can participate in creating it by choosing healthy attitudes and behaviors.

> "In Step Two we acknowledge a power that is doing for us what we haven't been able to do for ourselves and we realize that, as we learn to rely on that power, our lives are restored to sanity."
>
> *The Forum*, February 1989, p. 22

The process of making decisions sometimes causes me problems and gets me stuck. I want to make the "perfect" decision not only for the problem at hand, but also for any consequences that might arise from the original decision. I'll spend an inordinate amount of time thinking of dozens of hypothetical problems, some of them occurring 30 years down the road, which cannot be obliterated by one single, "perfect" decision I might make today.

Finally I'll catch myself and remember how the slogans help me make sound choices. First, I use "One Day at a Time" to bring myself back into the moment, which is the only place my Higher Power can really help me anyway. I tell myself this day is all I have to work with and that I have to make this decision using only the information I have today. Once I'm in the present, I use other slogans to sort things out. "Easy Does It" reminds me to slow down, breathe, and "Think." The slogan "Keep It Simple" reminds me that I have good, creative problem-solving skills. "How Important Is It?" puts the decision into perspective. If it's not that important, sometimes I find I've reached a conclusion just by following my process. If it is important, I wait until I've had time to pray, meditate, attend extra meetings, and talk about the situation with my sponsor or other program friends. Either way, I know I'll make a good choice because my decision came from a state of sanity brought about by using the tools of the program.

Thought for the Day

As long as I remember to use the slogans, the decision-making process can be a challenge rather than a chore.

> "It feels good to have choices, so I get to decide how important my serenity is to me."

The Forum, January 1999, p. 5

When I first heard the slogans at Al-Anon meetings, I considered them to be trite little clichés that couldn't possibly help anybody. They were far too simple to work, and I was far too skeptical to even attempt them. Then it dawned on me that I had been using my own slogans all my life. Unfortunately, they were slogans of *non*-recovery. I'd said many of them daily, and I had grown up hearing most of them from alcoholic relatives. They included "you should know how I feel", "after all I've done for you", "if you really loved me", "damned if you do, damned if you don't," and "I hope you're happy now."

I'd like to think these slogans didn't work, but they did just what they were supposed to do. They left me and everyone around me feeling hurt, guilt-ridden, and miserable. Soon I began to wonder. If these little phrases had such power to destroy, then maybe the Al-Anon slogans had the power to rebuild.

Now I think of our slogans as "instant Al-Anon." I don't always have the presence of mind to recall the Steps or Traditions when I'm in the middle of a problem. But usually with negligible effort on my part, applying those simple little words really helps. They certainly help me more than the slogans I used to say!

Thought for the Day

Today I won't discount simplicity until I give it a decent try.

> "Each slogan can be an easy reminder that we do have choices, that we can stop doing things that aren't working for us and that we can see things differently."

> *Alateen Talks Back on Slogans*, p. 3

Due to my distorted thinking, I made some regrettable choices in my life. I also held on to anger about being raised by unavailable, alcoholic parents. I was jealous of people who had normal parents who loved and supported them. I relived past circumstances and imagined alternative outcomes, thinking, "If only I had . . ." I wasted large portions of my day lost in daydreams, rewriting the past with happy endings and doling out justice to those who had caused me harm.

Reading little snippets of Al-Anon literature began to change how I thought about my past. At my second meeting, I picked up the pamphlet *Alcoholism, the Family Disease*. Every day for a year I read the page entitled "One Day at a Time." I read this page until I could recite it from memory. Then I strived to live its suggestions a little bit better each day. Sometimes I felt expansive and trusting enough to use all the ideas. Some days, when I was feeling overwhelmed with the strangeness of the recovery process, I clung to only one or two. Eventually I started using the page as a bookmark in every book I was reading, planting recovery suggestions for myself all over the house. Gradually these words became second nature to me and replaced my bitter and jealous thoughts of the past.

It hasn't been easy to let go of my remorse over yesterday. However, when I strive to do so, I can live in the present and create a new set of yesterdays full of good feelings and happy memories.

Thought for the Day

With time, patience, and practice of the Al-Anon program, I can create a future that heals and balances out the past.

"Let us remind ourselves each morning, that we will live this one day as fully and confidently as we can."

Alcoholism, the Family Disease, p. 18

As I've grown toward serenity with the help of Al-Anon, I've devised a quick and easy two-part summary of how I work my recovery. Distilling my program into two simple parts helps me remember the tools available to me during times when I may not be thinking clearly.

In the first part I take responsibility for my own life—my happiness, my growth, my choices and their consequences. What others say or do may bring up feelings, but I need to remember they are *my* feelings. I am responsible for what I do with them. Being responsible for my own life implies I am not responsible for directing anyone else's life. If asked, I can share my experience, strength, and hope, or I can just stay quiet and listen.

Taking responsibility for my life would be frightening if it were not for the second part—intimacy. I need another trusted person with whom to share the life for which I've taken responsibility. Actually I reveal myself intimately to several others—my Higher Power, my sponsor, and a few special Al-Anon friends. They all listen to and accept my feelings, reflect back to me what I say, and hold me accountable for my choices and actions. With firm compassion they help me grow into the person I long to be. They let me know I am never alone and that hope and help are always available to me if I ask.

Thought for the Day

Taking responsibility for my life can be overwhelming. I need intimate relationships with others. They help me make the hard decisions that move me in a positive direction and join me in celebrating the wonderful results of doing so.

> "I think that the fellowship of Al-Anon gives us two important qualities that are lacking in many of our lives as a result of living with alcoholics: intimacy and interdependence."
>
> *As We Understood . . .*, p. 27

Recently at a meeting I shared the grand plan of my life and how it has changed during my recovery in Al-Anon. In the past, my plan referred to my entire life, especially the future. It was a broad view in which I became the sum total of my achievements, viewed from a God-like distance. Over time my plan has shifted from the accomplishments of a lifetime to adjusting my attitude one day at a time. Instead of considering what I would do with my future, I now choose what I can do in the present. Instead of dreaming about tomorrow, I fashion it with the choices I make today.

Some of our slogans seem designed to help me stay aware of the present moment: "One Day at a Time", "Just for Today", "How Important Is It?" and "Keep It Simple." These slogans give me the means to let go of yesterday and tomorrow in order to focus on that small window of miracles called today. My first sponsor used to say that God works in the present moment. If I'm not in the present with God, what am I missing?

When I apply the slogans, I feel myself slow down. I become aware of my breath and how I might be holding it instead of letting it flow deeply through me. If I allow it, my muscles relax and my mind and heart open trustingly to the realm of possibilities my Higher Power has waiting for me. Finally I am resting in the only place my spirit will ever know—the present moment.

Thought for the Day

The slogans help make me aware of the present moment, where God and I are more likely to meet one another.

> "The first tools of the program I grabbed were the slogans. They helped me begin to learn how to live in the moment . . ."

> *From Survival to Recovery*, p. 250

Forgiveness is a process that often must be repeated. Even when I've worked through my feelings and forgiven someone who has hurt me, including myself, I may find pain from old wounds resurfacing. This signals me that it's time to do a spot-check inventory and run the resentment through the Steps again.

Awareness, the work I do in Step Ten, is mandatory; it warns me when old resentments creep back. When that happens, I backtrack through many of the Steps. Step Four helps me root out my reason for hanging on to the resentment. Step Five helps me get it out in the open. Then I can become willing to offer the resentment for removal in Steps Six and Seven. In Steps Eight and Nine, I make amends to myself and to the other person for damage caused by the resentment. In revisiting Step Ten, I make sure the resentment is truly healed, with no loose ends remaining. By the time I get to Step Eleven, I find that reworking my way through forgiveness has freed me to move beyond my pain. I can now establish a healthier and more intimate relationship with God. Finally I experience a wonderful freedom. Holding grudges keeps me trapped in self-centeredness. Forgiveness sets me free to focus on God's plan for my life.

Thought for the Day

The price of freedom is eternal vigilance. I'll stay aware of my attitudes so I can remain free.

> "From time to time, things that happen in the normal course of my life cause an old resentment or reaction to surface, and I have to work through the issue yet again."
>
> *From Survival to Recovery,* p. 171

I had recently moved to a new location when my car broke down one morning. There I was, sitting alone in a hot car, feeling sorry for myself while waiting for a tow truck. I found myself staring at a tree—a pretty ugly one at that. It was bare and stumpy, not at all like the beautiful, lush green trees I was used to back home. As I continued to stare, I noticed I didn't feel very good. In fact, I felt a little like that tree looked. I told myself it didn't matter because now my whole day was ruined anyway.

Just to occupy myself while waiting, I tried looking at that ugly tree from a different perspective. As I examined it more closely, I began to notice some interesting things. First, the tree looked different from the ones surrounding it. It had its own unique quality. The leaves weren't perfectly green, but they were a pleasing color. Its trunk was thin but strong looking, like a wiry, powerful man. The roots gripped the earth tenaciously. Suddenly this ugly, scrawny tree became an object of respectable beauty.

I tried the same experiment with my situation. Before I knew it, my perceptions changed right before my eyes. The plans I had made for the day had changed beyond my control. Suddenly the whole day was mine to fill as I liked—play tennis, hike, call an old friend, put my feet up and relax. My unexpected situation turned into a pleasure-filled gift, once I was willing to look at it differently.

Thought for the Day

God grants me the "wisdom to know the difference" each time I'm willing to change my perceptions.

> ". . . I look for the qualities I want to change in myself—the times during the day when either my attitude or my behavior was inappropriate."
>
> As We Understood . . ., p. 237

I remember the first time someone asked me to be a sponsor. I agreed to do it, and then I went home and read the Al-Anon leaflet *Sponsorship, What It's All About* to be sure I qualified. Even then I hesitated. What did I have to offer anyone? I was still at the "toddler" stage of my own recovery, stumbling and falling more often than not. I was convinced I had to be perfect before I dared try to help anyone else.

Then I remembered my early days in the program. What I had wanted most from my sponsor was acceptance, affection, reassurance, and a trustworthy listener. I certainly hadn't expected perfection. Suddenly my inadequacies seemed unimportant, and my heart swelled as I realized that someone saw me as a healthy and valuable human being.

My Higher Power showed me I didn't have to talk much to be a sponsor. What I really needed to do was listen. As I listened I became aware of blessings I had never counted, areas of my life that needed attention, and principles at work in my life I had not recognized. It amazed me how helping others gave me insight regarding my own situation.

Those I sponsor have helped me feel loved and needed. More important, they have helped me feel human. Because they reached out to me, I find it easier to ask for help myself without feeling weak. It's been a privilege and a joy to give back a small part of the immense treasure I have received from God and from the Al-Anon program of recovery.

Thought for the Day

Being asked to sponsor someone affirms I do indeed have something valuable to offer a fellow human.

> "Realize that a sponsor is only one channel for Al-Anon's message of hope, and avoid thinking that it is necessary to know all the answers."
>
> *Sponsorship, What It's All About*, p. 9

The Traditions serve as guidelines for establishing and maintaining good relationships, not only in our Al-Anon groups but also with family and friends.

The First Tradition, "Our common welfare should come first; personal progress for the greatest number depends upon unity," has helped me greatly in learning to deal with my family. Participating in Al-Anon meetings, in which our common welfare is an important condition of recovery, has enabled me to give voice to my own portion of the common welfare in family affairs. I've learned I have the right to initiate and contribute fully to discussions on matters concerning our common welfare.

Tradition Two, which states in part, "For our group purpose there is but one authority—a loving God as He may express Himself in our group conscience," gives me guidelines to follow when I *do* speak up during family discussions. Stating my opinion once is appropriate; any more than that is an attempt at governing those around me.

Using my Al-Anon experience of progress through unity, I have discovered a new level of patience in seeking common ground with family members. Although we don't always find that common ground, I am thankful I can now do my part to allow the possibility.

Thought for the Day

Tradition One helps me experience the benefits of participation in my family as well as in Al-Anon. Tradition Two reminds me that although I am a participant, I am not in charge.

"Today I know that for unity to exist in my family or in my group, all of us must have a voice."

Paths to Recovery, p. 139

Often in the quiet stillness of late evening, my mind begins to reel and the fearful projections of doom and gloom try to settle in. To gain some peace and perspective, I use the Serenity Prayer to break the cycle. First, I substitute the prayer for my insane thoughts and recite it as many times as necessary to focus on the here and now. Then I break the prayer down into its three parts and apply them to my jumbled mind.

I pray, "God grant me the serenity to accept the things I cannot change . . ." (it's late at night and I'm afraid to speak with anyone in the program right now) ". . . courage to change the things I can . . ." (I read from my shelf of Conference Approved Literature and write my problems down in my journal; I also ask to be guided by my Higher Power's will) ". . . and wisdom to know the difference" (I thank God for halting my confusion and ask for peace and restorative sleep).

I repeat this process until serenity settles over me like a warm and cozy blanket, encouraging me to relax in body, mind, and spirit until I finally fall asleep. When I awaken the next day, I often find something has changed during the night. Sometimes it's my viewpoint of the situation, and my course of action changes accordingly. Sometimes the situation resolves itself with no effort on my part. Either way it is fine with me. I'm just glad I use the Serenity Prayer to turn the problem over and prevent myself from suffering needlessly!

Thought for the Day

Have I tried breaking down the Serenity Prayer and using its three sections as healthy lenses through which to view my problem?

> "Reflecting on each thought in the Serenity Prayer can
> help put situations into a clearer perspective."
>
> *Purpose & Suggestions*, p. 5

The slogan "Let Go and Let God" strongly impressed me when I first came into Al-Anon. Many years later I still use it to distinguish my part from God's in the growth I crave and seek.

I recently read how a gardener must recognize powerlessness over the elements as they govern the success or failure of the garden. One can only accept the reality of the climate and do what one can to compensate for the plants' needs. First, the gardener gets on his or her knees to loosen the soil and nourish it with nutrients as well as to carefully plant the seeds. Then protective measures are taken. Barriers can be erected to discourage damage from strong winds. Protective coverings shelter the seedlings from too much rain or sun. Sprinklers can be used when there isn't enough rain. Then it's time to detach and wait to see what the harvest brings.

Similarly for me, it wasn't until I surrendered, fell to my knees, and asked God for help that I was led to Al-Anon. There, fellow members loosen my misunderstandings about alcoholism while the program offers me the nutrition and protection I need to grow. However, it's up to me to soak up that nutrition and use that protection. Every time I attend a meeting, read literature, call my sponsor, or volunteer for service, I take the raw materials the program provides me and use them for the feeding and growth of my spirit. Then I let go and let God bring in the harvest of peace, serenity, and love.

Thought for the Day

First I dream. Then I do. Then I detach and let God determine the outcome.

> "Looking back today with gratitude reveals my background as a rich garden of human possibility just waiting for the gardener with the right wheelbarrow full of tools—the Twelve Steps."

From Survival to Recovery, p. 201

In Al-Anon I've learned that, in general, it's healthier to keep the focus on me. However, there was a period during my early recovery when focusing on my parents' behavior was a means to a healthy end. I was grappling with my belief that I was inherently bad and that I couldn't change. As I explored this with my sponsor, I became aware that I had learned many self-defeating attitudes and behaviors from my parents, both of whom were preoccupied with alcoholism. It was a relief to know I wasn't hopelessly defective.

If I hadn't had a program at that point, I might have continued blaming my parents for passing such a legacy down to me. Fortunately I had already been exposed in Al-Anon to the idea that I was responsible for my shortcomings, no matter where they came from. However, I had this awareness only on an intellectual level. It took some emotional struggle to move it down to the heart. I had to let go of the hope that some day my parents would teach me differently. I needed to accept that they—like myself and others—were operating at the highest level they could at any given time. If they could have done better, they would have.

I owned up to my defects, without blaming my parents, in my Fourth and Fifth Steps. In Steps Six and Seven I became ready and humbly asked God to remove them. Then in working Steps Eight and Nine, I made amends by slowly changing my behavior while accepting my parents' right not to change.

Thought for the Day

As a child I may have learned some of my parents' shortcomings. As an adult I can unlearn them with the help of the Al-Anon program.

> "Behaviors we adopted to cope with alcoholism in our families became so habitual we thought they were part of our identity."
>
> *From Survival to Recovery*, p.17

In recovering from being raised in an alcoholic home, I've had to pay particular attention to "me-versus-them" thinking and how it keeps me immobilized. Such thinking often manifests in the way I relate to my Higher Power, particularly regarding the issue of my will versus Its will. Whenever I perceive myself as pitted against someone or something, my stubbornness comes out, and I don't want to change or grow.

I think much of it has to do with the words I use with myself internally. I tend to interpret the Third and Eleventh Steps in terms of a struggle because I gave up a great deal of myself to survive alcoholism. As an adult I still sometimes lose myself in certain relationships. Now I'm working hard to find out who I really am, and I don't particularly relish the idea of giving up my will.

It helps me to think instead of *aligning* my will with that of my Higher Power. When I look at it this way, I'm reminded that I don't have to lose myself again in the disease or in relationships. Developing a healthy relationship with my Higher Power is about teamwork, with an emphasis on my deference to Its will. This reminds me that my will isn't intrinsically bad, as I once believed. It's simply misaligned, and my Higher Power can make it straight again.

I have two prayers that feel comfortable to me: "Higher Power, please align my will with Thine," and "God, please help me to want what You want."

Thought for the Day

My Higher Power wants what's best for me. However, I need to want it, too.

"Our job is to cooperate with God . . ."

Paths to Recovery, p. 74

Recently I attended a meeting where the suggested topic for discussion was denial. I was struck by a broader awareness of denial than I had previously imagined. There is denial of the disease of alcoholism and its side effects. There is also denial of the pain inherent in betrayal, loss, disability, and death. In meditation I reflected on the way in which my upbringing in an alcoholic family had encouraged me to engage in other subtle but perhaps equally devastating forms of denial.

While growing up I had used denial to block myself from feeling pain, which also blocked me from experiencing pleasure. Now that I'm in Al-Anon recovery, working my program means letting go of my denial by opening my heart to daily sources of wonder and delight. It also includes practicing gratitude for daily miracles. I now savor the beauty to be found in each day, no matter how fleeting, and I give thanks to my Higher Power for allowing me to witness it.

Another form of denial is thinking I am the sum of my problems and limitations. Thanks to Al-Anon, I have accepted the truth: I am a spiritual being. My denial has been replaced by acceptance of an infinitely larger, more beautiful reality in which I rely on the strength and guidance of a Power greater than myself for protection and direction.

Thought for the Day

Today I let go of my denial, face the truth, and celebrate my recovery.

"Denial is a symptom of the effects of alcoholism."

Courage to Change, p. 146

I never thought that the Traditions applied to anything other than my Al-Anon group. Now I realize they pertain to me as an individual because I'm a member of my family and other groups.

Tradition Four, which speaks of groups being autonomous except in matters affecting other groups or Al-Anon or AA as a whole, has been especially meaningful to me. It tells me that I have choices and may make whatever decisions I desire in my best interests, provided those decisions do not harm another person. If I have the God-given right to make my own decisions, then it follows that other people have this same right. Therefore I need to respect their right to choose, free of my interference, judgment, and control.

Peacefully allowing others to make their own decisions can be difficult for me, especially when I think I know best for someone else's life or when I fear that someone's decision will have a negative impact on me. If I ignore this Tradition, the result can range from minor irritation to more serious repercussions, including ruptured relationships.

Thought for the Day

Tradition Four is about respecting others enough to let them make their own decisions.

> "Tradition Four is democracy in action. With it, we can step out into the world well-balanced between freedom and responsibility."

> *Paths to Recovery*, p. 166

My favorite great-aunt is dying, and I want to write to her daughter, my cousin. My hand shakes as I face the empty card. I was the black sheep, the runaway, and my father was the town drunk. I haven't seen my cousin since I left home, and I am still ashamed. This has been the legacy of alcoholism for me: no matter how much good I do in my life, how well I rear my children, keep my house, do my job, or how much community service work I do, I am still ashamed to talk to people who knew me as my father's daughter. Yet if I don't send the card, once my aunt dies, I may lose touch with a whole branch of my family. My children may never have the opportunity to know their cousins, which would continue the legacy of isolation and shame.

Three years of Al-Anon remind me to "Keep It Simple" and to change what I can. I write a brief note in the card and seal it. I mail it and let it go. Whether I receive an answer is not important. What is important is letting go of my shame and perpetual feeling of failure. Only by parting with them may I open the door to a new life filled with possibilities.

Thought for the Day

Hope leads me to the future. With the support of Al-Anon, I can free myself of the past.

> "If we live each day to the best of our ability, we will soon find we don't have time to worry about the future or regret the past. We will be too busy enjoying life."
>
> *Alateen—Hope for Children of Alcoholics*, p. 56

The serenity I am offered in Al-Anon is not an escape from life. Rather, it is the power to find peacefulness within life.

Al-Anon does not promise me freedom from pain, sorrow, or difficult situations. It does, however, give me the opportunity to learn from others how to develop the necessary skills for maintaining peace of mind, even when life seems most unbearable. The program helps me learn how to request, accept, and use the strength and wisdom of my Higher Power. My Higher Power, working through my fellow members, helps me maintain my sanity and sense of self-worth.

Al-Anon also gives me the opportunity to live a serene life free from the burden of responsibility for other's decisions. It teaches me that I can make choices to redirect my life toward personal growth and satisfaction. It increases my confidence, which comes from trusting that the Higher Power of my understanding will sustain me and guide me through life's ups and downs.

Thought for the Day

Serenity is not about the end of pain. It's about my ability to flourish peacefully no matter what life brings my way.

> "I felt utterly at peace with life and at the same time filled with joy. At that moment, I realized *this* was serenity, and I laughed out loud for the sheer, glorious pleasure of it!"
>
> *From Survival to Recovery, p. 268*

Our preamble to the Twelve Steps states in part, "that changed attitudes can aid recovery," and I can attest to this. My family situation has improved considerably because I've learned to mind my own business. "How Important Is It?" reminds me that my opinion doesn't have to be, and often shouldn't be, expressed unless it is requested. "Live and Let Live" reminds me that my life is separate from my adult children and that we are each meant to govern our own lives.

In the past I used to mind my children's business. I usually offered advice whether or not it was wanted. Now I hold my comments about the situations, problems, and conflicts my children share with me. I don't accomplish this changed behavior perfectly all the time. Often my first reaction is to tell them how I would handle the problem. However, my Higher Power has shown me that this behavior only alienates them. However, when one of them speaks of a decision affecting me personally in a negative way, I speak up and set my boundaries.

I've seen concrete rewards from my willingness to change and apply the program. My children tell me they appreciate being able to talk with me without being "fixed" or "bossed around." To have my children share with me today is testimony to the fact that the program works. The more I monitor my opinions and advice-giving, the more my children share their lives with me, and the more open and intimate we become.

Thought for the Day

It's not important for me to comment on everything I hear. It is important for me to let go and let others make decisions for themselves.

> "Al-Anon helped me to let live by teaching me about detachment and helping me to see that many of my problems stemmed from minding everyone's business but my own."

Courage to Change, p. 234

Learning to enjoy life and have fun has been difficult for me. I find it much easier to isolate myself and to resist taking risks. When I look at this defect, I feel incredibly flawed. When I look deeper, I see it is just fear.

As a child I was shamed for acting like a child and for not doing anything well enough. I quickly became afraid to do anything. It was, and sometimes still is, easier to stay home and fill my emptiness with food, television, and books. Yet I know if I do what I've always done, I'll get what I've always gotten. Al-Anon encourages me to apply new behavior and to trust the results. I can truly live my life, let others live theirs, and see the humor in situations by asking myself, "How important is it?" Through the process of working the program, I'm learning that I'm not flawed and that the source of my being is love. There is a Higher Power who loves me. While I encourage myself to take small steps in getting over my fear of enjoying life, I know that God loves me just as I am—a work in progress.

Now I have choices throughout my day. If I start feeling emptiness and shame, I know I've crossed back to that place of isolation. When I'm ready to return to self-love, all I need to do is practice "Let it Begin with Me" by finding the fun and humor already present in my life.

Thought for the Day

Anticipating enjoyment is a good way to begin my day. If I lose my place, I'll remember I can start my day over at any time.

> "I haven't succeeded in changing my past, of course, but the present is filled with promise, and, amazingly, I am discovering that it is fun to be me."

From Survival to Recovery, p. 185

After a recent Al-Anon meeting, two people commented that my voice was so soft they couldn't hear what I was saying. I felt quietly stunned that they would care enough to even mention this.

For days I wondered what God was trying to tell me. Thoughts of my alcoholic upbringing bubbled to the surface. It seemed as though my parents and I always misunderstood each other. Either they couldn't understand what I was trying to say, or they did understand but didn't like what I was saying. I learned to keep my mouth closed or to keep my voice quiet. That's how I protected myself. I eventually convinced myself that I had nothing worthwhile to say.

Al-Anon is gentle. I could have remained silent for a long time in meetings. No one ever forced me to speak or called on me like a teacher to a student. If not for the comments of those two people, it would have been easy for me to continue soaking in the sharings, never giving anything back.

Another aspect of Al-Anon's gentleness is that the option to share is always there. I began to see those two people as bearers of an invitation to let God speak through me. To do that I needed to believe that what I had to say was worth sharing. Often I had to go ahead and speak, even though I doubted the value of my words. Gradually other members told me they appreciated, even identified with my thoughts and feelings. My willingness to develop new behavior helped my voice, as well as my self-esteem, become "louder." Thank you, Al-Anon, for those two special people who challenged me to grow.

Thought for the Day

Speaking too little can be as self-defeating as speaking too much.

"Other people keep telling me I'm a worthwhile person. Maybe it's time I started to believe them."

Alateen—a day at a time, p. 88

I've found many helpful statements in the Suggested Welcome and Closing to our meetings, but the one that has helped me the most is "Let there be no gossip or criticism. . . ." When I take this thought and apply it to all the people I know, not just to my friends in Al-Anon, I stay more focused on my life, my responsibilities, and myself. As a result I have more loving relationships with my family.

In setting some boundaries for myself, I have decided that I will no longer hold a conversation about someone who isn't physically present in the same room. "News bulletins," such as my brother buying a new home or my sister returning to school, are allowed. Still I don't permit myself to judge their decisions or speculate about their motives or the outcomes of their choices.

My mother caught on quickly to this notion. Now we discuss our feelings about subjects applying only to us. When I was seriously ill, we talked about death and dying. Now that I'm well, we speak of our Higher Power, beautiful family memories, and our hopes and dreams for the future. Refraining from gossip and criticism keeps me focused on myself, and firmly established in reality. I like that much more than bemoaning the fates of my family members.

Thought for the Day

Whatever I concentrate on will become central to my life.

"Not only do we avoid focusing on ourselves when we gossip, but our disrespect for others reinforces self-defeating attitudes about relationships."

How Al-Anon Works for Families & Friends of Alcoholics, p. 97

One day I had to get a heavy box down from our attic. While carrying it down a ladder, I felt myself struggling and losing control. In a panic I told my boyfriend I was afraid the box would fall. Suddenly he reached up and supported the box. The struggle was over.

My labor with faith has been a similar experience. I grew up with an alcoholic father who considered himself an atheist. I took on his views and became a skeptic. Eventually I became full of despair. Life seemed meaningless.

Working the first three Steps in Al-Anon allowed me to discover a faith of my own. I heard members speak about their Higher Power, which ranged from the Al-Anon group to a female deity to the more conventional male figure. I found others who had adopted someone else's views only to find they didn't fit. Members spoke of undergoing a *process* in building a relationship with God. This was often described as being similar to the process one would go through in developing a friendship. It involved talking (praying), listening (meditating), and learning to trust, over time, that the friend would be there. These analogies struck a chord in me. I already had several well-trusted friends. As I examined my role in developing these connections, I saw that the common thread was consistent contact. Slowly I tried the same method with my Higher Power. Through my consistent prayer and meditation, God has become my best friend. Now I am able to pray for help during my struggles and to feel the hand of my Higher Power supporting me.

Thought for the Day

The Steps speak of a God of my understanding. Am I engaging in the behavior necessary to reach that understanding?

"... My life has changed completely as I have pursued spiritual development and turned to a Higher Power for help."
How Al-Anon Works for Families & Friends of Alcoholics, p. 172

Practicing Tradition Seven, which speaks of being fully self-supporting, has been difficult in my personal life. I grew up watching my father, who was a child during the Depression, spend large sums of money on himself and rarely on the family. I found it hard to buy gifts for my mother who grew up in an alcoholic home, because she had no wants. I often heard my parents say they had no savings. I learned this was acceptable.

Then I married. Within months I spent my husband's entire savings buying "needed" furnishings for the house. Then reality hit: My mother had spent her life in denial, and now I was doing the same. The only way I could change was to take some self-supporting actions. I started by authorizing automatic payments into a retirement fund, which is growing nicely. Now before I purchase something, I ask myself if it's something I want or something I need. If it's a want, I wait at least a week to see if the urge passes. If the urge doesn't pass, I inventory the desire and make an effort to detach emotionally so that I can see the real reason why I want the item. These practices and others give me the peace of mind that comes from being fully self-supporting.

Thought for the Day

I am grateful today that Al-Anon teaches me to support myself through my own voluntary contributions.

> "When individual members and individual groups under-stand that they are responsible for their own survival and progress, a great spiritual strength flows into each part as well as the whole."
>
> *Al-Anon's Twelve Steps & Twelve Traditions,* p. 116

Before I came into the program, I struggled with feeling numb and fragmented. Once in Al-Anon and exposed to Step Two, I had to ask the question, "What does it mean to me to be sane or insane?" There were some good indicators in my life of both sanity and insanity. Still I didn't believe I had anything to do with the presence or absence of either of them; they just happened.

In time I learned that the emotional numbness I had developed to cope with growing up with alcoholism contributed much to my sense of insanity. It forced me to see life as happening totally outside of and unconnected to myself. In Al-Anon, by learning to listen to my feelings, give them a name, and express them, I built a bridge between my broken self, my Higher Power, and my wholeness. Never in my wildest dreams could I have known that my insanity came from my lost relationship with myself and with God.

Thought for the Day

Al-Anon gives me the opportunity to retrieve all the broken, scattered aspects of myself and offer them to God to piece together into wholeness.

> "Sometimes slowly or haltingly, occasionally in great bursts of brilliance, those who work the Steps change and grow toward light, toward health, and toward their Higher Power."

From Survival to Recovery, p. 270

Serenity often comes and goes in my life depending on the effort I put into welcoming it or pushing it away. I can't will serenity, but I can create an environment where it's more likely to blossom.

Sometimes I slip back into character defects. Often these bouts are triggered because I've allowed myself to get too hungry, angry, lonely, or tired. During these times I'm likely to push serenity away. I might skip a few meetings or forget to call my sponsor. Perhaps I fall back into associating with people who reinforce my self-defeating attitudes.

Other times I do the things necessary to invite serenity into my life. I get a good night's sleep, read my Al-Anon literature in the morning, exercise, eat well, work responsibly, get to a meeting, and call someone in the program. I also continue to work the Steps, especially Four through Nine. I continue to make peace with my past and stay peaceful by practicing Step Ten. I feel more open to serenity.

So what makes me waver between the two attitudes? It's my degree of willingness to surrender. Sometimes I have days when I just don't feel like it. I act childishly and spurn my Higher Power by refusing to surrender to His will. On other days surrender comes easily. I used to think I was powerless over my willingness. Then I realized that it was up to me. When I don't feel willing to surrender, I can surrender that, too! Now one of my favorite prayers is, "God, please help me be willing to be willing."

Thought for the Day

My recovery either begins or ends with my degree of willingness.

> "By acting on our willingness, we make room for a Power greater than ourselves. . ."
>
> *How Al-Anon Works for Families & Friends of Alcoholics*, p. 105

At a recent meeting, the discussion topic was how to discern God's will. Someone shared her belief that even though God knows what is best for her and offers to reveal His will, she doesn't have to accept it. She can choose to forego good choices and remain in misery.

For me this program is a choice. It is my Higher Power's will that each day I have the option to accept the gift of Al-Anon or to refuse it and try to live life on my own terms. However, my experience is that my terms are not as good as God's. They aren't as loving, kind, or compassionate, nor are they as filled with opportunity.

As the saying goes, my best thinking got me here. I didn't go to Alateen and later to Al-Anon because my will worked so wonderfully that I was truly happy, serene, and joyful. I came here because I was so sick and miserable that I couldn't perceive God's will for me and ran into continuous roadblocks to the peace and serenity I craved.

Today I'm learning to make choices that feel like God's will. Although I still resist on occasion, more often I choose the simpler, more compassionate road God offers me. As I continue to select His will over my own, I continue to grow in health, happiness, and peace of mind.

Thought for the Day

My Higher Power believes I deserve the very best and wants me to have it, if only I will reach out and take it.

> "...I believe my Higher Power is waiting for me to realize that I need help."

> *The Forum*, November 1999, p. 30

I am grateful for the many blessings that have come my way since I joined Al-Anon. My gratitude is reflected in my attitude toward life today. In fact, I feel great, and I am full of joy. At a recent meeting on gratitude I stated, "I surely would like to know why the word 'grateful' is spelled that way, because I really feel 'greatly full.'" Many nodded their heads in agreement.

No matter where I go, Al-Anon's message of hope has been there. I have lived in two different parts of the country, and in both I attended the *greatest* home group in the world. My bookcases are full of great Al-Anon Conference Approved Literature. I have loving and tough—in other words, *great*—recovery and service sponsors.

My marriage has survived many seasons of recovery. My relationship with my parents is now better than ever. I have friends, the dear friends I longed for as a child. Today I am full of knowledge of their love and respect for me. All of this has come about because of Al-Anon.

Was I grateful in the early days when I came defeated into these rooms? No. Was I grateful for the epidemic of this cunning, powerful, baffling disease in my family? No. Yet I have survived and flourished. I am grateful that I did what I had to do to get to where—and who—I am today.

Thought for the Day

I will always be grateful for the alcoholics and alcoholism in my life. It is because of this family disease, and my recovery from it, that I am who I am.

> "...I want to thank my Higher Power for having given me the gift to live with an alcoholic and the opportunity to have arrived at an Al-Anon room."

> *Having Had a Spiritual Awakening . . .*, p. 164

I grew up believing that my behavior was supposed to be perfect and hating myself when it wasn't. No one actually told me I was supposed to be flawless, but that's what I believed. My self-esteem diminished whenever I made a mistake, didn't know something I was expected to know, did something wrong, or when something I unintentionally did or said ended up hurting someone. I believed my mistakes were proof of my failure at the one thing I was supposed to accomplish—perfection.

After some time in Al-Anon, I felt I needed to take Step Four, "a searching and fearless moral inventory" of myself. I felt fear in approaching the Step and shame over each imperfection for which I would have to take responsibility. I believed my inventory was a tally of my "goods" and "bads" that would soon prove to God, to myself, and another human being that I was a failure.

After thoroughly studying this Step in Al-Anon literature and speaking with my sponsor, I decided to change my attitude. Humility, not humiliation, is the long-term goal of the Fourth Step inventory. The moral inventory is not intended as a score-board or report card. There are many things in my life I can't control, but I do have choices about my attitudes and behaviors. The real purpose of the Fourth Step inventory is to help me develop a list of the things I can change to make my life more spiritual, sane, satisfying, and serene. In this context perfection is not an option.

Thought for the Day

Taking a Fourth Step inventory clarifies the things over which I *do* have power.

> "It may demand courage and self-discipline, but by freely acknowledging who we have been, we can make positive changes about who we are becoming."
>
> *Courage to Change*, p. 158

When doing my Fourth Step, I saw a major character defect that permeated my life. I had the attitude of "hurry up and get it over with." This phrase indicates the lack of peace I live with when I focus on my destination rather than on my journey.

When I live for results, I put all of my progress, achievement, and faith in the future rather than in the present. I miss the gifts today has to offer. These might include the fierce beauty of a storm-ridden sky, the spontaneous warmth of a child's hug, the self-respect which comes from making amends, and the joyful validation that arises from encouraging someone I sponsor.

Conversely, when I focus on my recovery journey, I honor my thoughts and feelings and pay attention to what they have to tell me regarding my path. I attend to the spiritual meaning embedded in the minute-by-minute details of my life. As I keenly notice the changes I undergo when I stretch myself spiritually by using a slogan, Step, or Tradition, I stay in today.

Thought for the Day

Living one day at a time, focusing on my best efforts rather than on outcomes, gives me a healthy framework for living.

> "Each moment of this day is precious, and I will make it count."
>
> *Courage to Change,* p. 257

When I first came to Al-Anon and heard the word "serenity," I thought, "Boring." My life thus far had been a roller-coaster ride of emotional highs and lows. It was pure madness, but at least it was exciting. Little did I know I was as addicted to chaos as the alcoholic was to alcohol. My life was insane and often painful, but it was comfortable in its own, strange way. It was all I had ever known.

In Al-Anon I attended countless meetings, shared with other members (particularly my sponsor), worked the Twelve Steps, and engaged in prayer and meditation. Gradually I experienced brief moments of serenity. I decided I liked this pleasant, albeit unusual, feeling of peacefulness.

Whenever my life became unmanageable, I turned to the tools of the program. Then I felt better, and my life became better. It never mattered what I shared at a meeting or with my sponsor, because the response I received was always unconditional love. In the embrace of this love, I was able to fully explore myself without fear of rejection. I was able to look at my defects of character, admit to them, and ask my Higher Power to remove them. Even more important, I was able to identify my character assets as well.

Serenity became my goal one day at a time. The process has been anything but boring! The growth I attained has been much more exciting than those chaotic roller-coaster rides of the past. I thank my Higher Power every day for this priceless gift of serenity. With the Twelve Steps, Traditions, and Concepts of Service, my possibilities for growth are endless, and my life is truly exciting.

Thought for the Day

Recovery may well be the most exciting ride I will ever take in my life.

> "Because of my commitment to my own growth . . . my life continues to exceed my wildest dreams."
>
> *Courage to Change*, p. 28

My unexpressed anger at living for years in a family deeply affected by alcoholism finally reached a breaking point during an argument between my parents and me. I left the house in a rage and refused any contact with them. Two years later I was still not on speaking terms with my parents when I walked into my first Al-Anon meeting.

In Al-Anon I received the things I needed so badly from my mom and dad. The sharing of other members; the Twelve Steps and Twelve Traditions; the Conference Approved Literature; the love that flows from my Higher Power through my sponsor—all of these gave me the wisdom, nurturing, discipline, acceptance, encouragement, and support my parents weren't able to give.

Receiving the nurturing I needed has freed me to see my parents in a different light. Today I can acknowledge that they are both individuals who themselves grew up with the insanity of active alcoholism.

I am grateful that in seeing the behavioral patterns of the disease in my parents, I have the opportunity to avoid their mistakes. My parents have saved me much pain through their examples. They suffered this pain because they didn't have the gift of Al-Anon. Now I have become separate enough, full enough, and whole enough to offer my parents the love I once craved from them. They don't always accept it, but it certainly feels good to have it to give.

Thought for the Day

Higher Power, please lead me to those who can give me what I need and grant me the compassion to love those who can't.

"No one's knowledge can go beyond experience."

Alcoholism, the Family Disease, p. 22

All of the Al-Anon tools I have learned and used have pointed me down the path to gaining wisdom. For me wisdom means knowing when to stop and listen to myself and to my Higher Power rather than rushing into a decision or action. I used to think I always had to do something and that waiting was a waste of time. Now I know God speaks to me while I'm waiting.

Wisdom means being patient with myself and others. I used to blame myself for everything. Now I can practice the slogan "Think." Maybe I don't need to be responsible for this situation. Maybe this other person doesn't need to be responsible for it, either. Maybe we are all doing the best we can with what we know right now.

Wisdom means knowing I can't live life in isolation. I need others. I need the love of other humans who make mistakes, understand my being human, and still love me. I also need the love and guidance of the God who created me. He is always with me, and when I call on Him, He will answer.

Wisdom means learning to mine the diamonds hidden in my problems. I used to waste precious time being depressed about how alone and unloved I was. I was blind to everything beautiful around me and ungrateful for my blessings. Now when life hands me rocks, I use the program to polish them into valuable gems.

Thought for the Day

Wisdom is the fruit of working the Al-Anon program.

> "When we ask for wisdom, we are asking God to share special knowledge with us."
>
> *Courage to Be Me*, p. 166

If there was nothing else I could do, I always prayed: "Dear God, please make sure this is not true," or "Help me find my keys." I took care of the rest. I did not tax God unnecessarily because I was a capable person and I didn't think He could achieve anything better. The possibility He would spend time on my problems was unimaginable. I was convinced the answer would be, "You can do it yourself" or "It's your own fault, so accept the consequences."

After a few years in Al-Anon, I came to accept my powerlessness over the alcoholic in my life. However, because I could not bear the powerlessness for long, I sought help in the Second Step. At that point I became aware that I perceived God as a cold, merciless being who could not spare time to help anyone as useless as me.

I heard some members talk of God as gracious, loving, and supportive. Could this be true? The Third Step asked me to do something new—to hand over control of my will and my life, not knowing exactly who this God was or whether He would help me. At that time in my life, I was drowning in problems. I figured God couldn't slip up too much in just one day. I tried Step Three and turned myself over for the first 24 hours. I paid close attention to how I was feeling that evening. I felt good, so He got my will and my life for another 24 hours. Each new day I turn myself over to God's care because what He does is well done.

Thought for the Day

I need only turn myself over one minute, one hour, one day at a time.

> "I began turning my life over five minutes at a time and watching God very carefully to see what happened."
>
> *From Survival to Recovery,* p.34

June 6

For many years in Al-Anon I practiced detaching from others, and I eventually became fairly good at it. I developed techniques that worked for me, such as excusing myself from a potentially heated argument to read some Al-Anon literature. I learned how to diffuse criticism by replying, "You may be right," and using the slogan "Think" to help me act rather than react.

However, I wasn't so adept at detaching from myself. During a maddening bout of reacting to my own emotions, my sponsor suggested I bring my mind to where my body was by doing something physical and repeating to myself whatever I was doing. I told myself, "I'm washing the dishes," or "I'm walking on the treadmill." I was looking for something more profound, and I dismissed her idea for eight years until I was tired of repeating the same behavior. I tried her suggestion, and it worked.

When something upsetting happens, old memories of previous hurts often come back to haunt me. This makes it difficult to stay in the present and I start living simultaneously in the past and the future. The outcomes of the past get projected onto present and future situations. I become trapped in hopelessness and find it difficult to make healthy decisions.

When I get lost in time, I ask what I need right then to care for myself. If I do something physical—such as make an Al-Anon phone call, write in my journal, exercise, or work on a project—I detach from myself. The past and future go back where they belong, and I come back, much calmer, to the present.

Thought for the Day

Have I experienced the power of detachment to keep my mind in the same place as my body?

"Detachment helps families look at their situations realistically and objectively, thereby making intelligent decisions possible."

Detachment

I rarely cried while I was growing up in my alcoholic family. I was sure it was a sign of weakness. However, my emotions came as a package. When I turned off one feeling, I shut off all the others.

When my mother died, I had been in Al-Anon a little less than one year. She was my primary reason for joining the program. She was also my best friend. My grief was, and sometimes still is, unbearable. If it weren't for the program, my sponsor, and the support of fellow Al-Anon members, I wouldn't be able to grieve at all.

Thanks to the program, I now realize that grieving is not a sign of frailty. In fact, it's the opposite. Sobbing, wailing, lamenting—all different ways of discharging my pain so that I can heal—allow me to experience the strength of my aliveness. They give me the freedom to miss an amazing woman and to carry her memory with me always.

The First, Second, and Third Steps helped me locate the threshold of recovery. Then they gave me the key to open the door to accepting and loving my mother. Now they accompany me as I walk down this dark and lonely hallway called grief. I'm glad I found Al-Anon in enough time to tell my mother I loved her just as she was. I may not have done it perfectly, but I did it. My mother gave me so much, and she continues to give today. Grieving lets me know that we were truly connected and that the love I felt, and still feel, for her is real.

Thought for the Day

The feeling of grief can be an affirmation of forgiveness and reconnection.

> "I know now that the grief I experience is normal. . . But if I use the tools of the program, I will be able to work through it."

. . . In All Our Affairs, p. 58

Even in my illness, I heard very clearly the suggestion at Al-Anon meetings to get a sponsor. As I began to experience the love and acceptance for which I had longed as a child, it gave me the courage to look for a sponsor. When I found her, she was just what my Higher Power ordered. Today she is my best friend. She works one of the best programs of anyone I know, and she helps me to work mine better, too.

My sponsor has always encouraged me to receive the blessings of service—first at the group level and then at the local and area levels. In service I found a group of people who truly accept and include me. They encourage me to develop new talents and to put my existing ones to work. It's hard to stay in my problems when surrounded by so many members striving to give back to the fellowship a portion of what they had received.

When I see people in Al-Anon service working the Steps, it encourages me to get busy and work them, too. When I see others take action in their lives, it inspires me to do the same. I've made amends to my parents, and now I'm working on having a better relationship with them. I've let go of some harmful associations and developed new ones with friends in the program. I've used the talents I discovered doing service to get a college degree, a better job, and a better place to live. I know commitment to this program works because today I'm living the results.

Thought for the Day

When I make a commitment through service, I really am making a commitment to myself.

> "As I join in maintaining a program that has spread around the world, I get a sense of hope for my own life's possibilities."

When I Got Busy, I Got Better, p. 25

I came to Al-Anon a broken, scared, and hurting person. I was afraid to say what was on my mind or in my heart for fear of being ridiculed, shunned, or criticized. When I realized that I had the freedom and the choice to say how I truly thought and felt, I began to feel my Higher Power's strength surge through me.

Now I have a reputation for being direct, honest, and open— all qualities I could never have found without the "permission" and experience I received from the Al-Anon program. Sharing in the rooms was the first time I really felt I was heard or had something valuable to offer. Today when I share my experience, strength, and hope with other Al-Anon members, they look at me in disbelief as I describe my former inability to express myself verbally.

Today I can let others know how I think and feel, and I can do it in a way that's courteous, polite, and dignified. I say whatever I like as long as I say it in a respectful and caring manner.

However, even with these skills there are times when I feel afraid to speak. As these times come, I remind myself that when uncomfortable topics are broached in my Al-Anon, social, or family life, I have a right to share what is in my mind and heart. Then I pray to the God of my understanding for help: "Should I speak? What should I say? Please direct me." I'm never left for long without an answer.

Thought for the Day

When it comes to speaking up, I need to let it begin with me. Al-Anon meetings provide a healthy environment in which to take that risk.

> "Sometimes I have to fight the old urge to keep quiet at all costs, but I have found that sharing is the key to healing."
>
> *Courage to Change*, p. 111

I find the lessons of Al-Anon appearing in the most unexpected places—for example, in preflight safety instructions. Along with the details of how to fasten the seat belt and where to find the nearest emergency exit, the instructions always advise how to deal with a loss of cabin pressure. The suggestion is that I apply my own oxygen mask, thus ensuring my survival, before attempting to help others.

For me, growing up with the disease of alcoholism was like suffering from oxygen deprivation. Because my parents didn't have "masks" to wear, I didn't get many of the things I needed to thrive emotionally and spiritually. Things like consistency, structure, encouragement, and acceptance of my feelings were missing, so I certainly didn't have them to pass on to anyone else. In Al-Anon, however, I learn these things and more. Practicing the Al-Anon program is akin to putting on an oxygen mask. I'm encouraged to do the things needed for my health, stability, and growth. These include eating well, getting enough rest, examining my behavior and correcting it when necessary, sharing my thoughts and feelings with others, asking for help, praying and meditating, and getting involved with my Al-Anon community. Only then, when I have taken care of these responsibilities to myself, am I strong and stable enough to help others.

Thought for the Day

Caring for myself first is part of caring for others. Am I taking care of myself today?

> "I pray for help to fulfill my responsibility to myself; only then can I help others."

One Day at a Time in Al-Anon, p. 91

After working the Al-Anon program for many years, I have learned that living the Steps requires two primary acts. First, I remain mindful of the suggestion that I *surrender* whatever it is about myself or someone else that I am trying to control. In other words, I need to let go of my ego. Letting go, turning it over, and keeping it simple all remind me that God is taking care of me and my life challenges. Sometimes when I feel exceptionally stressed, surrender does not come easily. Ultimately I must even let go of the surrendering process. I cannot control the moment my Higher Power decides to grant me the grace to feel and act serenely.

The second act in working the Steps is *faith*. This requires simply trusting that my Higher Power is there for me, sometimes in spite of myself and my best efforts. I need to choose the right action on the basis of that trust. I've found that I can surrender my control and my will endlessly, but surrender is meaningless unless I follow through with action based on faith. When I forget about the faith part, I take back my worries over and over again. When I doubt that God is listening, all I need to do is remember the countless times peace has surrounded me in the past. Faith takes over from there.

Thought for the Day

Al-Anon works. All I need to do is surrender my ego, act in faith, and follow the wisdom of the Steps. My Higher Power does the rest.

> "Whenever I trust God and surrender to Him, He has really helped."
>
> *Having Had a Spiritual Awakening . . .*, p. 94

I thought I could skip over Step One because I didn't live with my alcoholic stepfather anymore. Then I heard other members apply Step One in a different way. They substituted other words or phrases for the word "alcohol." Instead of saying they were powerless over alcohol, they mentioned other people or situations over which they were powerless.

I looked to my past and saw with new clarity the times I had tried to exert control without results. I hid my stepfather's booze. I avoided my mother's constant yelling by staying out late, often getting into trouble. I finally saw how these attempts at control had harmed rather than helped me.

I looked to my present and recognized how I sought to gain other people's acceptance by saying or doing—or in some cases not saying or not doing—the things I thought they wanted. Manipulation had become second nature to me. I discovered how much I wanted other people to change so I could be happy. I even saw how I took pains to control the speed and direction of my own recovery.

Sometimes it takes me a while to figure out whom or what I can't control. When I figure it out, I can put the appropriate word into Step One. Today the usefulness of Step One is broader for me because I can substitute all manner of people and situations for "alcohol." This breadth also helps me work Step Twelve because each and every one of my affairs contains elements I can't control.

Thought for the Day

Step One can be a multi-purpose tool.

"We can take Al-Anon's First Step, admitting that we are powerless over the facts of our situation and the other people involved and that our lives have become unmanageable."

. . . In All Our Affairs, p. 31

Step Two, "Came to believe that a Power greater than myself could restore me to sanity," used to be difficult for me. I was upset with the word "sanity." As a child growing up in an alcoholic home, I experienced insanity. I saw my mother taken to a psychiatric unit and labeled "crazy" by family, neighbors, and friends. She was blamed and criticized for an entire family's disease. As an adult I, too, was held responsible for my family's illness. When I came to Al-Anon and heard "sanity," all I could think of was the lack of it. I feared becoming like my mother.

What I had overlooked in Step Two was the word "Power." The day I started placing my attention on that Power instead of on insanity, I began to see miracles in my life. One such miracle was my ability to talk about my fears in Al-Anon meetings. Other miracles included taking the Twelve Steps that led me to serenity, and engaging in the process of forgiving and healing.

It has taken many years of hearing Step Two read at meetings for me to really hear the word "Power." Now I realize how much more awesome my Higher Power is than this disease. Instead of dwelling in fear, today I am striving to pass on the miracles of recovery to my children.

Thought for the Day

Dear God, when I get caught up in the craziness of my life, please help me to focus on Your awesome power to restore me to sanity.

> "Belief grows as we open our minds enough to consider
> that a spiritual resource could help us with our problems."
>
> Paths to Recovery, p. 18

When I first started going to Al-Anon meetings, the phrase "came to believe" struck me as nothing new. All my life I had been taught to believe in God, and I had always done so. To act on my belief, however, was an entirely different matter. When asked in Step Three to decide to turn my will and my life over to the care of God, I wasn't sure I could.

I felt frightened to turn over even the slightest thing, so I decided to start small. First, I turned over a reaction someone had to something I said. I was amazed to discover that although the person didn't react as I wished, I still felt at peace and was able to respond appropriately. Soon I was turning slightly larger issues over to God. In time, my trust in my Higher Power began to grow.

The following analogy helped me understand trust even more. A rock climber has a rope for safety. Unless he uses it, however, the rope does no good. Trust, through which I commit the action of turning over my daily challenges to my Higher Power, is my "rope," my lifeline. It allows me to be more serene and to take on life in ways that might otherwise seem reckless and ridiculous.

For me faith isn't a feeling. Rather, it's a reality, based on the results of my choice to trust. My belief transforms into faith as I take the action required by Step Three and make a decision.

Thought for the Day

If I don't take the action to trust, my Higher Power has nothing to work with.

> "... My actions demonstrate my willingness to be helped.
> And time after time, the help I need is given to me."

Courage to Change, p. 48

Why would I do a Fourth Step? Because I am worth it. I am worth the time and effort of pursuing recovery rather than stewing in my difficulties. I am going about the process of determining, with as much honesty as possible, just what makes me tick. I don't have to do it alone. My Higher Power is with me all the way.

How can I benefit from doing an inventory? I want to relieve myself of those self-defeating attitudes and behaviors that block me from living life to the fullest. I know my recovery is a lifelong journey, and I begin it by identifying troublesome areas right here, right now. I ask myself certain questions. What are the attitudes and behaviors that may have served me (or at least gave the illusion of serving me) in the past but now limit my capacity to experience joy and fulfillment? What are the resentments that keep me in bondage to the past? Can I honestly admit my part in my difficulties and strained relationships? Am I still holding on to situations in which I have no fault ? Do I have the courage to take responsibility for my own feelings and actions? Do I accept that although I am powerless to change anything from my past, I can claim happiness for my future? Am I coming to trust and value myself? Do I know that I am worthy of loving myself as my Higher Power already does?

Doing a Fourth Step inventory is something I do *for* me, not *to* me. Satisfaction for a job well done can only enhance my self-worth. As a result, I like myself better.

Thought for the Day

With the Fourth Step I begin the process of becoming not perfect but more perfectly at peace with myself.

> "Now complete honesty is required in order to know ourselves."
>
> *The Al-Anon Family Groups—Classic Edition*, p. 114

I was sure I'd never take Step Five. Step Four was nearly impossible, and Step Five seemed to require more strength than I possessed. Ugly character defects had sprouted on my written inventory like poisonous mushrooms, and I was determined they would stay there, never to be revealed to anyone else. I felt too ashamed. Besides, my alcoholic family had taught me all too well that no one was trustworthy.

One day an Al-Anon friend stopped by, and we began discussing Step Five. When she offered to help me with it, I panicked and searched desperately for excuses. After every pretext I cited, she told me, "Get your list." Finally I got my list. There wasn't a single positive word on it. As I read each defect, she told me quietly how *she* saw me. She pointed out my positive attributes and accomplishments. She asked me to do the same and suggested I write them down next to my shortcomings. Eight hours and several boxes of tissues later, she congratulated me on having the courage to stick with the task when it was obviously so excruciating. I was stunned that anyone could hear the horrendous things I'd done and still be gentle and loving toward me. That day I began to trust.

Since then I listen particularly closely to others' sharings. Hearing them describe their own irrational behavior, and sometimes even laugh at it, helps me keep at bay the insane denial that fooled no one but myself. No longer do I have to suffer in silence with my human imperfection.

Thought for the Day

Step Five invites me to leave the emotional prison in which I have spent my life and seek ongoing recovery through working the rest of the Steps.

> "It took my Fifth Step to really teach me I was ... a person who belonged on earth, at one with humanity."
>
> *From Survival to Recovery*, p. 193

Step Six says, "Were entirely ready to have God remove all these defects of character." Suddenly, after having heard and read this Step for three years, the word "remove" jumped off the page. I looked up its definition in the dictionary, and here's what I found: "a distancing or separation of one person or thing from another." Nowhere in the definition did it say there would be a complete disappearance of the person or thing.

So it is with my shortcomings. They are not magically, completely, and irrevocably banished from my life. If this truly were the case, I wouldn't take them back on occasion. However, my Higher Power does separate my defects from me. God shows me how to set them aside. The concrete action of setting them aside becomes apparent as I work the program on a daily basis. I now examine situations and determine my contribution to them. I remind myself I can make different choices in my words and actions and become willing to enact them. Then I let it begin with me by making amends for my part. If I'm willing to do these things and others, I can keep some spiritual distance between myself and my character defects.

Thought for the Day

Although God does not completely eradicate my defects, I am provided with Al-Anon tools to maintain my separation from them.

> "I expected to just say, 'Okay, God, take over,' and they'd be gone overnight. It didn't quite work out that way."
>
> *Twelve Steps and Twelve Traditions for Alateen*, p. 15

I struggled with the Sixth Step for two years before I finally got it. I was in the habit of blaming two particular people for all my problems. I would take turns detesting and obsessing about each of them instead of focusing on myself.

During this time I continued to work my way through the Steps. By the time I got to Step Seven, I finally understood that the best way for me to recover was to change my attitudes. I prayed to my Higher Power to remove my obsession with others and to help me focus on myself.

Many of my character defects improved as I continued to work my program, but I still struggled with keeping the focus on myself. One day an Al-Anon friend gave me a coffee mug with a special prayer printed on it, reminding me to ask my Higher Power to remove my character defects. She knew about my struggles and thought seeing the prayer every day with my morning coffee might help.

Every morning I saw that prayer, which encouraged me to practice Step Seven more intently. My friend's intentions didn't take too long to manifest. Within several days I had a spiritual awakening. In this matter, as in all others, I had to submit to the God of my understanding. I realized that I had been pray-ing—no, dictating—to my Higher Power which character defect I wanted removed most. As I finally surrendered, I knew in my heart what I needed to pray for. I asked to be relieved of what-ever character defects prevented me from being God's channel for this one day.

Thought for the Day

I pray to trust the decisions of my Higher Power, Who knows which of my shortcomings need to be removed and when.

"We learn to trust God's way and pace as we go about our business."

Paths to Recovery, p. 72

I listened intently as others shared on Step Eight. When it was my turn to speak, I mouthed the words I had heard so often: "My parents did the best they could. I made peace with them at their gravesite." The words hung hollow as vivid memories of my alcoholic mother still tortured me. In desperation I finally talked with my sponsor, who assured me I didn't have to make amends yet. I just had to become willing, and my willingness would allow me to move on. I held this thought for several days as memories flooded me with fierce intensity.

The longer I reflected on becoming willing, the brighter the light of understanding grew. I realized that my family had lived in the black-and-white world of alcoholism. I understood that my parents didn't have healthy parenting skills and were unaware I had done as well as any unsupervised 12-year-old could be expected to do.

With these thoughts, something melted inside of me. Perhaps it was my own hardened heart. I didn't have to go to my parents' graves to make amends. It happened when I softened enough to become willing.

Thought for the Day

When I can see the disease of alcoholism, rather than the alcoholic, as the cause of my wounds, the deep healing of recovery can begin.

> "Step Eight reminds us that only we can unlock the door of our past and walk away."

Paths to Recovery, p. 84

Step Nine, "Made direct amends to such people wherever possible, except when to do so would injure them or others," was a recent topic at my Al-Anon meeting. Members shared many painful stories about parent-child relationships that sounded as if they couldn't be repaired. I wondered whether mine could be. Then I heard my "magic formula" from another member—to ask myself what talents I received from my parents. That night I wrote down the many talents I had received from my father, the alcoholic, and I felt exhilarated.

The next night I sat down to write the talents I had received from my mother. The page was blank; my mind was blank; I could remember only the pain. So for the next few weeks I prayed. I sat down again, and this time my Higher Power wrote the words: genuine, thoughtful, patient, gentle, insightful. I knew I had those qualities, and my mother had them, too. Could I have received them from her? Yes, I could have, and I had. I felt humble and grateful when I realized that these gifts had come from my mother. My anger dissipated, and I felt close to her for the first time. Now I could begin to be the kind of daughter I had always wanted to be.

Thought for the Day

My parents have passed many of their talents, not just their burdens, on to me. Realizing this could be a step toward repairing my relationship with them.

> "Everyone who plays a part in our lives offers something we might learn."

Courage to Change, p. 335

June 21

Step Ten , "Continued to take personal inventory and when we were wrong promptly admitted it," reminds me that I have the right to be human. My sponsor tells me that God made me a perfect human being, not a perfect God. I certainly do engage regularly in a wide array of human behaviors—making mistakes, harming others, and hurting myself. No matter how long I am in recovery, I'll never progress beyond being human.

However, accepting my human condition doesn't mean I have to live with the uncomfortable feelings, such as guilt and shame, which often go along with making human mistakes. Step Ten invites me to regularly keep a finger on my spiritual pulse so I can cooperate with God in my spiritual growth and healing. It says that if I do or say something wrong, I can stop, turn around, and do something different now. Step Ten invites me to grow up, to be responsible, and to make amends—all for my own benefit. I take Step Ten because I want to be the best me I can be.

Thought for the Day

When I continue to take personal inventory and amend my wrongs, I can live my life peacefully with God's other children.

> "This Step continues the process which began with Step Four—being aware of the things we do, and taking corrective measures without delay…"
>
> *Twelve Steps and Twelve Traditions for Alateen*, p. 20

It took me many years in Al-Anon to get to Step Eleven, the "prayer and meditation" Step. When I finally got there, after wrestling with Steps Four through Ten, Step Eleven became my spiritual oasis. Working it made my life a kinder, gentler one.

During my time in Al-Anon, I went through a period of separation and eventual divorce from my husband. When this process began, I was working my way through Steps Nine and Ten. When my situation was at its most chaotic, I started on Step Eleven. I felt lonely living alone. Although I did not miss my husband's alcoholic behavior, I missed him. Through the prayer and meditation of Step Eleven, I became less lonely, less uncomfortable being single. Living on my own felt like less of a burden because I could relax and allow myself to be enveloped by the comforting presence of a Power greater than myself.

Through prayer and meditation, I developed a warm and comforting relationship with God as I understand Him. Sitting still gave me time to listen to myself. I sat quietly and explored my mind and heart. I asked my Higher Power to speak to me in the silence and reveal what He wanted of me today and in the difficult months to come.

As always my Al-Anon program did not disappoint me. The prayer and meditation suggested in Step Eleven helped me hear my Higher Power's voice within. Prayer and meditation helped me know myself and in so doing helped me discern my Higher Power's will for my life.

Thought for the Day

I never, ever need to be alone. All I need to do is make conscious contact with God as I understand Him.

> "When we turn to God, we find He has been facing us all the time."

As We Understood . . ., p. 200

Now that I'm in touch with my intuition, I don't hold back as much as I once did. Al-Anon has taught me that when something feels right, I can trust it is the right thing to do.

I take in typing projects at home and recently typed the family chronicles of an elderly customer. Because it was a 500-page endeavor, we worked together for several months. It was a delightful project, and I grew fond of her. When the project had been completed and we said our goodbyes, I reached out spontaneously to give her a hug.

She stiffened, however, and didn't return the embrace. Apprehension reared up in me, and I backed off. We parted company with just a few words. I questioned myself during the next few days. I was sure I had stepped unknowingly over an invisible line. It was a terrible feeling.

The customer returned later to give me something. During our visit, she shared with me how much the hug had meant to her. She said it had felt so good she started hugging others. She even began asking her husband, sons, and grandchildren for hugs.

I was astonished at how differently we had each perceived the same situation. My sponsor suggested that the more I healed, the more I'd become a messenger of the program while God chose the message. Who knew I'd be used in such a delightful way to spread a little warmth of the program?

Thought for the Day

There are as many ways to work the Twelfth Step as there are stars in the sky.

> "We who have lived in anguish for so long have discovered a way to live in serenity, one day at a time, and our greatest joy is to share this way of life with others."

As We Understood . . ., p. 231

For some time I struggled with the part of Tradition Five that says, ". . . encouraging and understanding our alcoholic relatives." I felt as if I were being encouraged to do what I came to Al-Anon to stop—aiding and abetting alcoholics.

After talking with a longtime member who once had similar difficulty with this Tradition, I clarified for myself what kind of encouragement and understanding I could provide. For encouragement I could practice detachment by doing my best to allow the alcoholics the dignity of making their own choices. For understanding I could work to recognize the disease and its effects, thereby improving my perspective.

Perhaps these forms of encouragement and understanding would provide cold comfort to some of the alcoholics in my life. In recovery, however, I've learned that I can set limits on what I am willing and able to contribute to others. By taking care of myself and slowly building positive relationships with alcoholics, I exhibit the message of hope found in Al-Anon meetings.

Thought for the Day

Today I give whatever understanding and encouragement I can to the alcoholics in my life. It is based on what I can provide, not on what they want.

> "I can have compassion for loved ones who suffer from the disease of alcoholism, or its effects, without losing my sense of self."
>
> *Courage to Change*, p. 194

As I was growing up, I felt unsure and afraid of life. In my alcoholic family, we didn't discuss thoughts and feelings, so I believed I was the only person who felt this way. I hid my insecurities for fear of being ridiculed and shamed by those who knew me. Although it hurt, keeping my secrets to myself made me feel safe.

I attended my first Al-Anon meeting at the persuasion of a college roommate. I didn't expect to get anything from it because, although my father was an alcoholic, his biggest offenses seemed limited to annoying philosophical ramblings. However, I was surprised and thrilled to hear others speak about their feelings. They shared in a large group of people the very thoughts I was afraid to admit even to myself. When I left the meeting, I didn't feel quite so alone.

After immersing myself in the open, honest atmosphere I found at Al-Anon meetings, I began to feel less vulnerable and started to open up. I found that there are many others like me. I learned that harboring secrets is one of the subtle effects of the disease of alcoholism.

My growth in this area has been about progress, not perfection. I sometimes still hide parts of myself from others, but keeping secrets no longer provides a sense of safety. When I share, I have an opportunity to experience the love and understanding of my fellow Al-Anon members. I feel more attractive, more worthy, more excited about life. I no longer feel there is something drastically wrong with me because I know I am not alone.

Thought for the Day

In Al-Anon I can set my secrets and myself free.

> ". . . In Al-Anon we find something available nowhere else—a community of people who share many of the same life experiences we have had and who understand as perhaps no one else can."

Paths to Recovery, p. 204

"Are you uneasy when your life is going smoothly, continually anticipating problems?" I identify with this question from the Al-Anon leaflet, "Did You Grow Up with a Problem Drinker?"

Today my life *is* going very well, thanks to the recovery work I have done in Al-Anon. I have a great job, a wonderful husband, and I'm finally working toward the graduate degree I've wanted for so long. Yet as great as this all feels, I'm still on edge. I'm still waiting for the other shoe to drop. It's as if I don't know how to handle happiness, so I start searching for difficulties to dwell on. I lie awake at night wondering if my car will break down. I try to guess what my employees are thinking, and I feel anxious if I'm not a week ahead on my schoolwork. The obsession is annoying, even to me.

Of course, none of this fretting serves any purpose. Even if I could anticipate all potential problems and have solutions in mind, my worry won't protect me from something that may never happen. When I have turned to my Higher Power in the past to remove my worries about *real* problems, She has come through for me. I need to remind myself that She can remove the *imaginary* difficulties, too. If I accept that I'm powerless over my mind's negative energy, if I desire to be restored to sanity, and if I ask my Higher Power to help me, She will do so. I can trust Her. All that's left for me to do is the footwork on each issue as needed. Then I can let go and enjoy my life.

Thought for the Day

When I've done all I can, I can "Let Go and Let God."

"...Worrying will not protect me from the future. It will just keep me from living here and now."

Courage to Change, p. 15

Tradition Eight says, "Al-Anon Twelfth Step work should remain forever nonprofessional, but our service centers may employ special workers." It shows us how to keep the spiritual part of our program spiritual. It defines the separation between the heart and the hands of Al-Anon. Certain work needs to be done to keep our program available to others—designing *The-Forum*, packing literature to send to various groups, emptying the wastebaskets at the World Service Office so that they don't overflow, etc. Additionally many specialized tasks need to be done as a necessary part of sustaining a large organization such as Al-Anon. It makes sense to pay people to do the things that need to be done.

However, Tradition Eight makes it clear that the true business of Al-Anon—its Twelfth Step work—remains nonprofessional and non-compensated monetarily. The love shared in this program between members is not something that can be bought; it's a gift, not a commodity. The great and wonderful paradox is that we give it away freely with no expectation of compensation, and we are nonetheless richly rewarded by receiving even more love and recovery than we give away.

Thought for the Day

Tradition Eight is a simple one. It provides for maintaining the body of Al-Anon so that the spirit of love can thrive.

"Tradition Eight guides us on how to carry the message of Al-Anon to others."

Paths to Recovery, p. 207

Before coming to Al-Anon, I spent most of my life having expectations of, and making unrealistic demands on, everyone around me. Anyone who didn't follow through on these demands invited my wrath. However, of all those I placed under my jurisdiction, the person I was hardest on was myself.

It felt strange, therefore, to come through the doors of Al-Anon to a place not governed by cruel dictators who gave harsh commands. Instead, I heard things like "Keep It Simple" and "Easy Does It." It was like entering a new and different world where I was taught to love myself and to treat myself with dignity and respect. Luckily I didn't have to learn these difficult lessons alone. Rather, I learned by watching other Al-Anon members treat themselves—and me—with love, dignity, and respect.

As other members modeled these approaches in relating to me, I was eager to use each one, right away! Quite often I stumbled while trying to implement too many changes at once by using my same old forceful self-will. Then I learned I could apply the slogans not just to the happenings in my life but also to the manner in which I worked my program. Members encouraged me to eliminate "have-tos" and "shoulds" and to slow down so that I could consciously choose which changes felt right to me. I've discovered that the only thing barely approaching a "have-to" in Al-Anon is willingness, and even that is optional. I can work my program at the speed and to the degree that suits my needs at any given time.

Thought for the Day

Bullying myself into recovery won't work. Loving myself into it will.

". . . While 'hard' doesn't do it, 'easy' often does."
How Al-Anon Works for Families & Friends of Alcoholics, p. 68

The word "we" used in so many of the Steps has become precious to me. It tells me that I am not alone and that I belong. It gives me courage to do things I would normally fear doing alone, like trying out new behaviors. "We" assures me that someone else is experiencing the same emotions as I am. Better yet, it means someone has lived through them and not only survived but thrived. It comforts me to know that others have walked the path I now travel. "We" acts as a beacon of light calling me to recovery.

My personal "we" is composed of my Higher Power, myself, and my Al-Anon community. Together we make up a simple majority needed for my protection, encouragement, and enlightenment along my recovery journey. This unified trio helps me fight my fears with faith and courage. "We" means my life is no longer a wilderness within which I am trapped, wandering aimlessly. Today serenity surrounds me on my journey. Signs and guideposts point me in the right direction, toward fullness and meaning. I no longer merely have to survive the hour, the day, or even the year in loneliness and isolation. Instead I can learn to trust someone else and take chances based on the wisdom of the Al-Anon program. "We" helps me learn to walk in freedom and dignity and to become the person my God designed me to be.

Thought for the Day

I need never again do anything alone.

"Together we're going to make it!"

Alateen—a day at a time, p. 170

As a child I seldom felt as though I had enough of any-thing—especially love, attention, and approval. It seemed no matter what my parents said or did, I always wanted more. As an adult I tried to get my needs met in other ways. I ate too much, thinking I could fill my empty spaces with food. I shopped in too many stores, searching for that elusive merchandise that would finally make me feel complete. I sought "substitute parents" whose attention and approval would make me feel good about my life and myself.

In Al-Anon I learned that when I expect more than oth-ers can give, I am setting myself up. Trying to get something or someone on the outside to make me content on the inside is futile. As my sponsor says, happiness is an inside job; it's my responsibility. No wonder my parents couldn't do, say, or give enough. Even if they hadn't been alcoholics, they still wouldn't have been responsible for my inner peace and contentment.

Today I find happiness in Al-Anon and in a close relationship with my Higher Power. Through daily prayer and meditation, I discover that I am exactly where God wants me to be. Whether times are good or bad, I can always count on my Higher Power to generously supply whatever I need. I've come to accept that my parents are exactly where God wants them to be, too. They cannot make me whole and complete. That job belongs to my Higher Power and me. This is powerful knowledge. It's a step toward a new way of life—rich with the love, attention, and approval from my Higher Power. Today I know I will always have enough.

Thought for the Day

What behaviors do I use to get my needs met? How are they working?

"Al-Anon members give me unconditional love and healthy attention."

From Survival to Recovery, p. 25

The last sentence in Tradition Two is, "Our leaders are but trusted servants; they do not govern." This prompts me to focus on an obstacle to success in Al-Anon—dominance. We strive to conduct our meetings as a fellowship of equals and to practice rotation of leadership. However, sometimes a member may keep a service position because no one else seems inclined to step forward to fill it.

Occasionally, I have held service positions too long. I've learned that sometimes it is necessary for me to let go whether or not a replacement has stepped forward. No one can pick up the ball until I've dropped it. I also have learned that what I view as a finely developed sense of responsibility may actually amount to a form of dominance.

I cannot attempt to direct the affairs of the group without standing in the way of the group's recovery or my own.

Thought for the Day

Today I will participate in Al-Anon's rotation of leadership.

> "One reason that rotation of duties is so important is that it gives everyone an equal opportunity for responsibility. Rotation also helps prevent a person from taking authority for a job."

Paths to Recovery, p. 216

July 2

In my search for help in coping with the effects of growing up with alcoholism, I accumulated shelves of books on psychology, religion, and a variety of self-disciplines. As a child I felt I could count on no one, and I was suspicious of asking others for help. I preferred to seek a solo form of assistance from books.

I started attending Al-Anon meetings sporadically, but I still didn't feel comfortable reaching out to the people there. Ironically, given my preference for the written word, I didn't grasp the idea that thousands of real-life Al-Anon experiences were available to me in Conference Approved Literature. It didn't dawn on me that this literature, right at my comfort level, could be my entrée into Al-Anon and into the experience of turning to others for comfort and guidance.

A friend of my family who attends Al-Anon meetings noted my struggle and gently shared with me the benefits she found from reading CAL. Aware that someone genuinely cared, I decided to buy my first Al-Anon book. I read it at home alone and pondered it for quite some time before I decided to give regular attendance at Al-Anon meetings a fair attempt.

Now I'm slowly accumulating a full library of Al-Anon publications by purchasing them at meetings and studying each one in turn. I've even mustered the courage to discuss my readings with other members. The insights garnered have turned my suspicion into trust. I've come out of my solitary personal library into the welcoming human world of Al-Anon.

Thought for the Day

Any entrance into Al-Anon is valid, even if at first it's not the door to the meeting place.

> "Our literature is a principal means by which Al-Anon growth, unity and service are facilitated. The influence of the many thousand books and pamphlets . . . is incalculable."
>
> *Al-Anon/Alateen Service Manual*, p. 182

If I'm going to get healthy, I need to attend healthy meetings. At my first meeting the members focused on problems rather than seek Al-Anon solutions. At first it was tempting to join them. After all, no one had really listened to me at home. Wasn't I entitled to a little sympathy because of all I had been through?

We all need to share some of our problems from time to time. However, I soon realized that dwelling on them week after week, with no movement toward recovery, was not helping me. Only after attending healthy meetings—ones focused on finding solutions through use of the Steps, Traditions, Concepts of Service, and Conference Approved Literature—did I finally begin to recover from the effects of growing up in an alcoholic home. These meetings, along with performing service work and seeking the help of a sponsor who was well-established in the program, helped me start taking responsibility for my choices.

I soon found that accepting responsibility in Al-Anon includes letting healthy meetings begin with me. When I look back, I realize my growth in the area of responsibility could have begun by speaking about my concerns at the first meeting. I don't punish myself for not having had those skills back then. Instead, I do my best to focus on sharing the positive rather than the negative. I follow the Traditions and encourage others to do the same, and I include the Steps and CAL in my sharing. I also support others in performing service at various levels. In Al-Anon I truly get back what I give.

Thought for the Day

What I get from and give to my meetings can change how I live my life today.

> "If a meeting doesn't go well, I speak up and try to put in my share to get it back on track."

Alateen—a day at a time, p. 208

July 4

Someone recently asked me to speak on my recovery in the area of intimacy and sexuality. The alcoholism in my family has impacted every area of my life, and my sexuality and enjoyment of intimacy are no exception. I fear intimacy as much as I crave it. I enjoy it for a while, but then I start feeling like I'm losing myself in the other person. I have some damaging perceptions about my body and its imperfections. Because affection was not easily expressed in my family, I often question my spontaneous inner urges to give someone a fond hug or kiss.

I didn't think my Higher Power wanted me to work on my character defects in the area of sexuality. However, I became aware that God already had been healing me in this area—quietly, gently, with great compassion and much love. Although I didn't realize it at first, this healing started when my sponsor suggested I take an inventory of my sexuality, sensuality, intimacy, passion, affection, self-expression, and desire.

I followed my sponsor's suggestion, and it proved to be a journey of surprises and discoveries. First, I learned to recognize, accept, trust, and enjoy my instincts and expressions. Then I learned how to set guidelines for myself and others regarding acceptable and unacceptable sexual behavior. Now I'm working on differentiating my physical sexuality from my mental, physical, emotional, and spiritual *sensuality* and passions. I now celebrate the gifts of my body, senses, and soul in intimate and sacred relationships with God, myself, my spouse, and others in my life.

Thought for the Day

Intimacy, sensuality, and passion are not limited to physical expression.

> "That was when I learned that sex is only part of intimacy—that intimacy encompasses caring and sharing, laughing, crying and praying together, touching and hugging, giving and taking."
>
> *Sexual Intimacy and the Alcoholic Relationship*, p. 40

When I first learned of Tradition Seven, which speaks of being fully self-supporting, I thought it meant I should support my group by donating when the basket is passed. Since then it has come to mean much more. I give support by attending and sharing at meetings, by setting out literature, by taking on a service position in the group, and by making calls when I need help. In short I support my group when I perform service.

While I've always attended other meetings to gain fresh perspectives, my home group is where I give back that little extra. At one point I considered changing home groups, but I decided to stay and focus my attention and energy there. In the long run, it is really up to each of us to make our home groups the best they can be. If I see that something could be strengthened in my group, it's up to me as much as anyone to help strengthen it. In this way I can live by Tradition Seven and keep my group self-supporting.

Thought for the Day

I have the responsibility to maintain the health of my home group, from which I derive my personal recovery—"Let It Begin with Me."

> "I had to make a contribution in order to get help. It wasn't a money contribution. It was I. I had to contribute a little bit of myself."
>
> *Courage to Be Me*, p. 230

July 6

Disappointments that come from growing up with alcoholism fueled my expectations that bad things would always happen. I came to expect the worst, leading to a deep fear that permeated my will and my life.

When I came to Al-Anon, I heard that faith replaces fear. However, I thought faith was something I either had or I didn't, as if it were granted or withheld by something outside myself. I didn't know faith is a spiritual skill to be cultivated. I didn't know my faith would evolve into a concrete awareness that God will always come through.

I practice faith using "Let Go and Let God" and Step Three. When I explore a new behavior and detach from the outcome, I experience the resolution of my problems—without intervention on my part. Such incidents form a repository of trust I can lean on the next time difficulty arises.

When fear overcomes me, I fall back on meetings. Whatever the threat, I know I can always go to a meeting where I'm reminded that this, too, shall pass. This puts me back on the path of faith and trust in my Higher Power.

I have also discovered something rather unnerving—I can easily possess faith one day and struggle with it the next. As someone who prefers consistency, it took me a while to become comfortable with the variable nature of *feeling* faith. Today I know my struggle with feeling faith is not an indication that I don't possess it. It's a natural part of the process. Faith exists whether or not I feel it.

Thought for the Day

When fear looms large, I can take faithful action to put the fear into perspective.

> "Now I have learned to rely so much on God that I can shrug off most of my fears."

> *The Forum*, May 1998, p. 24

I felt victimized by the alcoholics I lived with while growing up, and I carried this attitude into my adult life. I took pains to appear mature, successful, grown up, and in charge. Inside, however, I felt like a scared little kid who was completely out of control. I continued to feel and act like a perpetual victim—fearful, reactive, and unable to cope. My fear became even more intense when I learned that my son was an alcoholic. Fortunately when he sought recovery, I found Al-Anon.

In Al-Anon I learned that I have choices. I don't need to be a helpless, hopeless victim. Instead, I can take responsibility for myself each moment through the choices I make. I can attend a meeting, call someone in the program, ask for guidance, pray, and work my program.

It isn't always easy. Sometimes I need to ask God to grant me courage to ask for help rather than to wallow in self-pity and fear. I can ask myself what I need and then do whatever is necessary to get my needs met. I don't have to worry about what everyone else is doing; they have their own Higher Power who cares for them. I can ask for courage to change the things I can and for serenity to accept the things I can't. Reminding myself that I always have choices gives me hope and courage to leave fear and passivity behind. I am always held in the care of my Higher Power, who gives me security and inspiration to act boldly by changing the one thing I can—myself.

Thought for the Day

Acting like a victim is a choice, not a destiny.

> "Victims create victims. Fortunately, recovery works the
> same way—recovery creates expanding recovery."
>
> *From Survival to Recovery*, p. 205

The word I would most likely use to describe the atmosphere of the home in which I grew up is "angry." For a while my parents were inactive alcoholics, although uncontrollable rages and frequent beatings were a common occurrence. None of this made sense until my mother started drinking again. I was almost grateful; at least then the insanity made sense. I never thought, "If only she'd stop drinking," but I did spend a lot of time and energy trying to understand her behavior.

I finally made my way into Al-Anon. Once during the fellowship time after the meeting, I shared a little bit about my mom and our relationship. The person with whom I was speaking said my mother's behavior sounded crazy. I had a big laugh. "Oh, yes," I said, "she's sick, and if I spend my time trying to figure her out instead of minding my own business, I'll get sick, too!"

Mom doesn't drink anymore, but she doesn't have a program, either. Today I can enjoy the parts of her that are well and leave the rest. Then I don't make myself insane, and my anger toward her is replaced with compassion. By minding my own business, practicing the principles of the program, and participating regularly in my home group, the atmosphere of my home life is one of serenity.

Thought for the Day

How do I use the Al-Anon program to achieve peace and serenity in my relationships with others?

> "... I put the focus on me and what I could do to heal myself."
>
> *From Survival to Recovery*, p. 60

I came to Alateen because my father was an alcoholic. I was introduced to the Al-Anon ideas in Alateen, but my focus was on the bonding and acceptance of my peers. I always felt out of place at home and at school. In Alateen I felt as if I belonged. I had wonderful sponsors, and many of the teens I met became my friends with whom I enjoyed a variety of outings and pursuits.

I made the transition into Al-Anon and have been here many years. However, lately I have been feeling as if something is missing. I often come home from meetings feeling empty rather than filled with healthy suggestions and ideas. I feel as if my body was at the meeting, but my mind wasn't really there.

I realize I've been considering Al-Anon's primary purpose to be friendship instead of recovery. The reason I come home feeling empty is because I'm usually thinking of where we'll all go after the meeting, or whether someone might want to go to a movie later. When I'm thinking about personalities, my mind is too full to hear the principles being shared.

I don't want to deny myself the possible friendships I could make in the program. I don't want them to be my primary focus, either. After all, nowhere in the Steps, Traditions, Concepts of Service, or slogans does it say I will make friends. Friendships can develop as I devote myself to my recovery.

Thought for the Day

The Traditions help me focus on why I attend Al-Anon.

"Each Al-Anon group has but one purpose: to help families of alcoholics. We do this by practicing the Twelve Steps of AA *ourselves*, by encouraging and understanding our alcoholic relatives, and by welcoming and giving comfort to families of alcoholics."

Tradition Five

When I care about something, I willingly give it my time and attention. I care about Al-Anon, and I care about my groups. I have a vested interest in their health and growth. So I do what is in my power to do. I participate freely and with love. I do whatever needs to be done—set up, clean up, chair meetings, and speak with newcomers. I do these things not out of a sense of obligation but because I belong. I feel as though I am a part of these groups.

I feel comfortable participating in Al-Anon meetings because in them I find an atmosphere of trust and mutual respect. However, I wasn't always so open. There have been times in my life when I didn't trust and I didn't receive respect, so I withdrew. I didn't allow myself to stay and work through the challenges offered to me. Now that I'm in recovery, I don't want to limit my opportunities to grow by restricting my involvement with others, whether or not they are in the program. As always, Al-Anon teaches me to pray, look at myself and my attitudes, and then take action.

For me this action means detaching from people's behavior and giving them the same acceptance, consideration, and respect for which I long. To live more harmoniously with others, I practice "Live and Let Live." I endeavor to accept that people are human and have human frailties and limitations, as do I. When I don't expect perfection from others or from myself, I am free to participate and be a part of life.

Thought for the Day

A sense of belonging is as necessary to my spiritual health as air is to my lungs.

> "Recognizing this spiritual need to belong, the principle of participating has been built into our whole service structure."
>
> *The Concepts—Al-Anon's Best Kept Secret?*, p. 11

One of the oddest things I learned in recovery was to develop tolerance and even desire for feeling good. At first I didn't connect much with other people. I didn't let anything approximating intimacy occur. Later, I noticed a paradox. When someone accepted or cared for me, I felt pleasure and pain. I was perplexed. Why would I feel pain at the same time as happiness? I asked an Al-Anon friend about this. She wondered if experiencing the good feelings I yearned for as a child might stir up some pain. She said the "receiving" might, for a short time, bring up the "not receiving."

Her words proved to be true for me. I did go through a recovery phase during which receiving others' love, approval, and respect almost instantly recalled deeply buried sadness at not having received those things from my parents while I was growing up. In fact, I often didn't know such pain was inside until someone was nice to me. Then I would pour it out into my sponsor's loving ears and arms. Eventually I learned that my parents couldn't give what they didn't have, and I was able to feel compassion for them.

Practicing "Easy Does It" helped me. I sometimes chose to leave meetings before they ended. I had received as much "good stuff" as I could handle on that particular day. Sometimes I had to limit the number of hugs I accepted. I'd share my thoughts and feelings afterward with my sponsor. Gradually, I began to like, and even love, getting the "good stuff" that leaves me feeling serene and happy.

Thought for the Day

If recovery feels too painful, maybe I need to slow down and practice "Easy Does It."

> "'Easy Does It' and 'First Things First' help us to keep moving, but remind us we need only take small steps."
>
> *From Survival to Recovery*, p. 95

Thanks to Al-Anon's emphasis on self-awareness, now I know I've lived in fear most of my life. When I took Step Four, I saw my willfulness and how that quality related to my fear. The more scared I was, the more I tried to control. Fear reared its ugly head particularly in my belief that I wasn't good enough or smart enough to have joyful, trusting, and intimate relationships. Instead of allowing myself to connect with others, I would often avoid them.

For example, once while out walking, I noticed a neighbor striding toward me on the other side of the street. My first inclination—that urging from my Higher Power—was to holler and wave, but I instantly disregarded that thought. She turned the corner, and an opportunity to try out a new behavior and initiate a connection with her was lost.

After my walk I felt uncomfortable. I looked at my options, decided to let it begin with me, and called my neighbor. I felt as if I grew up a little bit by choosing to talk with her rather than to keep silent. I also felt good about taking the risk to move toward intimacy with another human being.

I'm beginning to recognize more occasions in which my choice to isolate hinders me from the opportunity to build healthy relationships. My Higher Power and my growing awareness of this character defect will surely help me develop the receptive, willing trustfulness needed to open up to others and allow them into my life.

Thought for the Day

I'm willing to learn new ways of relating to the world as I let go of my fear. I trust that my Higher Power is with me and within me.

> ". . . My Higher Power is the confidence within me that
> makes me unafraid . . ."

As We Understood . . ., p. 105

One of the questions in the Al-Anon leaflet, "Did You Grow Up with a Problem Drinker?" is "Do you have a need for perfection?" This question was very relevant to me. My compulsive need for flawlessness kept me from attempting or completing many projects because I believed the results would fall far short of my goals.

Fortunately from my very first days in the program, it was suggested that I never say no to Al-Anon. My fellow members assured me it was part of my job as a human to make mistakes and that few errors were so severe they couldn't be overlooked or mended. They also reminded me that they would be by my side to share their experience, strength, and hope if I needed it.

Although I was terrified, I kept saying yes. Consequently I eventually chaired meetings, became group representative, sponsored an Alateen group, and volunteered at our local Al-Anon information service. Each new opportunity led me to more self-esteem and to greater confidence. I gradually let go of the idea that I can or need to perform any job perfectly. I simply do the best I can at any given time. I found that giving myself permission to be imperfect gives me tremendous freedom, the freedom to be me.

Thought for the Day

There is only one area in which I can possibly be perfect, and that is in my human imperfection!

"I tried to ignore my mistakes, and I tried to be perfect. . I don't ignore my mistakes anymore. I've actually learned how to use them."

Courage to Be Me, p. 125

"God, grant me the serenity . . ." As I sit in the sunlight streaming through my kitchen window, I ask myself "What is serenity?" It's related to my understanding of my Higher Power, who is kind, gentle, understanding, and the source of serenity itself. The thread of striving to love myself in the same kind and serene manner in which my Higher Power loves me runs throughout my Al-Anon program. My perception of serenity is also related to part of a dictionary definition of "serene" I once came across: "a title of honor, respect, or reverence, used in speaking of or to certain members of royalty."

My serenity manifests in several ways. Whenever I realize I'm thinking of myself or others with less than the honor, respect, and reverence due a child of God, I practice being kind and gentle. I seek to expand my enjoyment of nature's beauty. I allow a gentle kiss on my cheek or on the top of my head to fill my heart and nurture my soul. I strive to talk my problems over with someone else without judging myself or others. I feel and express my emotions and allow others to do the same, practicing detachment if necessary. I remind myself that it's okay not to know everything. I pray for the ability to accept myself as a child of a loving Higher Power whose forgiveness is unlimited.

Thought for the Day

How can I work my program today to increase the possibility of feeling serene?

> "Serenity isn't freedom from the storms of life. It's the calm in the middle of the storm that gets me through. It's up to me to try to keep this calm, even when the storm gets worse."
>
> *Alateen—a day at a time*, p. 30

My sponsor once shared an idea about Step Eight that I found very helpful. She suggested I make my list in column format as described in *Paths to Recovery*. I put the name of the person I had harmed in the first column, their relationship to me in the second column, my harmful act in the third column, the reason for amends in the fourth column, and my willingness to do so in the final column.

That third column certainly was difficult! I discovered the same defects turning up over and over. If I had not become aware of these character defects and their destructive impact in Steps Four through Seven, I certainly had the opportunity to see them now in the walking-and-talking, living-and-breathing, full-dimensional color portrait of myself and my family, friends, and acquaintances!

Thought for the Day

Today I will be open to creative new ways to work my program.

"As I review the injustices I have done to others, do I see a significant pattern that indicated a character flaw I ought to try to correct?"

The Dilemma of the Alcoholic Marriage, p. 88

Because I grew up in an alcoholic family, I didn't understand the process of trust. I fully trusted people who had not proven themselves to be trustworthy. I would indiscriminately tell people intimate details of my life. This often left me feeling hurt or betrayed.

Through attending meetings and developing a relationship with a sponsor and with my Higher Power, I have developed a technique for trust. I've learned that it's healthy to allow people to *earn* my trust. I visualize this process as being similar to climbing a ladder, with each rung symbolizing an increasing degree of self-disclosure.

I climb these rungs slowly now—no more races to the top. Sometimes I start off by talking about the weather with someone. If I feel safe with the person's response, I might make myself more vulnerable and climb another rung, such as giving a compliment on his or her outfit. If I still feel comfortable, I can continue to climb the rungs of trust by gradually sharing more of myself. However, if I don't feel safe, back down the ladder I go!

Trust develops as I slowly reveal myself to others and attend to my thoughts and feelings about their responses to my self-disclosure. Through this process I learn to identify trustworthy people with whom I can develop intimate relationships.

Thought for the Day

Trust is a process over which I have some control. I don't have to form relationships any faster than I'm ready.

> "Facing reality means accepting that many of my experiences in Al-Anon demonstrate that there *are* people upon whom I can rely."
>
> *Courage to Change*, p. 232

The first limit I learned to set in recovery was in response to sarcasm. Someone had initiated a discussion with me regarding a conflict. Though I was attempting in good faith to arrive at an agreeable solution, I was met repeatedly with sarcasm. After a time I said that if the sarcasm persisted, I would not participate any further until the other party was willing to carry on the discussion in a respectful and productive manner. When the disagreeable behavior continued, I got up from the table and went about my business. After a few such occasions, sarcasm became rare in my discussions with this particular person. After an initially angry response, I gained respect from the other person when I matched my intentions with my actions. However, the most important result was the respect I gained for myself.

Being clear about what is acceptable to me is a tool I use to take care of myself. It falls under the category of changing the things I can, as stated in the Serenity Prayer. To set reasonable and effective boundaries, it's important that I discern the difference between my responsibilities and someone else's. The Serenity Prayer can help me with this, too. Then I can make choices about what action I will or will not take. I am free to take care of myself in any way I deem necessary, whether or not anyone else likes my choices.

Thought for the Day

I take care of myself today by setting reasonable boundaries with those around me.

> "You cannot set boundaries and take care of someone else's feelings at the same time."

The Forum, September 2000, p. 28

I have found "contentment and even happiness" by learning to let go of self-pity and to replace it with humor. I first saw Al-Anon as a place to complain about my lot in life. It wasn't long before this was dispelled.

At a meeting, I was relating how my spouse was treating me, and tears were streaming down my face. Suddenly, someone laughed out loud. The unexpected laughter stopped me.

I stepped back to consider what I was saying that had been so funny. As I did, my tears dried up, and my lips curved into a small smile. I realized my story really was a funny one. I wanted to "save" my marriage, but I kept insisting my husband move out and then demanding he move back in. In a flash, I saw the humor. How could we work on our relationship in the turmoil created by the packing and unpacking of boxes as he moved in and out? My indecisiveness about sharing a home with him obviously reflected a deeper uncertainty about my desire to remain married, but I couldn't see that at the time. It seemed to me now that to attempt reconciliation under such circumstances was ludicrous!

That day I began to develop a sense of humor. As I continue in recovery, I find more and more things to laugh about. Now I laugh with my husband because we did work through that stage and are still together. I laugh with my children, and I even manage to laugh out loud at myself!

Thought for the Day

What situation in my life today could I view with humor rather than self-pity?

> "If I take a step back and look at this day as if I were watching a movie, I am sure to find at least a moment where I can enjoy some comic relief."
>
> *Courage to Change*, p. 205

As much as I hate to admit it, even after years in the program I still yearn to have one other person in my life whose sole job is to anticipate and meet all of my needs without my having to ask. What a fantasy!

I think this fantasy has much to do with being a child of an alcoholic. Since infants can't speak, parents have the considerable responsibility of anticipating and meeting some of their infants' needs. Doing so requires an awesome amount of energy—energy my parents didn't have. Because of my father's alcoholism, I didn't get much of this special type of attention when I was an infant. Even as an adult I still sometimes yearn for it. My undertaking now is to grow beyond this childlike fantasy by taking responsibility for getting my wants and needs met instead of expecting others to do it for me.

The Al-Anon tools that help me most with this challenge are Tradition Seven and "Let It Begin with Me." Tradition Seven suggests being fully self-supporting. I need to remember to support myself emotionally. Even if no one else seems to notice or commend my growth and courage, I can pat myself on the back.

"Let It Begin with Me" reminds me that no one is a mind reader. If I want or need something, I have to let someone know. I need to ask, which means taking risks. Maybe my request will be granted; maybe it won't. If it is, great. If it isn't, I'll still feel better for having asked, and then I can move on to someone else who might be able to help me.

Thought for the Day

I am powerless over alcoholics and alcoholism. I no longer have to be powerless over me.

> "I actually got up in a meeting and asked people to call me and to help me."

> *From Survival to Recovery,* p. 34

July 20

The meeting topic was "Healing Ourselves." Healing ourselves? If I could have healed myself, I thought, I would have done so long ago. If I could heal myself, would I go to so many meetings even when I didn't feel like it? Would I inconvenience myself to work these Steps when I had other things I wanted to do? Would I tell my sponsor embarrassing things about myself and tolerate her loving confrontations?

After I calmed down, I thought about the topic from a different perspective. I recalled a story about a man who labored in his garden, plowing, planting, and weeding. The result was a beautiful and bountiful crop. His admiring neighbor commented on what a glorious harvest God had provided. The man replied dryly that she should see the garden when God is the only one doing any of the work.

This story tells me that I need to *want* to get well, and then I need to be willing to take some action, to do something differently, before I can make progress in my recovery. My action demonstrates my willingness to be healed, and then God can come in and do the healing.

Thought for the Day

Healing cannot happen without my acquiescence and cooperation. If I cooperate with God in my spiritual education, then I am truly a partner in healing myself.

> "The Al-Anon Family Groups show us the need to cultivate the gardens of our lives. . ."
>
> *The Al-Anon Family Groups—Classic Edition*, p. 57

Unity was a foreign idea to me as a child. I never felt as though I were part of a family. It felt more like a bunch of strangers living in the same house. At best my family had poor communication or none at all. It seemed no one was available to help me. In fact, I usually was the recipient of criticisms and complaints. Instead of feeling united with my family, I felt isolated and alone.

It felt good to be part of an Al-Anon group who shared many of my emotions and who had similar experiences. However, it also felt strange. It took a while to grow comfortable thinking of myself as part of a larger entity, knowing my personal actions could affect that entity.

Fortunately, Al-Anon has principles to foster that sense of unity and to show me how to enact it in my life. Tradition One spells out the basic purpose of unity—to accomplish the greatest good for the greatest number. The idea is that many can accomplish together what one alone cannot. I see Tradition One at work in the process of taking an informed group conscience. Tradition Four reminds me that I do not exist in a vacuum; I always need to consider the effects of my actions on those around me. Concept One tells me that the future of Al-Anon rests in the *groups*, not in one individual. The Alateens remind me that "Together We Can Make It." I'm so grateful that Al-Anon shows me how to be part of a group so I never have to feel isolated and alone again.

Thought for the Day

A feeling of unity is as close as the nearest Al-Anon meeting.

"When I see Tradition One applied at the group level, it reminds me again how important unity is in my life."

Paths to Recovery, p. 139

One of the most important things I've learned in Al-Anon is to be gentle with myself, especially with regard to attending meetings. I attend two meetings regularly, and sometimes I attend a third or fourth. Sometimes, however, I prefer to isolate. These are the times when I need to push myself to go, and I do. I keep in mind something I've heard at meetings: If I'm thinking of going to a meeting, it's better to go to the meeting and think about it afterwards.

I realize that there are times when it's not appropriate for me to go to a meeting. Some days I have other responsibilities that need to be filled. I might have homework, or I might have to study for a school exam the next day. Maybe I really just need to go to bed early and get a good night's sleep. Perhaps I need to connect quietly with my Higher Power by praying, meditating, and journaling. Other times I know I need one-on-one attention as well as a good cry, so I'll stay home and call my sponsor instead. Then there are always moments when I need to relax, have fun, and come back to my recovery work refreshed.

My recovery is a matter of balance. Al-Anon has taught me to concentrate on myself and to discern what I really need to do for me, not what I "should" do. That might mean going to a meeting, or it might mean something else. I need to remember that Al-Anon is a gentle way of life, not a military drill!

Thought for the Day

Attending Al-Anon meetings is but one part of a balanced recovery journey.

> "After hearing slogans like 'Keep It Simple' and First Things First,' I came to realize that I was no help to anyone when I wasn't physically or mentally taking care of myself."
>
> *Living Today in Alateen*, p. 76

Courage to Change states, "Resentments mark the places where I see myself as a victim." Occasionally I felt buried under my resentments. They drained my energy each day as I thought of them. My insides felt corroded from bitterness. Feeling resentment was like drinking poison and hoping the person I resented would die!

I often *felt* like there was nothing I could do, yet the truth was I *knew* what to do—work the Steps on my resentments, and let my Higher Power lift them from me. However, I felt such resistance to this that I needed to ask myself, "What do I get out of feeling like a victim?" As I pondered this question, my Higher Power slowly opened my awareness. I felt protected by my resentments. They acted as a barbed wire fence to keep away the people I felt had hurt me. The problem was I kept pricking my own skin on the barbs. I also was comfortable with my resentments. I wondered who I'd be without them, because they were as familiar to me as my own skin.

Realizing that my resentments are not necessary or protective opened the door to change. I began relying on my Higher Power to show me healthier ways to speak for myself in situations where I felt hurt or damaged. I took a deep breath and allowed my Higher Power to dismantle a powerfully self-destructive character defect. I became entirely willing.

Thought for the Day

Do I have a character defect I use to protect myself? Do I need it anymore?

> "It is not enough merely to see that we have faults and make vague resolutions to do better. It takes definite effort to make ourselves receptive."
>
> *The Twelve Steps and Traditions*, p. 6

The idea of "God *as we understood Him*" gave me some trouble about six months after I came into Al-Anon. I was at a point in my early recovery where some of the pain had lifted. I wasn't crying every day anymore, and I was beginning to question everything I heard at meetings. Everyone kept talking about this "Higher Power," which I thought was somewhat sacrilegious. My devout parents took me to church every time the doors opened, and *I* knew who God was! My thoughts told me I should set these people straight. If they only understood God the way I did, they would be just fine.

At that moment of smug self-righteousness, my Higher Power decided to send me a spiritual awakening. He told me that perhaps they understood more about Him than I did. After all, they were the ones who were happy and free, filled with peace. Perhaps I could learn something from them if I opened my mind enough to listen and opened my heart enough to risk getting involved in the program.

Listen and risk I did. After doing both for many years now, I am quite comfortable not "understanding" anything about God but rather experiencing Him by working the Twelve Steps, attending meetings, sharing with my sponsor, and serving the fellowship. Through these actions I have come to know the love and peace of relying on a Power greater than myself. It is in try-ing to understand less that I experience more.

Thought for the Day

There are many ways of understanding my Higher Power.

> "I had always known a religion, but now I knew the spiritu-
> ality that others talked about."
>
> *As We Understood . . .*, p. 88

Growing up with two alcoholic parents, I learned to hide from them *before* the trouble started. By the time I was a teenager, I was trained to the point where I would disappear as soon as I heard the sound of an ice cube hitting the bottom of a glass.

Now years later, the urge to escape can come over me just as suddenly and irrationally. A slight misunderstanding or awkward silence between another person and me is enough to trigger my fear and cause me to run and hide in one way or another. Sometimes I hide in obvious ways, like not answering the phone. More often I hide simply by not saying what I really mean so I can avoid becoming the target of expected criticism.

Al-Anon taught me to think before I run away from a person, a conflict, or an opportunity to share from the heart. When I react in fear, I give power to the unhealthy part of myself that tells me it's not safe to be myself and that I'll never be able to change. Today my search for new solutions to old problems begins with either self-acceptance or change.

Thought for the Day

The Serenity Prayer reminds me that I can always count on my Higher Power for help when I make an effort to face my fears by using the tools of the program.

> "I need courage to change *my* attitude and behavior. The Serenity Prayer can help me."
>
> *Alateen—a day at a time,* p. 247

As a child in an alcoholic home, I wasn't encouraged to share my viewpoints. When I did, I didn't feel as though anyone was listening. Someone always ended up walking away hurt or angry.

When I was promoted to supervisor at work, I finally felt I was in a position of unqualified authority. When decisions needed to be made and actions carried out, I never discussed options with the people who worked under me. They retaliated by doing their work poorly, which reflected badly on me. I felt confused about what I was doing wrong.

As a stepmother I also felt in charge. I listened with my head and not my heart. The teenagers in our home lashed out in anger and sometimes ran away. I ended up feeling publicly humiliated, and our home boiled over with controversy.

When I learned about the General Warranties in Concept Twelve, I felt hope. To me a warranty is like a guarantee. If my relationships aren't working, I can return to the General Warranties to adjust my attitudes. Through them I've learned not to use my authority to push my viewpoint or to punish someone for disagreeing with me. I've also learned to avoid controversy by listening and encouraging others to share their viewpoints when making decisions. Sometimes we can even come to a unanimous decision.

Thanks to the General Warranties in Concept Twelve, my relationships are smoother and filled with less tension. I am finally experiencing the peace I longed for as a child. Once again the Al-Anon tools prove useful in all my affairs!

Thought for the Day

Our Concepts of Service and the General Warranties are tools to aid my personal recovery.

> "Many Al-Anon members have also found that the Concepts [of Service] are applicable to home and work situations."

> *Paths to Recovery*, p. 248

As I recover from the effects of alcoholism, I'm discovering many things about myself. I instinctively want to fix problems, and they don't necessarily have to be mine. In fact, most of the time they're not.

If I hadn't taken on many responsibilities while growing up in a large alcoholic family, no one would have. I became a very dependable person. I believed it was my responsibility to help others who could not or did not want to help themselves. What one person would call caretaking, I called being responsible.

I didn't realize that doing for others what they needed to do for themselves was, in fact, doing them a great disservice. Doing for others didn't allow them to be responsible; it enabled them to be irresponsible. God has a plan for each of us. Caretaking robs others of the self-esteem that comes from struggling with and conquering the challenges that God has planned for their lives. Letting others face the consequences of their actions allows them to learn and grow from their choices.

Thought for the Day

Standing with my arms extended and turning in a full circle gives me a visual marker of the extent of my responsibility. If it doesn't come into my space, I leave it alone.

> "Today I will remember that I have choices, and so does the alcoholic. I will make the best choices I can and allow others in my life to do the same without interference."
>
> *Courage to Change*, p. 5

Al-Anon meetings are far apart where I live, and Alateen is nonexistent. However, one young person has been in desperate need of help, so my local Al-Anon group consulted the *Al-Anon/Alateen Service Manual* to see if we could assist. According to the *Manual*, Alateens are members of the Al-Anon fellowship. Because the *Manual* states, "Where there is no Alateen meeting available, teens seeking help are encouraged to attend Al-Anon meetings," our group decided to encourage her to attend our meetings. After a time she asked me to be her personal sponsor. I felt honored and humbled that this young person, so damaged from growing up with alcoholism, would choose to put her trust in me. Actually I really learned how to trust her and my Higher Power, who was leading me to more self-knowledge through this special relationship.

Today I feel I have learned much from this young person. She has taught me about the disease and reminded me how much it became a part of *my* daily life as I grew up with alcoholism. Her sharings have helped me recollect the pain and isolation. By guiding her through the Steps and listening to her share, I faced and felt all the childhood emotions that were once too great to bear on my own. When I started to work through these feelings with my own sponsor, my healing deepened and my recovery was enriched.

I've been in Al-Anon long enough to know that recovery is an adventure, but never did I expect to have such a young guide! I'm grateful that my Higher Power keeps me open to new and unexpected ways of healing.

Thought for the Day

I might start out giving when I sponsor an Alateen individual or group, but I end up receiving even more.

> "Sponsorship is not all giving. By helping others, sponsors find they help themselves."
>
> *Sponsorship, What It's All About*, p. 11

Step Two, "Came to believe that a Power greater than ourselves could restore us to sanity," filled me with hope that I could live a sane and balanced life. In my family, there was never a sense of balance, just extremes—poverty and plenty, power and helplessness, violence and an uneasy calm. I longed for balance, for a feeling of normalcy that might help me feel safe and connected to others.

When I first came to an Al-Anon meeting for adult children, several people assured me that the hope offered in Step Two was real. As I listened, I began to see the miracle of other members being restored to sanity and finding balance in their lives. I heard their stories change in tone from worry to faith and from confusion to clarity.

By witnessing these miracles, I came to believe that God could lead me to a saner way of life. I surrendered, asked for help, and relied on my Higher Power to restore me to sanity. The answer to my plea was to learn how to live the Serenity Prayer. With help from fellow Al-Anon members, I slowly began to define balanced manageability for myself. God helped me discern the difference between letting go of the things I could not control and changing the things I could.

I once thought balance was the privilege of those who had grown up in normal, nonalcoholic families. I thought I was permanently damaged by the chaotic extremes of my childhood. Now I know it's possible to be made whole, to be rebuilt, to be restored to sanity.

Thought for the Day

No matter how much I may have been damaged in childhood, Step Two gives me hope for healing.

> "Step Two offers us an option: sanity. With this new perspective in mind, we truly begin to experience the hope that so many speak of."
>
> *Paths to Recovery*, p. 20

Recently I began to realize that I harbored many illusions regarding the extent of my control. This awareness was sparked by a reading in *How Al-Anon Works for Families & Friends of Alcoholics*, which speaks not of giving up control but of giving up the *illusion* of control.

I implored my Higher Power to strip me of my illusions, even if it was painfully brutal. An emotional period of bitterness, disillusionment, and scorn followed. All the people I had put on pedestals—where my Higher Power should have been instead—came tumbling down to reveal their proverbial "clay feet." I cried to my God, "Where will I ever find true integrity?"

The answer was this: "If you want integrity in your life, you must express it yourself." My next thought was "Let It Begin with Me." This slogan took on a new, powerful meaning. Because I was familiar with how my Higher Power works, I trusted there would be opportunities to translate the words into action.

My appreciation for this slogan has called me to grow beyond my comfort zone. It has dared me to forgive my alcoholic father. It has challenged me to give my mother the kind of love I wanted to receive from her. "Let It Begin with Me" has also coaxed me to offer uncomfortable, albeit Tradition-based, viewpoints at group inventory meetings. Instead of losing myself in my reactions, it has given me a tool to come home to myself—by showing me how to place principles above personalities.

Thought for the Day

When I give up the illusion of control, I gain my *real* power by letting it begin with me.

> "But we *do* have a power, derived from God, and that is the power to change our own lives."
>
> *One Day at a Time in Al-Anon*, p. 86

While I was growing up in an alcoholic family, I clipped a magazine segment that suggested that the correct use of mind leads to wisdom and that the incorrect use of the mind leads to insanity. Little did I know then that I would eventually be working a program whose core was the right use of my mind as well as my heart.

Today the program provides me with the spiritual direction I crave. I've learned that everything about my recovery begins and ends with me. I've found that the power of my own mind and heart can either help me or hurt me, but it's my choice. The highest way for me to use my heart and mind is to focus on my Higher Power through prayer and meditation, asking only to know His will for me and the power to carry it out.

I learned in my study of Step Three that "will" refers to our thoughts and feelings and that "lives" refers to our actions. When I pray in accordance with the Eleventh Step, I am asking to know what thoughts and feelings God wants me to have and praying for the power to translate them into action.

I am comforted by the simplicity of my Step Eleven understanding. I reaffirm that God is a Power greater than myself with thoughts and feelings very different from mine. This allows me to set my thoughts aside and take time to focus on His thoughts and how He wants to express them through me. In this way I can set my mind and heart on the right path.

Thought for the Day

Are my mind and heart focused on my recovery, or do they linger somewhere else that does me less good?

"Only God knows what I need."

Having Had a Spiritual Awakening . . ., p. 46

I grew up in an alcoholic home. My parents argued a lot, and they told me not to talk. I had no voice or say about anything. I often felt scared, and I became a quiet, isolated child who was unresponsive when asked a question by a relative or friend.

As a result, when I first came into the Al-Anon program, I found it difficult to share openly. However, as time passed and I continued attending meetings, I began to open up. Listening to other members gave me the courage to reveal myself a little at a time. It felt good to learn that it was okay to communicate my feelings and thoughts at meetings.

Now I share frequently. My spirit is set free each time I take the risk to express myself to people who understand how I think and feel. Several years ago a sponsee shared a phrase that highlighted my growth in this area—"Now you're talking!"

Thought for the Day

Sharing is the doorway through which we discover and impart our special gifts. In return we gain self-worth and a sense of who we are.

> "I'd just like to thank you for listening . . . If it wasn't for you, I'd probably still hide my feelings. I'd never really go after my dreams."
>
> *Courage to Be Me*, p. 53

Once I was able to stay up all night and sleep all day. Now I rarely make it to midnight, and I seldom sleep through the night without awakening in the wee hours for an unscheduled bout of restless alertness.

I used to have trouble knowing what to do with this time, but at the suggestion of a fellow Al-Anon member, I now use this unexpected free time to pray. I believe it's okay to pray in bed or anywhere else and it's okay to pray whether or not I feel composed. In fact, when I'm angry, confused, upset, or worried, I'm most likely to have the energy for late-night or early-morning prayer.

With no elaborate ceremonies or rituals, I do my best to open my heart to God. If I fall asleep before I finish, I know God can accept even a prayer that is incomplete.

Thought for the Day

It's okay to be creative with my prayer life—different times, different places, different words, even no words at all.

"In Al-Anon, I learned that God meets me where I am."

As We Understood . . ., p. 196

I've always wanted my mother to accept me for who I am. I know she loves me, but she seems to become so disappointed with little things. In Al-Anon I found the acceptance I craved. I truly began to believe that I am totally lovable and that although I make mistakes, I'm not a mistake. Although I do things differently than my mother, I am still a worthy person. However, it wasn't long before I found myself wishing for the same kind of acceptance from my mother that I get from the members of Al-Anon.

With the help of some of my Al-Anon friends, I discovered that I don't accept my mother as she is, either! I want her to embrace my way of thinking, start saying no to people, and not get so upset about unimportant issues. Basically I want her to think as I do, and Al-Anon has given me some words for this attitude: self-righteousness, arrogance, and control.

I've started to work on these character defects of mine by practicing "Live and Let Live." I attempt to keep the focus on myself and to embrace Tradition Eleven, which encourages me to exercise attraction rather than promotion. This change in my attitude has had a tremendous effect on our relationship. Since I stopped giving my mother unsolicited recommendations on how to improve her life, she no longer finds it necessary to try to reshape mine.

Thought for the Day

When I point my finger at someone, three fingers are pointing back at me. Could this suggest that for every defect I want to correct in another, there might be three of my own that need some attention?

> "Sometimes the things that bother us most about others
> are the very things we do ourselves without realizing it."
> *How Al-Anon Works for Families & Friends of Alcoholics*, p. 71

As a child of alcoholic parents, I grew up in a violent environment. My parents physically and verbally abused me, and I became angry with them. When I expressed my anger, they abused me even more. I learned to shut down and to be silent. Our communication broke down.

My family could not support me financially, so at 17 years of age I became self-supporting. I entered the job market with severely impaired perceptions of authority figures. Since my parents were the main authorities in my life until then, I expected my boss to treat me the same way my parents did. I acted on that expectation by shutting down in fear. If I felt uncomfortable about something in the workplace, I kept quiet. When I felt my employee rights were being violated, I stuffed my anger. As a result my responses to life and to my loved ones became irrational and out of control.

Step Twelve tells me I can apply the tenets of the program to all areas of my life, whether or not they directly involve alcohol. As a starting point, I had to admit my fear of authority figures and that my life had become unmanageable. Then I practiced communicating about my anger at meetings, where I received acceptance, validation, and understanding. Based on my positive experiences with sharing at meetings, I decided to risk expressing my feelings at work. When I did, sometimes I met opposition and that felt uncomfortable. Sometimes I met acceptance and a change in the offending behavior. Either way, I felt better because I had spoken up for myself with respect and self-esteem.

Thought for the Day

When I suppress anger, I give it room to fester in my heart and mind, and it unravels my recovery.

> "In the Al-Anon group, I found something I needed very badly—permission to get angry."
>
> *From Survival to Recovery*, p. 133

For a number of years, I worked at a job that drained me emotionally, mentally, and physically. I didn't like my job, but I didn't hate it enough to take a risk and find something better. As with every other aspect of my life, I didn't believe I deserved better. Many times the only way I got through the workday was to read Al-Anon's "Just for Today" wallet card. One line in particular always helped me: "Just for today . . . I can do something for twelve hours that would appall me if I felt that I had to keep it up for a lifetime."

Then I went to a meeting where the topic was "Just for Today." After listening carefully to fellow members' comments, I realized that if I continued to do something day after day, year after year, then essentially I *was* keeping it up for a lifetime! Perhaps I *should* be appalled by my acceptance of an unacceptable situation. Getting through temporary difficulties by reminding myself they are short-lived is not the same thing as continuing to suffer with the hopeless resignation that "this is as good as it gets."

As I searched my heart, I knew the only thing really keeping me at my job was fear. By applying the wisdom contained in a small piece of Al-Anon literature and asking my Higher Power for help, I gained the courage to change the things I could. Reciting the Serenity Prayer each step of the way, I finally let go of my old job and found employment that suited me better.

Thought for the Day

The Al-Anon tools work best when the right one is used in the right way for the right task.

> "I needed to learn how to use those tools so I could put them into action."

The Forum, May 2001, p. 25

When my home group started an Alateen meeting, they asked the two youngest Al-Anon members to be sponsors. I was one of them. My group thought that because we were closer to the teens' age, we could relate better to them. I didn't even like teenagers. However, my sponsor taught me to always say yes to service.

An amazing and sometimes painful journey awaited me. I soon found that I didn't dislike adolescents—I was just afraid of them. Most of my fears arose from the fact that I had never allowed myself to be a teenager, so I felt I didn't understand them. My adolescence was spent hiding from the world and the chaos created by my mother's drinking. I didn't socialize, date, or even rebel. I just hid.

Listening each week to young people still coping with alcoholic parents stirred up all the feelings that had scared me into hiding. As I continued to sponsor the teens and learn about my feelings, Al-Anon gave me the strength to face my childhood honestly, and the wisdom to see other options besides isolation.

I went through many changes in a short time. My behavior was a lot like a teenager's. I questioned everything! Fortunately the emotional roller-coaster ride was short-lived. Thanks to traveling belatedly through my teen years, I now have a much better sense of who I am. I don't know how much I helped the Alateens, but I know how much they helped me.

Thought for the Day

Opportunity for growth can come from the most unexpected places. All I really need is willingness, courage, and an open mind.

> "Alateen allows me to 're-wind the tapes' to my own teenage years."
>
> *A Guide to Alateen Sponsorship*, p. 20

Depression, compulsive overeating, and low self-esteem are some ways my father's alcoholism affected me. I had to attend many Al-Anon meetings, however, before I understood that the root of these shortcomings was my inability to be true to myself. I became aware of my tendency to let people take advantage of me because I wanted to please them. Yet I often felt depressed when I did something expected of me that ran counter to my goals or values. When I did stand up for myself, I felt guilty. My life was like walking a tightrope.

Al-Anon helped me discover my rights as a person. It began with being given the right to speak at meetings without interruption or advice. I was told my anonymity would be respected and that only I had the right to disclose it. This was possibly one of the first choices I had ever been given.

Eventually I heard that "no" is a complete sentence and that I had a right to refuse without explanation. I learned the value of applying the Serenity Prayer to relationships and to my people-pleasing. If nothing I do or say can make people like or dislike me, then I might as well do what is in my best interest as long as it hurts no one else.

Lastly, through service I learned how to set realistic goals and achieve them step-by-step. I learned that success is irrelevant. Failure can be an opportunity to grow, not to beat myself up. This is how positive self-esteem is built. I never experienced the process of personal growth until I came to Al-Anon.

Thought for the Day

With every meeting attended, with every Al-Anon tool worked and applied, the ability to value myself expands.

> "Al-Anon taught me that I am worth something … but—most of all—that I can choose how to live my life."
>
> *From Survival to Recovery*, p. 276

My dad asked me to go camping. I felt thrilled that he wanted to do something with me. It made me feel special. Shortly before we were to depart, he called. His plane was in need of repair and he wouldn't be able to fly up after all. My immediate reaction was, "Oh, that's okay, Dad." As the weeks passed, I recognized my reaction was an old pattern for me. I got excited about plans with my dad, they fell through, and I didn't share my disappointment with him.

However, I did share my feelings about the cancelled camping trip with my home group. I cried during my sharing, which felt good. People came up to me after the meeting and thanked me for opening up. One member said the greatest gift he ever received was when his children told him that he had hurt them.

I felt terrified to talk to my dad about my emotions, even though he'd been in AA for more than ten years and in Al-Anon for more than one. I talked to my sponsor, and she suggested I tell my father how I felt. After we finished talking, I called my dad. I told him I loved him and that spending time together was important to me. Then I started to cry and he let me. He didn't cut me off. I told him I felt disappointed that he cancelled the trip. He listened to me and when I was done, he told me he was sorry I felt hurt. Then he said, "I'm glad you told me."

Thought for the Day

When I talk openly about my emotions at meetings and other members thank me for my honesty, it gives me courage to do so in other areas of my life.

> "With a change of attitude, I have choices about what to do with my feelings."
>
> *Courage to Change*, p. 270

By the time I found Al-Anon, my self-esteem was very low. My sense of unworthiness stemmed in large part from having little experience being valued for my thoughts or ideas. I was convinced that who I was and what I said or did was unimportant. The alcoholism in my home told me many lies and whispered repeatedly that I was not worthy of sharing and being heard. I had opinions, but I kept them inside where they just stagnated. Even when I did have the opportunity to talk, I usually forfeited it.

I am grateful for Al-Anon's Concept Five, which states, "The Rights of Appeal and Petition protect minorities and assure that they be heard." This Concept lets me know it is important to share my views at group business meetings even if I disagree with the majority perspective. For an Al-Anon group conscience to work with spiritual effectiveness, every voice must be heard. It might just be my voice the Higher Power uses to further inform the group regarding a decision at hand. My lone voice *can* make a difference.

Once I have some experience sharing, it might be tempting to use this Concept as an excuse for imposing my opinions on others. However, this enticement is tempered by the lesson of Tradition Two, which states that our group has only one authority—a loving Higher Power as expressed through our group conscience. With these two legacies in mind, I can stay balanced, in true humility between silence and dominance.

Thought for the Day

Can I express myself today, free of expectations of how others will react?

> "In caring for the smaller and seemingly weaker members of the fellowship, this Concept provides security and continuity for all."

The Concepts—Al-Anon's Best Kept Secret?, p. 13

As a child I lived in a fantasy world where to think it so would make it so. Combined with my need for perfectionism and self-control, I believed I could think myself out of reacting emotionally to people and situations. I carried these misperceptions into adulthood. In my denial, I thought I could make myself not feel anything. I had practiced being tough for a long time.

In Al-Anon the emotional truth of my life surfaced as I accepted my past. At first I felt terrified. Ugliness locked deep inside me—anger, fear, and resentment—poured forth like boiling lava from an erupting volcano.

As I continued to feel and express my emotions, the lava cooled and reached calmer, level ground. I went through a period thinking I must apply perfectionism and self-control to my now-out-in-the-open emotional life. This was short-lived because life kept happening, and so did my emotions. I was healthy enough to know that stuffing my feelings would impede my recovery. Anything less than honesty wouldn't work.

I'm learning to be comfortable with my feelings as I accept whatever life brings my way. I use the Serenity Prayer and the slogans "Think" and "Keep It Simple." Using "Easy Does It" and "One Day at a Time" helps, too. I'll never forget when I chose to face my dark side. When I did, my gentle side became available, and my emotional life grew more balanced. Today, instead of veering between extremes, I'm living a life of stability and serenity.

Thought for the Day

In order to heal, I need to feel. It might be rough going at first, but I know my Higher Power and the program will help me find an emotional center point.

> "The more we accept and share our feelings, the closer we come to experiencing the full range of our emotions, from sadness to joy."

Alateen's 4th Step Inventory, p. 32

When I first started coming to Al-Anon, I found that I wasn't alone in trying to meet the challenges from growing up in an alcoholic home. That discovery was a blessing in so many ways. Being a member of the Al-Anon fellowship removed the crippling burden of shame that I carried on my shoulders for decades. I also came to believe that alcoholism truly is a family disease, affecting everyone close to the drinker. In addition the program took my recovery a step further and gave me tools for coping with the disease. A daily dose of the Steps, slogans, service, sharing, and spirituality—when taken day after day, month after month, year after year—has kept my disease in remission. No amount of professional therapy, although helpful, had replaced the profound relief of hearing others share their similar experiences, strength, and hope.

"The healing is in the hearing" is a simple yet weighty truth in Al-Anon. I hear myself in others' experiences and find myself in our shared emotions. In learning to feel compassion and acceptance for my fellow members, I learn to feel the same for myself. I receive strength from their strength and hope from their hope, believing that if they can heal, so can I. Nothing can take the place of personally witnessing the healing, change, and growth of other Al-Anon members. That's all the encouragement I need to keep working my program together with others who struggle with this insidious disease.

Thought for the Day

The mutual sharing of experience, strength, and hope at Al-Anon meetings releases us from individual isolation and loneliness.

> "It is, in fact, in the sharing of our diversity and unique experience that we break down our walls of isolation, grow in understanding, realize we are not alone and learn we are entitled to full, happy, and productive lives."
>
> *Al-Anon Is for Gays and Lesbians*, p. 2

I learned very little about respect in the household of my youth. There was talk of respect and a demand for respect, but there was little to show for it. Fortunately my Higher Power eventually led me to choose a path in which I could explore a new concept—earning respect.

In my work I decided that earning respect would be both essential and desirable. Still, I was very much on my own. Learning by trial and error, I soon discovered that to earn respect I had to give it—with sincerity. Miraculously, whatever I gave out returned to me.

In my personal life, however, the effects of alcoholism still made it difficult for me to maintain respect for the alcoholics in my life, and so for myself. I repeatedly encountered difficulty until again I was fortunate and found Al-Anon.

During meetings we take turns sharing, giving everyone a chance to speak, and thanking one another for doing so. We refrain from advising, criticizing, arguing, or judging. We let one another's words hover in the meeting room without contest, waiting for whoever needs them to absorb them. We give each other time to learn difficult lessons. We respect one another and thus ourselves.

Thought for the Day

The very framework of an Al-Anon meeting gives me a chance to practice giving and receiving respect.

> "I found myself in the midst of groups that treated me with trust and respect ..."
>
> *Having Had a Spiritual Awakening . . .*, p. 124

Step Twelve encourages me to ". . . practice these principles in all my affairs." Some of my affairs are financial ones, and a part of me thought I could manage them without the help of a Higher Power.

Not only did I think I could handle my finances alone, separate from the principles of the program, but I also thought that if I made a certain amount of money from my work, I could tell God to go jump in a lake. I was still clinging to the notion that something—in this case a sum of money—was going to allow me to manage my life in my own way and on my terms.

The end result was ironic, but it made sense, too. The more I asked God to help me achieve the goal that would finally eliminate my need for a Higher Power, the crazier I became. Finally I realized what I was doing and went back to the first three Steps. Once again I accepted that my Higher Power would always be in charge of me and all my affairs.

Thought for the Day

When I rely on self-will, I severely limit *all* of my resources. When I turn to my Higher Power, those limitations fall away.

> "We become capable of directing our destiny by surrendering to a will other than our own."
>
> *Forum Favorites,* Volume 3, p. 40

Before Al-Anon I sometimes made choices in reaction to uncomfortable emotions such as confusion, anger, and fear, none of which are good foundations for decision-making. I was reacting, and my life felt completely unmanageable.

Al-Anon showed me how to respond appropriately to my emotions. In terms of reacting, I learned to deal with my feelings first so that I could clearly consider the facts of a situation. Now when I experience intense emotions, I call my sponsor to talk out the problem and to defuse my feelings. Sometimes I write in my journal or do something physical, like swimming. Prayer and meditation also help me calm down and get perspective. When I want to take drastic action, I ask myself, "How important is it?" Is my proposed behavior proportionate to the aggravation? Often it's not. Each of these tools helps me gain space and time to untangle the threads of intellect and emotion. Then I can act rather than react.

It helps to keep in mind that *getting better* doesn't always mean *feeling better*. When I need to walk through pain to let it go, I remember "This Too Shall Pass." I tell myself that just as thinking doesn't make it so, neither does feeling make it so. My life is going to work out according to God's will regardless of how I feel, so why try to manipulate situations to avoid the unavoidable—human emotions? Such behavior only creates more pain, and I certainly don't want more of that!

Thought for the Day

Am I working with my feelings or allowing them to work against me?

> "The true nature of my problem was my stubborn refusal to acknowledge feelings, to accept them, *and* to let them go."
>
> *Courage to Change*, p. 249

Fear is the energy that activates my character defects. Sometimes my shortcomings lie dormant like a bumper-car ride with the electricity turned off, and I don't even notice them. When I'm afraid, however, my fear acts like a charge that causes the cars (my defects) to start moving. I spend my mental and physical energy running in circles, trying not to get bumped or run over.

What triggers my fear in the first place? Trying to control things over which I have no power is always one reliable switch. How do I disengage it? Using the Serenity Prayer helps me calm down. I make a list, with one column titled "can change" and another titled "can't change." Then I break the problem down into elements and put each into the appropriate column. When I'm done, I ask my Higher Power to redirect my energy toward those elements I can change.

Leaving the present and worrying about the future is another trigger. When I feel like my mind is ahead of my body, it helps to refocus on my body, and my mind often follows. I remind myself to let go and let God handle the things in my "can't change" column. I focus on what I'm doing at the present moment: I am washing my hair; I am cooking dinner; I am driving my car. It might feel silly, but I'm willing to do what I can to bring myself back to the present moment. Such action sets the tone for a more serene and grounded day.

Thought for the Day

My fear is a natural human emotion for which there are many triggers. Al-Anon tools help me sort out and turn off the source for each one of them.

"My fears about alcoholism can keep me thinking in circles. The program helps me break their hold on my mind."

Alateen—a day at a time, p. 144

Tradition Six, which cautions us against diverting ourselves from our primary spiritual aim, can be condensed into three simple words—focus, focus, focus. How does this apply to me in Al-Anon? I choose to accept that Al-Anon's one purpose is to help families and friends of alcoholics. How do I do this? Focus. If I get sidetracked on some other mission, cause, group, or ideology—no matter how worthy—I divide my energies and am less likely to achieve my goal.

Is it all right to read other materials to meet my emotional and spiritual needs? Of course, but I don't call it Al-Anon. May I go to open AA meetings to search for a better understanding of the alcoholics in my life? Absolutely, but I don't call it Al-Anon. May I attend counseling or therapy? Certainly. I can do whatever I choose, *as an individual*, but I don't call it Al-Anon, and I don't bring it to my meetings. I come to Al-Anon to learn Al-Anon. There are as many wonderful adjuncts to recovery as there are members, but if I let myself get distracted, I'll undermine my own program as well as my ability to help others.

Thought for the Day

If I forget my focus, I may fail to achieve my primary spiritual aim.

". . . If Al-Anon were to involve itself in every worthwhile cause, where could we draw the line that would keep our fellowship intact to do its job?"

The Al-Anon Family Groups—Classic Edition, p. 174

I was excited when I came to Al-Anon and found the Twelve Steps. I felt as if I finally had permission to live life my way, but instead I found myself using the program to dissect other people's lives. I knew many people who could benefit from the wisdom I was receiving in Al-Anon, and I decided it was my job to enlighten them!

Then I came to a new understanding of Step Three, in which I turn my will and my life over to the care of the Higher Power of my understanding. I finally realized I don't have to enlighten anyone. Part of turning my life over to my Higher Power now includes turning over my loved ones and all of their words, actions, and attitudes as well. Allowing my loved ones to make their own decisions and learn from their mistakes gives them the gift of dignity and gives me the gift of serenity. When I'm not spending my energy trying to figure out other people's lives, I have the insight to make the everyday decisions that bring me peace.

Thought for the Day

Today I'll stop minding other people's business and create some business of my own to mind.

> "Al-Anon helped me to . . . see that many of my problems stemmed from minding everyone's business but my own."
>
> *Courage to Change*, p. 234

Steps Four and Five healed my shame. Steps Six through Eight healed my guilt. Shame is about my thoughts and feelings, my inner self. My shame says that *who I am* is not okay. Guilt is about my words and actions, my outer self. My guilt says that *what I do* is not okay. Before Al-Anon, I dragged around so much shame and guilt I couldn't imagine that these emotions ever would help me. I didn't know shame and guilt could warn me when my behavior was incompatible with my values. In my alcoholic family, I didn't learn healthy, consistent values. Shame and guilt were used to punish and control me. I ended up feeling ashamed and guilty about almost everything.

Al-Anon and my sponsor helped heal my shame by providing a safe atmosphere in which to share my thoughts and feelings. When I took my Fourth and Fifth Steps with my sponsor, I received the gift of having someone I trust and respect see my whole self and love me anyway. I never dreamed this would happen. The Sixth through Ninth Steps healed my guilt by giving me guidelines so I could identify my part in situations, discern my mistakes, and make amends. Now that I've admitted my mistakes and shortcomings to God, to myself, and to another human being, my normal feelings of guilt and shame guide me in Step Ten, where I continue to take personal inventory. Those uncomfortable emotions let me know that I may have said or done something contrary to the values I've developed in Al-Anon. Then I can make appropriate amends to protect my self-esteem.

Thought for the Day

Have I considered that *normal* feelings of shame and guilt might help my recovery instead of hinder it?

> "What we do with our feelings and how we respond to them is what's important. Alateen shows me how to respond."

Alateen's 4th Step Inventory, p. 32

I began my habits of controlling, butting in, and focusing on others at an early age. I believed I had to protect the well-being of my family. As a child, these behaviors provided a false sense of power that helped me feel secure in the inconsistent, chaotic atmosphere of alcoholism. When I carried these behaviors into my adult life, they began to destroy my health and well-being.

I became tired, cranky, depleted, sapped of spirit. I suffered from constant headaches, stomach pains, and mild depression. Did I consider seeing my doctor about these problems? No, because my focus was elsewhere. However, I did mention them to a friend who is familiar with my childhood. She had mentioned Al-Anon before, but now that I was physically falling apart, she became even more persistent in encouraging me to attend. My body hit bottom, and I took her suggestion.

The idea of self-care caught my ear as I immersed myself in Al-Anon meetings and just listened. It was a foreign concept, but I was willing to attempt it. I established a "self-care account" in an old notebook and made two columns: "meddling" and "self-care." In the self-care column, I listed things I needed to do or would like to do to nourish myself mentally, physically, emotionally, and spiritually. Each day I wrote down the minutes and hours I spent meddling and considered the cost in terms of my health and well-being. For example, instead of spending 30 minutes nagging my adult son, I could have been making a doctor's appointment to address my headaches. Finally I had a concrete way to keep the focus on me.

Thought for the Day

It's an illusion that depleting myself will help someone else.

"... Making a life for ourselves, regardless of what others are doing or not doing, must be a top priority."
How Al-Anon Works for Families & Friends of Alcoholics, p. 75

Steps One, Two, and Three opened doors to profound and meaningful changes. The effects of being raised in an alcoholic family seemed as fixed in me as my eye color. Two traits come to mind—turning to emotionally unavailable people for support, and engaging in self-doubt and self-hate. With the help of my sponsor, I now see that these and other traits, not other people, are the source of my anguish.

That insight, however, was only the beginning. The real freedom came when I finally admitted I couldn't get better on my own, which lifted my denial. My powerlessness filled my lungs, brushed my skin, beat in tandem with my heart. I stood at the edge of acceptance, took a step, and free-fell into Step One. I realized that if only I could remember I was truly powerless over these effects and not try to pretend otherwise, I would be fine. Why? Because of Step Two. A Power greater than myself can help me. What that Power is and how it can help me doesn't matter. It is only important that I can place my restless hope in this Power. In Step Three I then surrender my thoughts, feelings, actions, dreams, needs—my whole life—to the care of this Power.

I bought myself a special ring to wear, and I touch it sometimes hourly to remind myself that I am not alone and that these three Steps are my stepping-stones to surrender, sanity, and eventual serenity. I have used them in quick sequence many times since. My life has changed for the better and continues to improve. I feel more like "me" than I have in 20 years.

Thought for the Day

This is the prayer of powerlessness: to ask only for guidance.

> "The more I feel my smallness and powerlessness, the more I grow in spirituality."
>
> *Having Had a Spiritual Awakening . . .*, p. 159

In my family, my parents were always telling me what to do. My response was usually angry compliance or rebellious refusal. Either way, I was reacting, not acting, and feeling controlled.

I had the opportunity to change when I came to Al-Anon. As a new group representative headed for my first area assembly, I wanted to vote the way my group told me. We discussed the issues on the ballot. Members spoke in favor and against the issues. Before it was time to choose, the outgoing group representative made a motion to let me use my best judgment. He said I would receive more information at the assembly, and I wouldn't have the opportunity to check with my group on every matter. Several members reminded us of Concept Three, "The Right of Decision makes effective leadership possible." I couldn't believe my group trusted me to speak for them. Nevertheless, I "Let Go and Let God" and trusted myself to make good decisions, at the assembly.

When I returned, I shared how I had voted. Not everyone agreed with my decisions, but no one wanted to vote me out of office. They thanked me for my service and paid me for my expenses. After my term, I offered the same support to the group representatives who succeeded me.

The support I receive from Al-Anon goes far beyond what my parents were capable of giving me. Today I know there is something more important than always doing, or refusing to do, what I am told. Instead, I can learn to trust my own judgment and let others trust me, too.

Thought for the Day

Al-Anon service gives me the opportunity to make decisions, which helps build my character.

"Being allowed to make appropriate decisions, to act freely without being hassled or second guessed, gives dignity to the person who is doing the job."

The Concepts—Al-Anon's Best Kept Secret?, p. 8

When I came to Al-Anon, I was waiting for instruction on something I badly needed. I wanted to know how to become an adult with sound values, self-respect, and self-esteem. I sought this lesson from everybody—my parents, employers, spouses, children, friends, etc.—everybody except my Higher Power and myself.

After attending meetings and listening to others share, one much-needed change became perfectly clear. I had to stop sabotaging myself by looking on the outside for something that exists only within.

Trying to find self-respect and self-esteem from inside felt like pulling a rabbit out of a hat, and I didn't have a rabbit or a hat! Growing up with unavailable alcoholic parents left some gaping holes in my childhood development. I couldn't figure out how I was going to fill myself with characteristics I had never seen in my home.

Al-Anon has repaired those holes by giving me tools to develop the qualities I desire and by showing me healthy people who already possess them. The program offers me sound, healthy guidelines—values—for life. As I let go and trust God to work things out without forcing my will, I become more mature. As I take responsibility for myself by making amends, I grow in self-esteem. As I conduct my social behavior according to the Traditions, I develop self-respect. Working my program helps me become the adult I always dreamed of being.

Thought for the Day

Four things are true for me. I have needs. I have parents. Sometimes my parents can't fulfill my needs. I *can* get my needs met elsewhere.

> "With help we can develop a new sense of living, as we become, one day at a time, the people we want to be."
>
> *Al-Anon Sharings from Adult Children,* p. 6

Being a sponsor has been an important part of my recovery from growing up with alcoholism. In fact, as a sponsor I never give as much as I get. For example, seeing a sponsee blossom in the sunshine of encouraging words shows me the importance of being gentle with myself and gives me an opportunity to practice the comfort-giving spoken of in Tradition Five.

When I have the privilege of hearing the secret a sponsee expected to carry in silence for a lifetime, I am reminded of how relieved I was to finally lay down the burden of my secrets with *my* sponsor.

Conversations in person or over the phone with sponsees often generate laughter, reminding both of us that our tragedies have elements of exaggerated comedy as well.

When a sponsee whom I have seen grow in leaps and bounds shares discouragement over seemingly slow progress, I become open to the possibility that my own discouragement may be a case of distorted thinking rather than actual lack of growth.

Thought for the Day

In becoming a sponsor, I cultivate a listening heart for others as well as for myself.

> "The interchange between sponsor and sponsored is a
> form of communication that will nourish both of you."
>
> *Sponsorship, What It's All About*, p. 11

Holding on to anger, resentment, and a "poor me" attitude is not an option for me today. Growing up with two alcoholic parents created many painful memories. However, until I was able to let go of my past by forgiving my parents, I was unable to enjoy the present.

Among Al-Anon's many healing tools, I found learning about alcoholism as a disease and how it affects families to be particularly helpful. It enabled me to see my parents in a different light. Today I know they were *unwilling* victims of the disease of alcoholism. I have no doubt that had they been given a choice, neither of my parents would have picked up that first drink and continued on such destructive paths. I saw them try to fight the disease in countless ways as I grew up—making promises, going through rehabilitation, etc.—but the disease won. My parents suffered, and my siblings and I shared the outcomes of their suffering as a result. In the battle with alcoholism, no one wins, not even those who seem to be "perpetrators."

Today I know in my heart that my parents were the best mother and father they could be, considering what they went through. As I imagine what they must have endured, I have gained empathy for their struggle. I have envisioned walking a mile in my parents' shoes, and I now have nothing but compassion for both of them. I am grateful to Al-Anon for helping me fully forgive my parents, and for helping me accept and enjoy them for who they are.

Thought for the Day

Remembering that alcoholism is a disease helps me see the person struggling beneath the burden of illness.

> "With the help of friends in Al-Anon, I could see my parents as. . . two people gravely affected by a disease."
>
> *From Survival to Recovery*, p. 170

I grew up in an alcoholic home where I felt no one was caring for me, so I decided I had to do so myself. Soon my vision became shortsighted. It took all my energy just to protect myself or figure out the bare necessities I needed to survive. I felt confused and overwhelmed by my environment, so I limited my awareness.

In Al-Anon I'm learning to look all around me, not just in front of me. My first experience with widening my awareness occurred in meetings. I took the risk to look at the people around me and listen to them. My reward was a bond with others who understood me, accepted me, and wanted to help me. In the course of attending just one meeting, I finally knew I was not alone.

Later, I began to see how the Traditions encouraged me to look around myself. Tradition One taught me that I am not the only one seeking recovery, because all of us attend meetings for the same purpose. The fulfillment of that purpose depends on choosing what is best for the whole, not just what is best for me. This was my second experience with wider awareness. My growth benefits from the growth of others.

My third experience with wider vision followed naturally in the form of Step Twelve, especially the part about carrying the message to others. Here I was encouraged to look around me with the intent of bringing the healthy light of Al-Anon to others who are still suffering. My gift for doing so was the affirmation that I am a worthwhile person who is capable of sharing experience, strength, and hope with others.

Thought for the Day

What recovery gifts might await me if I widen my circle of awareness just a bit?

> "I kept going to meetings and gradually my perspective changed."
>
> *Alcoholism, the Family Disease*, p. 10

It wasn't a coincidence, but a miracle of Al-Anon, that I began my Fourth Step and undertook a major overhaul of my garden on the same day. I had moved too late for planting, but I decided to remove all the overgrowth in preparation for next year. I removed weeds, leaves, and dead plant material. Then I began to dig, turning dirt over to loosen it. My progress was halted by a clump that had once been a tiger lily. I dug around, delving deeper, to reveal a tangle of roots binding the mass to the earth. My attempts to remove it in one clump proved futile. I tugged, pushed, and kicked, but it refused to move. My frustration mounted and I regretted embarking on a project that seemed impossible to achieve.

I took a break. I rested and thought of using a different approach to removing the tangle of roots. I got up and went back to work. This time, slowly and meticulously I began disentangling the mass one tiny piece at a time. After I had finished, leaving behind a large hole in the ground, I filled the hole with new earth. I gazed satisfied at the result of my persistence—a garden prepared for new growth.

That's when it came to me. This is how Al-Anon helps me today. Al-Anon showed me how to detangle myself, sift through the debris, and humbly ask my Higher Power to prepare me for new growth by removing the clumps in my way.

Thought for the Day

If the work of sorting myself out in Step Four seems daunting, I'll ask God to show me a different approach.

"... New weeds will sprout and some plants will forever need pruning. The Steps equip me with weed control and garden manuals."

From Survival to Recovery, p. 201

For some time I had difficulty detaching. When I tried it, my focus shifted to me, and I had a hard time just being with myself. I began to understand that my skill in detaching rested on my ability to accept my own thoughts and feelings and to become comfortable with myself.

As I felt accepted in Al-Anon, I grew in self-acceptance, which gave me courage to practice detachment. I tried it with the active drinker. When my spouse went drinking after work and was late for dinner, the kids and I ate and went to an early movie. I didn't stay home waiting with anger and bitterness.

When someone struggled with a dilemma at work, I learned to offer my experience and then to let go of whether the person tried my ideas. I didn't lose my focus or productivity by taking over someone else's problem.

Then I began detaching from my alcoholic parent as well as the sober one. When they argued, I learned to say, "I'm sure you'll find a creative solution," and then leave the room. To increase my self-care options, I rented a car when I visited them. If one of them tried to draw me into a disagreement, I got in the car and drove somewhere safe until I could calm myself enough to return.

Now with lots of practice, I find it easier and easier to detach. The more I detach, the more time I get to know, accept, and spend time with a really wonderful person—me!

Thought for the Day

Detaching from others and getting to know myself go hand in hand.

> "Because my fate—my very life—was no longer tied directly to theirs, I was able to accept them for who they were and to listen to their ideas and concerns without trying to exercise control."
>
> *Courage to Change*, p. 199

Before Al-Anon, I had a false sense of self. Because of their diseases, my alcoholic father and my mother who grew up in an alcoholic home couldn't see themselves clearly. They weren't able to help me, either. As I grew up it seemed that my parents couldn't see me at all. I felt invisible and voiceless. I had no idea of my likes and dislikes, let alone what I would or would not accept in a relationship. I felt empty inside. When there did seem to be something inside me, it felt like someone else's experience.

Al-Anon changed all that. I heard suggestions such as "Keep the focus on yourself," and, "Take your own inventory instead of someone else's." These ideas perplexed me. Who was I? I didn't know myself. The person I knew was the teenager my mother considered a burden. My father criticized me incessantly. There had to be more to me than that.

By working the Steps, especially the first four, I came to know who I am. In Step One I experienced myself as someone who insanely tried to control alcoholism but couldn't. I came to know my powerlessness. In Step Two, I considered the existence of and possible help from a Power my senses couldn't define. I came to know my God as I understand Her. In Step Three I experienced my yearning to trust that Power, who was greater than me. I came to know my surrendered self. And in Step Four I experienced my ability to define myself rather than let others do the job. I came to know me.

Thought for the Day

In Al-Anon I can safely do the work of defining myself rather than allowing others to do the job.

> "The real truth might be that we are far more valuable
> and loveable than other people have led us to believe."
>
> *Courage to Be Me*, p. 122

My mother's behavior was my original reason for joining Al-Anon. She was the first and most important alcoholic in my life. A talented and creative woman, she was also troubled by the effects of growing up in her own alcoholic family and by the death of my brother. As I grew older, her drinking became more obvious as did the wall she erected between herself and the rest of the family.

By the time I came to Al-Anon, my mother was living alone and isolated, although apparently not drinking. The effects of the family disease of alcoholism continued to invade our relationship, however, until I finally began to detach from her with love. I stopped trying to help her take care of herself, which also stopped the fights we had. I put the focus on myself, realizing that in my disease I didn't know where my mother ended and I began. Finding out who I was, apart from my mother, was my first Al-Anon challenge.

In those early days detaching with love from my mother meant setting limits on our face-to-face contact. For more than a year, our only communication was through notes sent by mail and gifts dropped off without seeing one another. This is what I needed for recovery at the time.

Today my mother and I have an honest and loving relationship based on mutual respect for each other's boundaries. When we speak, I keep the focus on myself and share my experience, strength, and hope rather than telling her what to do. My recovery has become healthier and stronger, as has my relationship with my mother. This is the miracle of Al-Anon in my life.

Thought for the Day

Detachment helps me set limits and untangle myself from the other people in my life.

"Choosing to set boundaries and create wellness for ourselves is our primary responsibility . . ."

From Survival to Recovery, p. 204

The rustling leaves outside my window betray the presence of a visitor. It's a chickadee enjoying the sun. I stand watching—yet fearing the loss of time from doing so. I envy her unhurried preening and obvious pleasure she takes in rubbing her head against her feathers, fluffing them out and then returning them to their correct place. "Not like my morning routine," I think as I rush to get ready for work—ironing, showering, and coaxing my hair into some presentable form.

I am brought back to the window by the persistent shaking of a leaf under the first bird, revealing a second I hadn't noticed before, and then a third and a fourth on a branch nearby. Again, I feel jealous. They have so much time to do each task, getting ready for their day. I'm getting ready for my day, too, but I'm not calm like they are.

Then I laugh. I've just detached for ten minutes from my "too busy" life to watch some birds just for pleasure. Before the program I never would have noticed these diminutive specks of pure movement. The lessons I'm learning in Al-Anon are finally taking root. My mind is now calm enough to notice them. Appreciation for their uncomplicated life seeps into my soul, echoing my need for simplicity and restoring my sense of balance.

Today I have a choice. I can seclude myself from the outside world, or I can slow down and appreciate it. I can feel the sights and rhythms deep down and allow them to nourish my soul, trusting that everything under the sun is in my Higher Power's care.

Thought for the Day

In Al-Anon I've learned to savor the tiny, specific, beautiful moments of my life.

> "I will set my problems to the side for a little while and appreciate what it means to be vitally alive."

Courage to Change, p. 325

I am the adult child of two alcoholics. Before I came into Al-Anon, I had no dreams or hope. I saw my life through my husband's drinking. I had heard about Al-Anon, but couldn't conceive how it could help me. As long as my husband was still drinking and had no intentions of stopping, how could going to meetings and focusing on myself make a difference in my life? My existence felt like an out-of-control whirlwind that nothing could stop.

I decided to go to a meeting and do whatever they suggested. "What could it hurt?" I asked myself. I attended meetings regularly whether or not I felt like it. I asked someone to be my sponsor and started applying the slogans and Steps to my life. When I still couldn't and didn't believe Al-Anon could help me in any meaningful way, my sponsor suggested, "Perhaps you could try believing that *I* believe." I decided to lean on my sponsor's faith in the program until I could develop some of my own.

After a few months, I was able to call my sponsor and tell her I no longer needed to rely solely on her faith because I had my own! After giving the program a real, fair chance by applying it to my life, I had gathered an impressive collection of my own miracles and spiritual awakenings. This came about by living one day at a time, practicing faith, and working our simple but difficult Steps. Today I am grateful to be alive, strengthened by my ever-growing belief and faith in my Higher Power, the Al-Anon program, and myself.

Thought for the Day

Without Al-Anon I would be on a dead-end road. Instead, my path is one of belief in the gift of recovery.

> ". . . I have grown into a believer who daily thanks my Higher Power and asks for help."

The Forum, May 1998, p. 24

After attending Al-Anon for a while, I realized that self-care didn't mean as much to me as it seemed to mean to other members. I thought I was doing a decent job of keeping myself clean and healthy. After talking about it with my sponsor, I became aware that although I did things to take care of myself, I did them with a focus on other people. I did them because other people expected me to do them, not because I cared about my own well-being. Gradually I realized that while growing up in an alcoholic home, I chose to ignore my natural feelings of self-love and self-worth because they didn't stop my parents from drinking or from criticizing me.

The more I work my program, the more I come to understand that I am rebuilding my relationship with myself. Self-care is for me, not for others. Now that my motives for self-care are in proper perspective, I make an effort to ask myself what matters in my life. I ask for my Higher Power's guidance before jumping into action. I pray for help in learning to love myself as my Higher Power loves me. The serenity I feel today when I do things to take care of myself is proof that my prayers are being answered.

Thought for the Day

Self-care reflects acceptance of my Higher Power's love for me.

> "In Al-Anon we learn to pay attention to our own behavior, thoughts, and feelings. We deserve this attention, and we need it."
>
> *Courage to Change*, p. 359

When I did my Fourth Step, I was amazed to discover that my stealing a ten-cent comb at age seven was fairly inconsequential. I had carried guilt for this minor infraction for many years. I identified with the concept of an overdeveloped sense of responsibility, but I had no idea it was a shortcoming. I considered my omnipotent accountability a sterling asset. The results of my inventory suggested I consider otherwise.

As I sought this defect's true nature, I found an underlying pattern of perfectionism. I wondered why I felt the need to be perfect all the time, to the point that no one had to punish me for doing something wrong. I punished myself before they could get to it. It surprised me to discover that my perfectionism covered a deep fear of abandonment. When I had done something incorrectly as a child, my alcoholic father wouldn't speak to me for days. I can still remember feeling tense, sad, and alone until he resumed communicating with me; then everything would be okay again. I felt as if I were being abandoned over and over. I didn't know my father's alcoholic thinking and behavior had nothing to do with me.

Fear of abandonment is probably universal, but fear of abandonment is not abandonment itself. Only when I hold onto my childhood perception of the past do I think I can control the possibility of being abandoned. Working the program and trusting my Higher Power gives me a fresh view of myself and of my past, thus freeing me from its grip.

Thought for the Day

It's natural for a child to want to control. As an adult in recovery, however, I have healthier options.

> "With a relationship with a God of my understanding ... I no longer fear abandonment."

From Survival to Recovery, p. 83

Recently I reacted to a situation. I started to get angry—really angry. I felt like a victim. Thank goodness for all the meetings I've attended and for the slogans and phrases I've heard over and over. I've also heard that the word "anger" is just one letter short of "danger." I knew my anger was leading me in a hazardous direction.

In remembering this warning, my Al-Anon lessons came back to me and I switched quickly from anger to gratitude. I considered things I could be thankful for at that moment. From anger to gratitude is a huge leap that I could take only with Al-Anon's help. I sought the place in my heart where I could find peace and serenity and move toward acceptance. I took a spot-check inventory on anger. Then I was able to begin to accept the things I could not change.

In a matter of hours, I found myself in a safe place, the place Al-Anon has created within me. I realized that there was little I could change about the situation. All I could change was my response to it. As I continued to work through this, I grew even more aware of the potential danger to be found in anger, in both word and deed. That one-letter, one-second choice between working my anger or working my program meant the difference between creating a cavernous gap in my relationships and creating connections based on unity and harmony. I thank my Higher Power for gently repeating my healthy choices to me through the sharings I've heard at many Al-Anon meetings.

Thought for the Day

The value of regular attendance at Al-Anon meetings becomes evident when I least expect it but need it the most.

> "One might think that reading the same Steps, Traditions, and prayers over and over at meetings would reduce their impact, but that is not true."
>
> *The Forum*, November 1999, p. 4

Once I was diagnosed with a stress fracture in my foot. I had already been handicapped for 20 years. Needless to say, having a fractured foot posed many problems. Because it was severely painful and even dangerous for me to walk, I ended up stuck alone in my apartment during a severe snowstorm and unable to get to meetings.

It wasn't surprising that I fell back into my old attitudes, mainly self-pity. I like to be coddled and pampered when I'm sick, and my friends and family members weren't "reading my mind" and meeting my expectations. I'm usually a very independent woman with good, creative problem-solving skills. However, when I'm mired in negative thinking, I become a different person.

As all things do, this too passed. My foot healed and I was able to get back to my meetings. When I did, I asked myself, "Do *you* take note when others are sick and offer them the same attention you crave?" My answer was no, and I promptly asked my Higher Power for an opportunity to practice "Let It Begin with Me."

Within weeks, two neighbors had surgery. I didn't wish for either of them to be ill, yet I was gladdened by the promptness God displayed in answering my request. Here was my chance! Funny thing is, by nurturing my neighbors—asking if they needed anything from the store and calling to check on them—I felt as though I were nurturing myself. I guess what they say about Al-Anon is true. I often get back more than I give.

Thought for the Day

I've heard it said that to keep this program, I have to give it away. When I give it away, I'm also giving it to myself.

> "Joy and peace of mind are among the rewards we seek when we decide to 'Let It Begin with Me'."

From to Survival to Recovery, p. 95

The first slogans I heard were "Just for Today" and "One Day at a Time." I thought they applied to other people, not to me. It took Step Three work and faith in my Higher Power to become honest.

In Step Four I realized I was stuck in the past. My daily thoughts were usually about plans for the next day, week, or even month. I always anticipated tomorrow to the point where it *became* my today. I'd get so caught up in what I was *going to do* that I often wasn't aware of what I was doing *now*.

After realizing this character defect and asking my Higher Power to remove it, each day I have is usually better than the one before. I give thanks for the little joys in each day. I still make plans, but I don't let my thoughts erase the present. Anticipation is sweet, but not at the cost of today.

When I look back on this in the context of alcoholism, I understand why I behaved as I did. With all the awful happenings at home, there were many todays I didn't want to experience. As a child I had limited options, so the best way to escape was to flee into the possibility of a better tomorrow. I have different choices now. I know enjoying my day and doing the right thing for myself and my Higher Power is the best plan for an even better tomorrow.

Thought for the Day

Just for today I choose to enjoy all this day has to offer. If I don't like the offering, I'll ask my Higher Power to help me adjust my attitude.

"I will keep always in mind that *today* is my sole concern, and that I will make it as good a day as I can."

One Day at a Time in Al-Anon, p. 79

Nearly two years ago I tried my first Al-Anon meeting. I realized that I truly belonged there and decided to attend a minimum of three meetings each week. However, life had other plans for me. Within days, my life changed dramatically. Attending meetings under my new circumstances would be nearly impossible.

Fortunately I had accumulated an assortment of Al-Anon Conference Approved Literature, some of which I read daily. It was in CAL that I learned of the Lone Member Service. Through this service, people who can't attend meetings for geographical or physical reasons, etc., are put in touch with Al-Anon members for correspondence. Soon I was exchanging letters with members all over the United States.

About one year after I first reached out to Al-Anon, I realized that the written word in the form of CAL and writing to lone members was not just my primary tool for learning and living my program. It had become a kind of Power greater than myself—a guide and a good, reliable friend. It helps me even when I don't fully comprehend the weight or wisdom of what I read or write. When I keep coming back to CAL it helps me ensure the serenity I've worked so hard for in Al-Anon.

I still hope someday that I'll be able to attend meetings and give back in service the magnificent gifts I have received from reading CAL. Until then I'll rely on CAL and the Lone Member Service to carry me through.

Thought for the Day

If I can't get to a meeting and a crisis strikes, sanity and serenity may be only a page away.

> "Between meetings and when other people are not available, Al-Anon literature can offer us the comfort of knowing that our problems are not unique and we are not alone."
>
> *How Al-Anon Works for Families & Friends of Alcoholics*, p. 40

When I first came to Al-Anon, I was willing to do anything to make those around me happy. I believed I was a born follower. If told to jump, I asked, "How high?" I certainly didn't recognize any personal leadership skills. Mine were more like "followship" skills. I carried this attitude with me to my meetings.

It wasn't long before I found myself involved in one Al-Anon service project after another. I didn't think I was capable of performing these projects, but that didn't stop anyone from asking me. When I admitted I was afraid to make mistakes, fellow members told me that we all make them and that I would learn from them. It helped immensely that other Al-Anon members with more experience were at my side, guiding me with love and acceptance. It was all right to learn and grow at my own pace.

Eventually I felt more comfortable with my abilities and discovered talents I didn't know I had. I even began to feel capable of doing what was asked of me. Before I realized it, I was the one giving loving guidance. It took some time to see, but I had become a leader.

Concept Nine states in part, "Good personal leadership at all service levels is a necessity." My leadership style is different from the strict authoritarian style in the alcoholic home of my childhood. I simply present my experience, strength, and hope to others and provide support and encouragement for them to do their best. I strive to let it begin with me, which is true Al-Anon leadership in action.

Thought for the Day

Al-Anon encourages me to develop as a leader in my Higher Power's time, in my Higher Power's way.

> "In Al-Anon we learn we can take charge of our lives. We are the leaders of ourselves."
>
> *The Concepts—Al-Anon's Best Kept Secret?*, p. 20

After coming to Al-Anon, I have finally found peace. My father's alcoholism and my mother's reactions to it caused much pain in my childhood. I passed this pain on to my own family. My marriage was clearly and deeply affected by my feelings of abandonment and distrust. I expected my husband and children to fill the deep emptiness in my soul. When that didn't work, I tried church, work, community service, and being the perfect mother, volunteer, employee, and shop owner. The list of things I tried is endless. Finally in Al-Anon I found what worked—my faith in a Higher Power. The empty feeling is gone now.

My mother died knowing I loved her and that I was grateful for everything she did for me. Al-Anon taught me she had done the best she could with the tools she had. My father suffers from alcoholic dementia. My other family members move him from institution to institution, hoping it is just Alzheimer's. I tell myself, "Live and Let Live."

I am not on this earth to change or control others. I am here to change and grow the best I can in order to serve my Higher Power. Sometimes I slip and make another person my "higher power." Then I pray, read Al-Anon literature, attend meetings, and talk with my Al-Anon family about letting go. It is in letting go that I know peace and freedom, the "priceless gift of serenity." I belong in Al-Anon, where I never have to feel abandoned or empty again.

Thought for the Day

If I "keep coming back," I'll get what I need to fill my empty spaces.

> "We see that none of the time that passed was wasted; although we didn't know it, we were quietly absorbing the program."
>
> *Courage to Change*, p. 135

Al-Anon suggests I "Keep It Simple." I used to think keeping it simple meant doing whatever I needed to do to keep people from being angry with me. Not so! Keeping it simple means I don't have to do ten things at once so that everyone is happy. The slogan indicates I don't even have to *think* of ten things at once. Keeping it simple also implies that I can make decisions with my own best interests in mind. I don't need to complicate my life with guesswork about others' actions or feelings. Keeping it simple helps me say great phrases like, "I need some time to think about that" and "I'll need to get back to you with my decision." "I'm not sure," or "I don't know the answer to that" are also responses that work well.

Keeping it simple denotes I don't have to respond to the face of anger. I don't have to explain my motives to an irrational person. Keeping it simple suggests I don't have to take on someone else's guilt and frustration. It signifies that my integrity is protected and remains intact. Keeping it simple gives me time to enjoy the lovely, carefree things in life—like breathing deeply, smiling broadly, and laughing out loud!

When I practice "Keep It Simple," my decisions and responsibilities become clear so I can deal with them quickly and get on with enjoying my life.

Thought for the Day

What happens when I practice "Keep It Simple"?

> "I look at the simple things around me—a smile, a beautiful sunrise, a warm feeling about a friend—and try to *Keep It Simple* in my life today."
>
> *Alateen—a day at a time*, p. 46

A member asked, "So, what does one *do* with a sponsor?" Sponsorship *is* a tool—a tool to pick up and use. Sponsorship can only help if I ask a sponsor to help me build an Al-Anon-based life.

While the alcoholic picked up a drink and became drunk on alcohol, I picked up the alcoholic and became drunk on control and approval-seeking. My sponsor was the first person I picked up based on a healthy motive. I liked her enthusiastic faith and admired her commitment to unconditional love. I wanted to know how she used the program to get where she was in her life.

How did I use sponsorship? I phoned my sponsor to talk. I took little steps by sharing minor details about myself. Once I knew we both desired and were willing to maintain a high degree of privacy, I felt comfortable to confide more intimate thoughts and feelings. When our relationship began to glide on the wings of trust, I asked if we could meet regularly twice a month for several hours at a time. I wanted her support and insight while I explored more deeply this person whom I didn't even really know—me.

Gradually and together we built roots and a pair of wings so I could soar and feel connected at the same time. I borrowed her faith until I acquired my own. I leaned on her Higher Power until I began to connect with mine. It all happened because I took the risk to love myself enough to ask for help.

Thought for the Day

Do I love myself enough to use the tools of the program that have been laid in front of me?

> ". . . Sponsorship is one of the most important tools of the Al-Anon program. The rewards are reaped when the tool is put to use."
>
> *Sponsorship, What It's All About,* p. 11-12

I've come to think of my recovery as a triangle with my Higher Power at the top. Underneath my Higher Power are the basic, core Al-Anon tools—the Steps, Traditions, Concepts of Service, slogans, meetings, service, sponsorship, and Conference Approved Literature. Next comes me and my physical, emotional, and spiritual health. At the base of the triangle are my job, my family, my friends, and my hobbies.

As long as I keep everything in that order, with my Higher Power at the top as my sole focus, everything in my life works serenely, even joyfully. God provides strength, wisdom, and guidance, which flows down to me through the Al-Anon program. With the help of Al-Anon and my Higher Power, I receive what is necessary to maintain a good, balanced life and I attend honorably to my various needs. Then when these things have been taken care of, I use whatever time and energy I have left on work, family, friends, and hobbies. This is how I keep "principles above personalities" and practice "First Things First."

If I put something or someone else at the top of my recovery triangle, such as concerns about an alcoholic loved one, my life becomes unmanageable. I cannot make a thing, an event, or another person my Higher Power without becoming starved in all areas of my life. Such replacements simply do not nourish me. Often when my life does start to feel unmanageable, all I need to ask myself is, "Who or what is at the top of my triangle?"

Thought for the Day

How balanced is my life today?

"The program has helped me to set my priorities straight."

Alateen—a day at a time, p. 222

I can still hear my sponsor's voice as she suggested I feel my feelings. Trusting her, I obediently began to feel. Uncomfortable emotions surfaced. I thought I had come to Al-Anon to get rid of the pain, not to increase it.

As I kept coming back, I realized the message in my alcoholic home I had learned was, "Don't feel." Whenever I expressed anger, fear, or sadness, I was told I shouldn't feel that way. Consequently, I grew up with distrust not only of my feelings but also of my entire being. If I shouldn't feel what I was feeling, then something was terribly wrong with me.

To keep my emotions in check, I had learned to focus elsewhere—school, overworking, promiscuity, and experimenting with alcohol. Nothing, however, worked as well as trying to control the uncontrollable—alcoholism. I focused all of my attention and energy on the crisis at hand and lost myself in it.

Al-Anon helped me heal this insane self-denial by providing me with a safe place to get to know my emotional self. I saw others share their feelings at meetings, and slowly I started to reveal mine. No one criticized me or told me I shouldn't feel anything. Al-Anon also gave me concrete tools for dealing with these newly felt emotions. The slogans helped me respond appropriately at the moment particular feelings arose, and Steps Four through Six let me take a deeper look at them. Then I could decide which ones I wanted to keep, such as joy and serenity, and which ones I wanted to release, such as fear and resentment.

Thought for the Day

Al-Anon gives me a safe environment to experience and let go of the painful feelings I hold deep inside me.

> "We will begin to feel and will come to know the vastness of our emotions, but we will not be slaves to them."
>
> *From Survival to Recovery*, p. 269

Why does a dog bark? I feel terror when I'm on the receiving end of ferocious barking. I suspect that a dog barks because of his own fear. If the dog really wanted to attack, he'd dispense with the barking and lunge for me.

My alcoholic father often flew into rages that he seemed to direct at me. I lived in constant fear of him, and I defended myself by attacking him first. Our behavior then escalated into an ugly fight. I carried this behavior into other relationships. When I didn't bark, I defended myself by feigning indifference, leading others to believe that I was a snob. Sure, I protected myself, but I deprived myself of any real friendships in the process.

When I finally made it to Al-Anon, opening my mind and heart was a challenge. As I sat in the Al-Anon rooms week after week, I gradually came to trust that I could speak my heart and not be scorned. I heard meeting topics about fear and anger, and I connected with the reason behind my need to attack others first. I was afraid. It didn't take me long to see that perhaps my father had barked at me because he had been afraid, too.

This realization didn't mean I could ignore my feelings about past verbal abuse. By the time I worked through my fear and anger at my dad, I realized he was just a person with the same emotions as I. Instead of snarling dogs, we were just two people with shortcomings. It's a great deal easier to make friends when I'm not barking at them!

Thought for the Day

Never underestimate the power of self-awareness to put past experience into a new perspective.

> "Until we take the time to look at ourselves honestly, we may never be free of the bondage in which alcoholism holds us captive."
>
> *How Al-Anon Works for Families & Friends of Alcoholics*, p. 26

I was raised by two alcoholics, and I felt angry that I had to attend a support group to deal with this fact. I had not chosen my parents or their problems. Yet I was faced with the repercussions of their drinking. I resented my parents and begrudged giving up time to attend Al-Anon. At least the spouses of alcoholics had the choice of marrying the person. I had no choice about who my parents would be.

My group allowed me to stew in my resentment.. They let me rail against Al-Anon, and no one insisted I be grateful for alcoholics or for the program. They simply told me to keep coming back. I shared my discontent, complained that it wasn't my fault, and ranted and raved about my parents. Gradually I found myself actually looking forward to my meetings. I was glad I could go to a safe place where people understood and accepted me. I became a grateful, recovering member of Al-Anon.

With the group, the Al-Anon tools, and my Higher Power, I learned that although my parents may initially have been responsible for many of my problems, the solutions were up to me. I finally grew up in Al-Anon. I've grown so much it's hard to remember the old me. Although my parents have not chosen recovery, my relationship with them continues to improve considerably as I apply the Al-Anon principles to my interactions with them.

Thought for the Day

I may not have grown up the way I wanted to the first time, but I can grow up all over again in Al-Anon.

> "Today I am growing by leaps and bounds. I've learned to
> focus on myself, not the alcoholic. Al-Anon has given me
> many things—from friends to tools for living—but most
> importantly, Al-Anon has given me a life of my own!"
>
> *Al-Anon Sharings from Adult Children,* p. 19

One of my most notable experiences of the power of making amends as described in Step Nine came not from amends I have made to others but from amends made to me by someone in the fellowship.

I remember feeling confused, fearful, and defensive when this person asked to meet with me. In the past we had had a difference of opinion about how to accomplish a task and had not parted on particularly cordial terms. Although I tried to keep an open mind about our meeting, I felt some uneasiness.

When I realized my fellow Al-Anon wished to make amends, I was amazed. I was deeply moved by this demonstration of humility and courage. This person had exercised great patience and open-mindedness in coming to understand and accept my point of view. I realized that I had received the precious gift of being heard and accepted without being judged. I also was given the opportunity to see what making amends looks like and how it can be done, which is a valuable frame of reference for me to use in making my own amends.

Thought for the Day

The process of making and receiving amends invites new acceptance and respect in all of my relationships.

> "Now I know if I make amends to someone, he probably will think a lot more of me for it, and I'll feel a lot better when I'm with him."
>
> *Twelve Steps and Twelve Traditions for Alateen*, p. 19

Rules were meaningless in my alcoholic family. I couldn't count on them because they changed. I had an 11:00 PM curfew. Some nights I'd come home early, and my mother would rage at me for making her wait up. Other nights I would call to let her know I'd be late, and she would yell at me for waking her up. Still other nights I could come home hours late, and no one would notice. No one seemed to notice that my mother also had a problem with alcohol.

When I came into Al-Anon, I viewed the Traditions the same as the rules in my alcoholic home. They were meaningless, so I ignored them. However, I was drawn to groups that stuck to the Traditions. At those meetings I felt an extra measure of safety and solidity.

It took me a while to see the value of the Traditions. I needed to establish myself in Steps One through Three and get a sponsor. As I began to gain some clarity, I started to notice and appreciate how the meetings were different from my earlier alcoholic environment. Consistency and structure replaced chaos and erratic behavior. Somehow I found it easier to heal when I knew what to expect. I had more energy for recovery when I didn't have to spend it trying to make sense out of turmoil.

Wherever I attend Al-Anon, I know I'll find the same Suggested Welcome and Closing, the Twelve Steps, Conference Approved Literature, unconditional love, and respect. This stability and structure is possible only when groups adhere voluntarily to the suggested Traditions.

Thought for the Day

Thanks to the Traditions, I have more energy for recovery because I don't get depleted from coping with inconsistency.

> "Now I think that the Twelve Traditions are just as important to me as the Twelve Steps'"
>
> *Alateen—a day at a time*, p. 318

As far back as I can remember, fear has clouded my vision. To cope with the active alcoholism in my family, I became a worrier. Worry gave me a false sense of being in control. I tried to fret my way out of the maze of alcoholism, judgment, and lack of support that characterized my upbringing. When I was able to leave my family and establish a home of my own, my habits came with me. Worrying soon became characteristic not only of my childhood but of my adult life as well.

In Al-Anon I learned it's fruitless to worry about things I cannot change. However, simply knowing that didn't help me quit worrying. I had to find a positive behavior to replace the fretting. Today if I catch myself worrying, I write down my specific fears, no matter how preposterous they may seem. Once I get them out of my mind and fix them on paper, I ask my Higher Power to show me which ones are real and which are imagined. Then I ask for clarification regarding which ones I can change.

This process reminds me of wearing my sunglasses inside a building. The glasses are useful in the sunshine, but once inside they make everything look dark and gloomy. So it is with worry. It helped me while growing up, but today it can make even a bright, shiny gift look tarnished. Small shadows become big monsters, and I waste my energy worrying about nonexistent problems. When I invite my Higher Power to help, it's like saying, "God, please hold these sunglasses for me. Help me to see as You do."

Thought for the Day

God, please clear my vision so I can let go of fear and worry.

"He is a God of my awareness who serves as a guide in all areas of my life."

As We Understood . . ., p. 93

When I first came into Al-Anon, I didn't care one way or the other about a Higher Power. When I read the Steps with all those references to God, I was a little skeptical. I wasn't even sure I wanted a relationship with a Higher Power or what to do with one if I had it. To my amazement, everyone let me approach the program in a way that reflected where I was at any given moment. They shared their experience, strength, and hope as I struggled with whether and to what degree I wanted to connect myself with a Higher Power. I stumbled around, moved forward, and fell back for months. Yet no one told me I had to believe as they did to get what the program has to offer.

Gradually, by keeping an open mind and heart, attending meetings, and using the program tools, I became willing to have, and then actually yearned for, a relationship with a Higher Power. This relationship allows me to share honestly, set boundaries, and express a full range of emotions. I will be forever grateful to all those people in all those rooms who, while knowing their own truth, allowed me to find mine.

Thought for the Day

Al-Anon lets me grow in my own way, at my own pace.

"As Al-Anon members, we are encouraged to define spiritual concepts in our own terms and are free to arrive at our own spiritual truths."

As We Understood. . ., p. 69

Growing up in an alcoholic family, I did not escape without experiencing various forms of mistreatment, including sexual abuse. By the time I came into Al-Anon, I felt like a victim and I had become an extremely angry, resentful person.

Whenever the subject of forgiveness came up at our meetings or in our literature, I shut it out. I thought resentment would prevent me from ever being hurt again. It took some time in the program, and a lot of work learning to love myself, before I began to understand that living my life under the heavy burdens of rage and resentment was hurting me. It affected every relationship I had, including work contacts, friends, family, and social acquaintances. I knew it was likely to color future connections as well, yet many of the people I resented weren't even alive. I surely wasn't hurting them! However, in my vehement determination to no longer be a victim, I held the hostility that perpetuated my pain.

Once I realized this, I experienced a spiritual awakening in the form of a deep desire to let go of those feelings that were poisoning my life. I accomplished this by going to extra Al-Anon meetings, praying, sharing with my sponsor, and working Steps Four through Nine. Thanks to Al-Anon, I gave up my bitterness and regained my life.

Thought for the Day

Today I see forgiveness as an action I take to love myself more fully.

"No one ever found serenity through hatred."

How Al-Anon Works for Families & Friends of Alcoholics, p. 86

When I came to Al-Anon, I only could see how different I was. We shared many of the same problems, but I couldn't see that we were alike. I was confident and capable. They all seemed to be whiners or perfectionists.

Nevertheless, something attracted me to Al-Anon. I continued to attend regularly and to read literature every day, but I certainly didn't give anyone a call. How could "those" people help me? So I kept my distance. When I felt enough pain, I admitted I needed a sponsor's help to understand and work the Steps, but I had no one to ask. Who would be good enough for me? Or worse, what if they judged me as I had judged them?

I squirmed through the next few meetings and finally had to admit the truth. As confident and capable as I was, I was afraid to speak up and ask for help. At that moment I heard someone straining to speak. Her voice trembled as she admitted she desperately needed a sponsor but was afraid to ask anyone. She began to cry.

Another member passed a box of tissues, and as I took the box in my hands, I realized that the frightened voice was my own. After the meeting, several people came over to offer me hugs and assurance. The same people I had once looked down upon now appeared to me as angels. When I see all the different faces at my Al-Anon meetings, my heart soars with gratitude for the rich mosaic of recovery that now includes me.

Thought for the Day

How do I contribute to my own feeling of being different?

"Each of us is unique and each of us is valuable. But as long as I held myself apart from or above other people, I denied both myself and others the rich interchange that is possible."

The Forum, April 1998, p. 30

Sometimes as I struggle with the effects of having grown up with the disease of alcoholism, the path seems too difficult to travel. I forget that there are ups and downs to any journey, and I feel overcome with disappointment with my seemingly slow progress. Then my Higher Power reminds me of a history lesson I once learned, and I regain hope.

An expedition of the Grand Canyon traveled along the Colorado River. Halfway through the canyon, the explorers encountered dangerous rapids. Some of the explorers were killed as the thrashing waters hurled them about. The others managed to get ashore where they gathered their wits to assess the situation. Although the river ahead looked choppy and menacing, some of the crew decided to forge ahead. They felt they had traveled too far to turn back. The others decided to return home on foot. The explorers who went ahead faced dangerous waters for a short period, but the remainder of their journey was safe, calm, and beautiful. Those who turned back actually faced greater dangers, and they did not survive.

This story reminds me how valuable it is to persistently move forward in the program. When the road ahead looks threatening and I want to turn back to my old attitudes and behaviors, I remember that I'm not alone on my path. I have the wisdom of a Power greater than myself, the tools of the program, and the experience, strength, and hope of my fellow travelers in Al-Anon to support me.

Thought for the Day

During bleak periods of my recovery, my Higher Power reminds me that the best way out is through.

"Today I will pause at a crossroad and listen for my Higher Power's voice."

Courage to Change, p. 81

Talking openly and honestly with my family members is difficult and at times downright painful. Saying to people I love that I'm no longer willing to be around their intense negative energy is a frightening experience. Sometimes I'm afraid I'll have to separate from my family members to maintain my quest for healthy living, especially when they deny and justify their unacceptable behavior.

I'm aware that I still want the people I love to change and mature, so I can be more comfortable. I am also aware that this may or may not happen. Today it's okay for me to want this to happen. However, I am slowly learning that trying to change someone else's behavior to suit my needs is an exercise in futility and frustration. Truly profound power and peace lie in the ability to change *my* behavior to suit my needs.

Thought for the Day

With the help of Al-Anon, I can accept people as they are and find serenity, even if I'm the only one who changes.

> "We need to recover, and, when we do, we sometimes
> find that others are motivated to get better, too."
>
> *Does She Drink Too Much?*, p. 4

I suffered from the compulsive need for perfection that I developed while growing up with an alcoholic mother. I found that trying to be perfect was the best defense against her anger. There was no way of knowing what would upset my mother next, and I believed perfect behavior and achievement would protect me from her dangerous responses.

A friend who often witnesses my destructive habit of criticizing myself told me of a mistake she made one morning. Instead of pouring her orange juice into a glass, she poured it into her coffee as if it were cream. She knew if I had made the same error, it would have been occasion for intense self-derision at my imperfection, and she was right. I was completely mystified by her casual dismissal of the mistake. I envied her ability to simply pour the coffee and juice mixture out of her mug and start over again. How could she laugh off the incident so easily? I had no idea how to treat myself in such a gentle, forgiving way.

A particular Al-Anon tool showed me how to apply the lessons of my friend's story to my own life. The repeated hearing and reading of the slogan "How Important Is It?" helped me to work this question into my daily experience. I finally understood that no serious damage is done when orange juice is poured into coffee. I learned to distinguish which behaviors result in consequences that need serious attention, and which ones do not. I came to understand that actions are about responsibility, not judgment. I have now learned to be as gentle with myself as I am with others.

Thought for the Day

What is my barometer for determining "How Important Is It?"

"Most of the time I find that what I might have viewed as a disaster is really insignificant."

Courage to Change, p. 228

When I came to Al-Anon, I was ill-prepared to accept that my "perfect" parents were full-fledged alcoholics, and that I suffered from the disease in the form of emotional sickness and spiritual starvation.

I believed that if Al-Anon would give me the answer book and allow me to study it, I could fix my family and we'd live happily together. I soon learned that there is no answer book. However, there is plenty of helpful Conference Approved Literature and a great deal of experience, strength, and hope. Most important, there are Twelve Steps that can help me find the answers.

As I became involved in Al-Anon, my family continued to deteriorate because of my parents' and my brother's drinking. In spite of my efforts, I grew despondent and disinterested in working Al-Anon's Twelve Steps and in living life.

Then the miracle commonly shared by others in the program happened to me. When I could not do another thing for myself, the loving God of my understanding wrapped me in protective care and began to teach me that I am worthy of joy and serenity. I became receptive to what living the Al-Anon program could achieve for me—joy and serenity in the face of chaos.

Today I live with the knowledge that I am worthy and deserving. If I cultivate my spiritual awareness and remember to avail myself of each moment's opportunities, I experience many hours of joy and serenity.

Thought for the Day

My Higher Power is looking out for me even when I can't.

> "I believe that God's grace also means that God is doing for us what we cannot do for ourselves. He floods my life with His grace, doing things for me and through me that I could never do myself."

As We Understood . . . pp. 97-98

My parents are due to visit. Nothing promotes my relapse into compulsive, controlling behavior better than the anticipation of their judgment. Although these days they are kinder than when I was a child, I can still react. I began the obsessive battle to make my life, house, and yard perfect. The more I struggle, the more distant I feel from my Higher Power.

Today I humbly asked for help. "Show me the way off this merry-go-round," I prayed. "Draw me closer and show me how to trust You." Immediately I saw the image of a sailboat steered by a tiller. With the tiller under my Higher Power's hand, the boat of my will and my life glides cleanly through the waves. Without wise, steady, and consistent guidance, the tiller swings wildly, and the boat is tossed by each wave. Although I cannot do anything about the waves rolling into my life, I can hand the tiller of my life over to God and trust that I will be steered to safety.

There is a path for me each day, just as there is a path through the water for each boat. My Higher Power can read the signs better than I. When I feel a nudge to do one task instead of another, I strive to respond willingly. Although another route may seem more appealing, I choose to trust that the course suggested by my Higher Power is the best for me.

Thought for the Day

Each time I doubt that my Higher Power knows the way, I'll remember how chaotic and complicated my life becomes when I try to take control.

> "In Al-Anon I have come to know that I have a resource within me and all around me that can guide me through the most overwhelming fears and the most challenging decisions—a Higher Power."
>
> *Courage to Change*, p. 327

I wanted to create a perfect family, and that was all. At 20 years old, the idea didn't seem crazy. My parents had divorced, and I wanted to prove I could do marriage differently. So I married someone who needed me. At our wedding ceremony, the minister said, ". . . and the two shall become one," and we did. "We" became "him."

We had problems immediately, but I associated them with my husband's drinking. I thought if I loved him enough, he wouldn't drink. I went to great lengths to smooth over bumps in his life. In the process I lost my dignity. I spent 14 years trying to be more loving, and I ended up in total isolation and spiritual poverty. I failed to build my perfect family.

In Al-Anon, I began by facing the truth about my alcoholic upbringing. My husband was not the sole cause of our troubles. I had been denying that my illness, acquired as the daughter of an alcoholic, was deeply affecting our marriage. Granted, the manifestations of my father's drinking had been less obvious than my husband's, but subtlety hadn't spared me the effects of the disease. It only lengthened the time it took for me to recognize and accept them.

Alcoholism still surrounds me. What is no longer present is the illusion that I have control over anyone's drinking. Now I spend my energy on seeking healthy solutions, which do not include trying to create the perfect family!

Thought for the Day

If I am experiencing difficulty in a relationship, the root cause may be in my alcoholic upbringing. Once I find that root, I can use the Steps to weed it out.

> "In Al-Anon, children of alcoholics find the tools that
> enable them to put the past to rest, to forgive and go on
> to meaningful adult lives."
>
> *Al-Anon Sharings from Adult Children*, p. 3

Many of us came into Al-Anon feeling as if we were on the outside looking in, never quite feeling a part of anything. This was the first place we finally felt our opinions mattered and were as good as anyone else's. We learned to participate first by setting up chairs or reading one of the Steps, and gradually we became more confident in our abilities. As fellow members encouraged us, we found we could expand our participation and need never do it alone.

Those of us who were perfectionists discovered that our participation did not have to be perfect. If we had problems relinquishing control, we found others in the program who had great ideas and needed to participate as well. I've heard it said in other settings that nothing great ever came out of a committee. Apparently that person never worked on an Al-Anon committee!

We all have an obligation as well as a need to participate. In Al-Anon we are offered a rare privilege to do so. Service expands our world and brings new friends into our lives. It presents us with new experiences and helps us grow immeasurably. Not everyone in the program will serve as delegate, area chairperson, trustee, or World Service Office staff. However, each of us has something unique that we bring to the program. Whether our participation includes setting up chairs, chairing a meeting, attending an area assembly, working on a convention, or being there when a newcomer calls, participation is not only the key to harmony, it is the key to growth and recovery.

Thought for the Day

Today I'll consider enriching my recovery by participating in Al-Anon service.

> "But the Right of Participation in our service structure is of such high importance to our future that it is urged we preserve this traditional right in the face of every attempt to whittle it down."

Al-Anon/Alateen Service Manual, p. 159

Even after coming to Al-Anon for a while, I harbored some secret thoughts and feelings I thought were far too personal to share with the group. However, other members had suggested that saying those difficult words out loud would help me recover. One night I shared my confusion over how to heal these parts of my life.

Soon after, my home group held a meeting on sponsorship. Several longtime members spoke about their experiences. From these individuals I learned sponsors are Al-Anon members who work with another member on a one-to-one basis to explain the program's tools and encourage their use. Sponsors respond to the needs of the sponsee in a loving and constructive manner. They listen to the situations presented by the sponsee, and if they have lived through similar experiences, they share how the Al-Anon principles helped them cope. Even if they have not gone through something similar, they can help the sponsee apply the Steps to the problem. I also heard that receiving a sponsor's support during a difficult situation can magnify whatever help the group has offered.

This meeting on sponsorship was helpful to me. I didn't feel as confused afterwards, and I even gained the courage to ask someone to be my sponsor. Now I understand more about how such a relationship works, and my sponsor has become yet another recovery tool for me. Her patient listening helps fill in the gaps when sharing at meetings is not quite sufficient for my needs. Together, meetings and sponsorship help me express myself to the fullest.

Thought for the Day

We honor ourselves when we ask an Al-Anon member to be a sponsor and to walk beside us on our path to recovery.

> "Certainly, pent-up resentments need release, and sponsors can be extremely helpful in working on those areas and putting them into perspective."
> *How Al-Anon Works for Families & Friends of Alcoholics*, p. 114

I can remember a time when sex was as easy as rolling off a log. Now even rolling off a log is not as easy as it used to be. I'm mature, and my body has more limitations than it used to have.

I also have more responsibilities than I once had. My life is more structured and less spontaneous. The positive aspect of responsibility and structure is that both allow me the pursuit of interests that bring me pleasure. Still, I find it difficult to allow intimate and spontaneous time with my wife.

What to do? Surprising to me, the most glaring oversight in my intimate experience is a failure to include my Higher Power. My sense of practicing Al-Anon's principles in all my affairs, as suggested in Step Twelve, invites me to ask for guidance from my Higher Power even in matters I once might have considered too personal.

Thought for the Day

My Higher Power is my partner in everything I do. Today I can include God in my entire life, even areas I once considered off-limits.

> "I don't mean to imply that I have found a magic formula for sexual enjoyment, but I do believe in changing the things I can. In my particular case, that meant putting the whole issue in the hands of God."
>
> *In All Our Affairs,* p. 115

I was ready to confront my alcoholic father. I wanted to let him know that I remembered every detail of all the times in my childhood when he hurt me. That way he could apologize to me and I would be healed. However, he refused to talk about it. He said it was water over the dam! I was furious. How could those wrongs be righted if he didn't admit them and tell me he was sorry?

By applying the tools of the Al-Anon program, I slowly tried to accept the thing I could not change—my father's refusal to apologize—and to change the thing I could—my attitude toward the situation. Learning more about alcoholism as a disease taught me that my father wasn't a bad person. He was a person with a disease that made him do bad things. Practicing "Live and Let Live" and keeping the focus on myself taught me to attend to my own behavior. I needed to make sure I wasn't practicing the very behaviors that had caused me so much anguish. By seeking my part in the hurt I felt, I learned that my hold on the pain of the injury, not the injury itself, was what I could do something about.

Eventually I realized I didn't need my father's apology in order to get better. I could move on by praying to lose my resentments and to replace them with forgiveness.

Thought for the Day

Forgiveness is something I do with my Higher Power's help, and I do it for me. I don't need anyone's apology to begin my healing process.

"By releasing resentment, I set myself free."

Courage to Change, p. 289

I spend most of my time at Al-Anon meetings engaging in a very important activity—listening. Part of what I do when I listen is described in our slogan "Listen and Learn." By listening, I learn about the program. I learn about alcoholism, how others apply the Steps and Traditions, and I learn that practice of the Al-Anon principles allows me to achieve a degree of serenity.

By listening at an Al-Anon meeting, however, I do more than learn. I may borrow experience, strength, and hope from fellow members, but I also lend my own dash of detachment, acceptance, and understanding. I join with others in forging the bond of unity that helps us heal. I strive to contribute to the unconditional acceptance that invites our Higher Power to join us.

Thought for the Day

An important part of what I give to my fellow Al-Anons is my willingness to listen.

"Al-Anon's slogan, 'Listen and Learn' reminds us that if we have the self-discipline to be quiet and pay attention to others' words, we can learn a tremendous amount about ourselves and our world."

How Al-Anon Works for Families & Friends of Alcoholics, p. 99

I often heard, "You'll never amount to anything. You'll end up barefoot and pregnant. Colleges don't accept dummies like you." These statements were imprinted on my mind and heart from a very early age while growing up with the chaotic, inconsistent, and abusive behavior of my alcoholic father. I wanted to prove him wrong, but no matter how hard I tried, I always seemed to fail to reach my goals of academic success after I graduated from high school.

I came to Al-Anon on my knees, willing to live a different way. I asked someone to be my sponsor after I had been in the program for six weeks. She directed me into service work right away, and I accepted the first position that was available in my home group. I felt afraid of doing the job incorrectly and being criticized, but I accepted it anyway. My fears were quelled because the criticism never came. Instead, I received praise from other members for a job well done. This gave me the courage to raise my hand the next time a position became vacant. The next thing I knew, I was part of our assembly board and a district representative.

Being of service to Al-Anon gave me the courage to finish college and to enter the teaching profession. I am truly grateful for the confidence and self-esteem Al-Anon has given me. The old negative messages have been replaced with courage, self-respect, and happiness. Al-Anon service work has helped me become the person my Higher Power and I always knew I could become.

Thought for the Day

Al-Anon service work provides a supportive training ground to find out the best of who I am and who I can become.

"... I can, I can, I can! And I do."

When I Got Busy, I Got Better, p. 22

Have you ever had the opportunity to watch preschoolers put together a puzzle? If a piece doesn't fit immediately, they often push and shove to make it fit, making lots of sound effects along the way.

This is how I lived most of my life. I never felt like I "fit" in my alcoholic family or anywhere else. I felt like the puzzle piece in a preschooler's hand. Instead of forcing myself to fit, I forced those around me. I tried to manipulate and control everybody in my life to change the shape of their personalities to suit mine. I even attended workshops so I could make changes happen. My personal slogan became "I have to make things happen." My life was unmanageable.

Fortunately I made it to Al-Anon before I wrecked the entire beautiful puzzle of my life. The program taught me first that there's nothing wrong with the way I'm shaped mentally, emotionally, physically, or spiritually. There's nothing wrong with other people's shapes either. Then I learned that the only piece I can change is my own. I have choices now. Instead of spending time with people and situations where I don't fit, I can look for the ones where I do. Regarding the puzzle of my family, I can't change the fact that I'm a member who doesn't always fit. However, Al-Anon gives me tools, such as detachment and the Serenity Prayer, to use when I'm around family members. I can change what I can and remember that this family gathering, too, shall pass. Soon I can move on to gatherings where I feel more comfortable.

Thought for the Day

My goal is not to change others to fit me. I aim to change myself to fit my Higher Power's will.

> "Our thinking becomes distorted by trying to force solutions and we become irritable and unreasonable without knowing it."
>
> Suggested Al-Anon/Alateen Welcome

My kitchen wallpaper has been the same since I moved into my house 20 years ago. I never liked the pattern, but it was something I learned to tolerate. I wanted to change it and thought about doing so many times over the years, but I was afraid to find out what was behind it. If I took the paper down, would the walls crumble? Would I find something I couldn't fix? This reminds me of my life. I've learned to live with, put up with, and tolerate many things I wanted to change but was afraid to try for fear of the unknown.

I finally tore the wallpaper down. It came off in little pieces. There were some cracks, a few holes, and lots of nicks and bumps. When I had to move the refrigerator, it seemed too big and unmanageable. Later that day my sponsor suggested that I put cardboard under the front and slide it. It seemed impossible, but I tried it and it worked!

The kitchen is going to need a lot of patching. I'm not going to repair it overnight, but with the right tools I know I can fix it. This can be true for me, too. With the help of Al-Anon, my sponsor, and my Higher Power, change need not be so scary. If I don't at least make an effort, I may never know how much I can accomplish.

Thought for the Day

My Higher Power may be inviting me to walk further down my spiritual path by giving me a desire to change. Today I take a risk, understanding that God loves and guides me through the process.

"... God's will will never take me where His love cannot protect me."

From Survival to Recovery, p. 111

I did not choose an alcoholic mother and a workaholic father, who were unable to express love. I did not decide to have an older brother who beat me and a younger brother whose love and attention I craved.

I did choose to give my younger brother things I wanted myself in order to win his love. I did decide to shut off my feelings from my family. I did pursue an occupation that allows me to be a workaholic like my father. I did ask a woman to marry me who, I thought, was nothing like my mother. She didn't smoke or drink, and she worked hard—as hard as my father. She worked hard when I wanted her company, when I wanted to go places with her, and when I was lonely in bed.

I joined Al-Anon when my wife and I separated. Although I had become depressed and unhappy by trying to live my life through her, it still hurt to let her go. By immersing myself in Al-Anon, I gradually learned I was responsible for my choices. I had to stop focusing on my ex-wife's emotional unavailability as the source of my problems. I had to look at why I chose to become involved with unavailable people.

I am learning to like and take care of myself. Today my choices are based on loving myself rather than on fear or control. I'm learning that when I try to make others love me, it becomes harder to know who I am and what I want. I'm discovering that I can make progress only by living in the moment. I am realizing that some choices are more beneficial for me than others.

Thought for the Day

My choices reflect my opinion of and relationship with myself.

"I can learn to respond with love, caring, and respect for myself . . ."

Courage to Change, p. 172

I recently had an enlightening experience at an A1-Anon convention. When I arrived at the meeting site, some fellow Al-Anon members told me of a special path through the woods. If I followed it, I would be led to a secluded space of calm beauty for private prayer, meditation, and contemplation. During the previous week my life had been chaotic and stressful, and I dearly wanted to do something nice for myself. I needed some quiet time with my Higher Power, so I decided to be adventurous and start down the path.

After walking for a little while, I came to a fork in the road. Faced with two paths, I felt anguished at the thought of not getting where I desperately wanted to be. I pondered which direction would lead me to my destination. Which one should I choose? What if I chose wrongly, got lost, and missed the special spot? Finally I decided to travel the left path and was delighted to find the place of serene beauty for my solitary meditation with God.

I returned along the same path, feeling refreshed and grateful for how well my Higher Power takes care of my needs. When I returned to the convention site, I happily reported my good luck to the group, only to be gently informed that either branch of the path would have led me to the same destination! I realized then that no matter which direction in life I choose, I will always be in my Higher Power's care.

Thought for the Day

Whichever way I turn, my Higher Power will be there if I ask.

"Any way I choose, my Higher Power is choosing for and with me."

Having Had a Spiritual Awakening . . ., p. 68

I remember finding my first sponsor. I had met her years before when I made the transition from Alateen into Al-Anon. I thought she was odd. She always smiled and laughed. At that point in recovery, I thought people who didn't take the healing process seriously had nothing to offer.

I saw my sponsor-to-be a few years later at convention. I didn't think of her again until I was desperate. Someone close to me had moved away, and I thought I wouldn't survive the loss. I had been in Al-Anon for three years and still didn't have a sponsor. My anguish brought me to my knees. I begged God for help, climbed into bed, and promptly fell asleep.

I awoke to birds singing. Clear as a bell, a voice deep within told me to ask the "odd" lady to be my sponsor. I knew this voice was my Higher Power's. "You've got to be kidding," I said. My Higher Power kept repeating the instructions.

I was in enough pain to try anything, so I asked her to be my sponsor. She was open to the idea and suggested we both pray on it for a week, and then talk again. When I said I still wanted her to be my sponsor, she agreed.

This experience taught me about listening to and acting on God's will, even when it seems to say something strange. My first sponsor and I ended up together for eight years. She became the key to my program. Her love led me toward a sense of belonging. I will be forever grateful for her presence in my life.

Thought for the Day

A sponsor is a special person who helps me make the program come alive.

"... Experience shows that sponsorship is a valuable aid to personal understanding and use of the Al-Anon program of recovery."

Sponsorship, What It's All About, p. 3

Growing up in an alcoholic home, I experienced a high degree of uncertainty in my young life. One day I would come home to open, loving arms that met my needs and allowed me to feel safe. The next day would be filled with verbal and emotional abuse. Living with these extremes, my feelings tried to keep pace. Eventually they resembled a roller-coaster ride filled with extreme highs and lows. I learned to cling to the extremes and to hold on for dear life.

When I reached Al-Anon, I slowly but surely climbed off the roller coaster and placed my emotions and my life into the hands of a Power greater than myself. Through attending meetings, reading literature, and practicing the Steps and slogans, I learned there's a lot of middle ground, or "gray areas," to my feelings. I learned to let go of my emotional extremes and to allow God to show me a more serene and peaceful way of life.

Thought for the Day

By improving my conscious contact with God, I find that emotional balance and inner peace can be a part of my daily life.

"Al-Anon helps me to come back to center."

Courage to Change, p. 194

My Higher Power gives me situations where I can choose to grow or not to grow. These situations seem to occur more frequently when I practice the Al-Anon principles. They usually involve unresolved issues with my family and reappear in the form of conflicts with colleagues, friends, and neighbors. These conflicts tend to repeat until I gather the awareness, courage, self-love, and willingness through the Twelve Steps to stop suffering. Then I can live life in a different way with healthier attitudes and choices.

When I faced people who reminded me of the alcoholic behavior in my childhood home, I used to be so afraid that I panicked, ran away, or shut down. This behavior perpetuated my old cycle of suffering. I didn't realize I was actually having flashbacks from my alcoholic upbringing and that my reactions to these people were extreme, as if I were still that frightened little girl.

Today, when I'm faced with unhealthy and unacceptable behavior, I don't run away. I use the program to help me. I remember to stop and "Think." I use my intellect instead of my emotions before responding. I detach from the person or situation until I can calm down and think rationally. I call my sponsor to defuse my emotions and help me figure out which program tools apply.

When I apply my Al-Anon wisdom in these types of situations, unacceptable behavior comes into my life less frequently. When I'm willing to let my Higher Power help me face my problems today in a healthier manner than I did in the past, I'm not as likely to recreate them.

Thought for the Day

If I don't take the time to recover from the past, I'm bound to repeat it.

> "Thanks to Alateen, I can talk to and understand people better, and I live what I call a happy, normal life."
>
> *Alateen—Hope for Children of Alcoholics,* p. 78

Sometimes I need to work Step One backwards. I don't always recognize when I'm powerless, but I certainly notice when my life becomes unmanageable. Then I remember that usually when I'm feeling insane, I'm forgetting my powerlessness and trying to control outcomes or other people.

My life quickly deteriorates when I indulge my ego and recklessly set out to change someone or something over which I have no control—in other words, when I try to get my way. I can be stubborn about it, too, spending an inordinate amount of time and effort to that end. The inevitable result is pain, frustration, and utter failure. Even if I acknowledge my powerlessness, until I accept it, I still experience pain.

When I accept my powerlessness and surrender to my Higher Power's will, however, I gain some measure of serenity and humility. I become spiritually teachable. I wish I could say I always recognize and accept my powerlessness. If only I asked my Higher Power for guidance, let Her do Her part while I do mine, and then went on from there. Often this process really does happen, but I'm human. Sometimes I need to go through the experience of struggling with someone or something before I become willing to surrender and accept reality once again.

My recovery is about progress, not perfection. Each time I practice accepting my powerlessness, it comes closer to being a natural response. The good news is that with surrender and acceptance comes release from my pain.

Thought for the Day

The pain is not in the surrender and acceptance. It's in the resistance.

> "I can hold onto my will until the situation becomes so painful that I am forced to submit, or I can put my energy where it can do me some good right now, and surrender to my Higher Power's care."

Courage to Change, p. 269

My method for dealing with the insanity and chaos while growing up in an alcoholic environment was *not* to deal with it. I escaped into a fantasy world of books and art and remained physically and emotionally removed from what went on around me. My family could argue all day long, but it didn't touch me because I was far away.

By the time I found my way to Al-Anon, years of isolating myself had left me with scars that couldn't heal overnight. I suffered from low self-esteem, impaired social skills, and lack of self-knowledge, to name a few. Being young, gay, and male added to my sense of being different at the meetings I attended. I was sure no one could help me unless they were just like me.

Finally I found what I thought I was looking for—an Al-Anon meeting for gay, male adult children. As I sat at that meeting week after week, finding new reasons to feel alone and separate, I began to realize two things. No matter how different we feel, we're all very similar. No matter how similar we seem, we're all very different. It was then that I knew my problem had nothing to do with which meeting I went to, and it had everything to do with keeping an open mind.

Thought for the Day

Making myself available to help and be helped by a wide range of people is a key to my recovery.

"Now I understand my uniqueness. There may be no one else on earth exactly like me, but with God as my partner and as a member of such a fellowship, I am not alone."

. . . In All Our Affairs, p. 117

When I think of boundaries, it helps if I think of a castle in a lake. Boundaries are the drawbridge connecting the castle with the world. Usually the drawbridge is down, and people can walk freely back and forth. However, when danger is sensed, the drawbridge rises to protect the castle.

To protect myself from the dangers of my alcoholic family, I shut down and kept my drawbridge closed to guard my feelings and thoughts. Eventually my castle grew musty and foul inside. When I reached Al-Anon, I couldn't distinguish between real and imagined threats. By listening to members share, I learned how to recognize danger signals in the behavior of others and how to respond appropriately.

On occasion, the danger signals are not clear. Sometimes what I perceive as a threat is something I've conjured up in my own mind. If I immediately shut down my feelings in reaction, I usually end up hurting myself or someone else. In the end I might lose an opportunity to grow or a chance to love and be loved.

With the help of my Higher Power and the Serenity Prayer, I've learned to distinguish between real and imagined threats. I've learned to recognize and respect others' boundaries. I'm also able to discern when it's wiser for me to remain open to some-one I love and trust even when I want to close up out of fear. I remind myself that I can't experience love, joy, and trust, and completely abandon myself to my Higher Power if I can't risk feeling the other extremes of sadness, hurt, and fear.

Thought for the Day

Knowing when to open and when to close my boundaries is a learning experience.

> "Boundaries are flexible, changeable, removable, so it's up to me how open or closed I'll be at any given time."
>
> *Courage to Change*, p. 201

"One Day at a Time" seems so simple, yet it is the most challenging slogan for me. I often worry about tomorrow. I don't worry so much about how other people will react to me. Instead, I worry about how I'll handle myself in a given situation. Will I have the courage to stand up for my beliefs, my rights, or my needs?

Step Eleven encourages me to seek my Higher Power's will for me and the power to carry it out. The essence of knowing my Higher Power's will for me in the context of living one day at a time means I'll know the right thoughts, feelings, words, and actions *at any given moment.* Having the power to carry it out means I will be provided with those qualities needed—willingness, courage, patience, etc.—to transform the knowledge into action *at any given moment.*

The real test came when I was faced with a frightening situation in a courtroom. I didn't know what to say, but my Higher Power did. I turned my fears over and asked for the right words, and they were supplied. I survived the ordeal because I trusted that my Higher Power would give me what I needed when I needed it.

Thought for the Day

My Higher Power already has the answers to all the questions or needs I'll ever have. To ask is to open the door and let the answers into my awareness.

> "We can rest assured that the answers, choices, actions, and thoughts we need will come to us when the time is right because we have placed them in the hands of our Higher Power."

How Al-Anon Works for Families & Friends of Alcoholics, p. 76

After my father died from alcoholism when I was nine and my mother died when I was twelve, I felt abandoned by God. I felt confused, and I existed in a daze that permeated all aspects of my life.

I sought solace in nature by spending most of my free time in the woods and fields around my home. I rested in the fields and watched the streams. I observed animals in the woods and learned about birds and their calls. I discovered many different kinds of life existing in small, stagnant ponds, and I collected bugs in the fields. The peace I felt when alone with nature helped me forget my pain.

Many years later I joined Al-Anon. It seemed as though every meeting contained mention of God, with whom I no longer had a relationship. The more I kept coming back, the more apparent it became that I needed to find a Higher Power of my understanding. If I couldn't accept and work the first three Steps, I knew my recovery would reach a standstill.

By the grace of prayer and meditation, I was blessed with boyhood recollections of my times in nature. The beauty of nature—warm summer breezes and the invigorating snap of cold winter air—had comforted me as nothing else could. Without me knowing it, God had allowed me to heal slowly in His natural world. In time I finally realized that God had not left me. Rather, He had just stepped back until I was ready to reestablish conscious contact with Him in my recovery.

Thought for the Day

My shifting thoughts and feelings cannot comprehend the breadth and depth of my Higher Power's care for me.

> "...It is quite easy to look at my past and see that God was working at all times in my life."
>
> *The Forum*, February 1998, p.7

I used to spend a lot of time doing nothing. I watched the world pass by as I berated myself for not accomplishing anything. When I did take action, it was often a reaction. I reacted impulsively and compulsively to the words and behaviors of everyone around me. It seemed as though I was always ricocheting off two walls, one marked "inactive" and the other marked "reactive."

I use Al-Anon tools to work on these character defects. To stop reacting, I use the slogan "How Important Is It?" and Tradition Twelve's suggestion of placing "principles above personalities." The Serenity Prayer, the slogan "Let It Begin with Me," and the Eleventh Step help me to transform dreams into reality by choosing actions wisely.

I need to remember to cultivate a balance between action and inaction. Impulsiveness can be as much a trap as immobility. I avoid this by praying to my Higher Power for guidance before I take action. It is important to wait—to be inactive—until I feel that guidance.

It helps me to remember that a period of inner waiting and preparation, what I used to call doing nothing, takes place before I can realize which action to take. When my Higher Power and I are ready, everything falls into place in a way that never could have happened had I acted alone.

Thought for the Day

My Higher Power's guidance suggests it's best to leave decisions about my times of rest, preparation, and action up to God's infinitely perfect sense of timing.

"I will realize that, even in doing nothing about my problems, I am actively practicing the Al-Anon idea."

One Day at a Time in Al-Anon, p. 143

One winter afternoon a friend and I took a stroll along a frozen lake. The lake was covered with a thin sheet of ice, but it showed cracks in some places where the ducks had been busily swimming. Most of the ducks were in a large area of open water, but two of them were in a smaller area that was separated by a barrier of ice. One of them tried repeatedly to get to the other side. She frantically tried to scramble over the thin wall of ice, but it broke under her weight as soon as she approached it. The duck didn't give up, however, and continued her crazy ice dance.

At first my friend and I burst out laughing at the hilarity of the duck's antics. Before too long I grew philosophical. The duck's situation seemed strangely familiar. How often had I tried in vain to be happy by always using the same unsuitable means, much like the duck that had forgotten she could fly over the wall of ice? What constitutes the "wings," that I have forgotten? Perhaps the tools of Al-Anon can help me over the legacy of my alcoholic family where I never learned to overcome my weaknesses—only to deny them or to blow them out of proportion.

I want to stop reproaching myself for my human frailties. Instead, I will use my Fourth Step inventory to determine my strong points, my wings. My confidence will grow as I build on my strengths and use them for my good as well as for the good of others.

Thought for the Day

In Al-Anon I have the opportunity to mend my "wings" or even to fashion a new pair if I choose.

> "This program has shown me that I have choices. I could stay the way I was, or I could change."
>
> *Living Today in Alateen*, p. 55

My father died long ago. For many years I didn't think of him. When I started in Al-Anon, long-buried memories of his alcoholic behavior surfaced. I angrily thought of him as "The Drunk." I continued attending meetings, though, and started my Step work, prayed, and talked with my sponsor. She listened gently and carefully, but she didn't say much. She gave me time and space.

A few months later, my mother asked me to pick up a box of my belongings. I took the box home and opened it. Inside was my father's wallet. "Here's 'The Drunk's' wallet," I thought, as I looked through it.

Inside the wallet were a number of things, including old pictures. There were lots of them, snapshots carefully trimmed to fit the plastic sleeves of the wallet. There was a picture of me and him on my prom night, and another of me with our dog. There was a picture of his boat and a picture I had taken at a football game. There were several pictures of him drinking with his buddies. He loved them, too.

Suddenly I saw my father apart from his alcoholism. He was a normal, everyday guy who had people and things he loved. All of my Al-Anon work, my studying, and praying fell into place. I realized I was ready to forgive him. I cried long and hard, missing my father for the first time in years. He was no longer "The Drunk." Now he was just Dad.

Thought for the Day

I know I'm recovering when I can see the alcoholic in my life as a human being.

> "Al-Anon has also given me my father in a new and wonderful way. It has helped me accept him as he was. He was sick, but also he was loving and he did the best he could."
>
> Al-Anon Is for Adult Children of Alcoholics, p. 17

The guidance embodied in the Serenity Prayer was a foreign concept when I walked into my first Al-Anon meeting. I soon realized it must be important because every meeting I attended since has used it as part of the opening. Applying it to my recovery seemed a worthwhile endeavor.

In the Serenity Prayer I ask my Higher Power to grant me "wisdom to know the difference" between the "things I cannot change" and the "things I can." Before Al-Anon I was unable to distinguish between the two. In fact, I think I had them absolutely backwards, often struggling to manage events that were beyond my ability to influence, let alone control. Such behavior usually led to mental, physical, and emotional fatigue as well as feelings of depression, failure, and worthlessness. These feelings became familiar as I matured in my alcoholic family, and I grudgingly came to accept them as normal.

Now, thanks to Al-Anon, I know I'm powerless over alcohol and alcoholic behavior. I know I'm a valuable, worthwhile person whose struggles resulted from the seemingly senseless events in my life. My illusion of control helped me survive, but I don't need it now.

Although uncomfortable feelings and the urge to rule crop up occasionally, I remind myself that this is part of my disease and that feelings aren't facts. I admit my powerlessness once again and turn my unhealthy reactions over to my Higher Power. Not only can He manage my life better than I can, He can also restore me to sanity.

Thought for the Day

When I take my hands off the controls and "Let Go and Let God," my life runs smoothly, and I feel serene.

"Let Go and Let God, He sees the world true,
Rely on Him, and you'll never be blue ..."

Alateen Talks Back on Slogans, p. 15

For me, giving and serving are selfish acts. Whenever I give, I get so much more in return. If I give ten minutes of my time to listen to someone share what is going on in his or her life, I gain new perspective on my own situation. I gain an opportunity to grow and to add to my understanding of how the Steps apply to my life. Just a few words of welcome to a newcomer can leave me feeling warm and uplifted for hours. In offering help, I have never felt taken advantage of, or as if I did something I didn't really want to do.

On the other hand, despite my growth in Al-Anon, sometimes I give for the wrong reasons. I need to distinguish between giving out of love and giving to please others in order to gain their attention or approval. It's a matter of motivation and degree. If I do something for the wrong reason, or do it to the extent that it detracts from my own recovery, then it's worth examining in Steps Four and Five.

The more I give out of love, however, the more I get back. Imagine a lottery that pays off every time! I buy a ticket for a dollar, and I get back five. So why wouldn't I buy a ticket when I know I'll win every time?

So it is with helping, serving, and carrying the message of recovery. When I do these things for the right reasons, it's my ticket to increased growth, self-esteem, and serenity. I always get more than I give. I'm a guaranteed winner every time!

Thought for the Day

Serving Al-Anon allows me to take risks and grow at the same time.

> "Most of all, I wanted to receive and keep recovery. What I found was the joy of giving it away . . ."
>
> *Paths to Recovery*, p. 126

In my first Al-Anon meeting, I listened intently to other people share. One woman spoke of feeling as if she were in a dark and lonely place, like the bottom of a well. The tools of the program helped her see the light at the top of the well, but it was still going to be a tough job scaling the walls to get out.

After a time, I came to understand through reading Al-Anon literature, listening to other members, and practicing the slogans, Steps, and Traditions in my personal life, that I could begin to climb out of my own well. Little by little, I stopped focusing on the alcoholic's problems and started concentrating on my own. I found that facing my responsibilities meant developing the ability to choose my responses to my problems.

To be responsible for myself meant keeping the focus on myself and not letting fear become a motivator for my actions, even when my fear felt huge. The strength I needed to climb out of my well had to come from my own self-respect. Without it, I didn't have the courage to scale those walls. Because my self-esteem was so low, I didn't think I had any courage. However, my sponsor told me I had a great deal of courage. She told me that by taking the risk to walk through the doors of Al-Anon, I had already taken responsibility for my self-esteem.

Thought for the Day

Fear is a feeling, not an action. Courage is not the absence of fear. It's choosing to act with love in spite of the fear.

> "If my fear had simply been removed, I might never have known that I am capable of acting on my own behalf."
>
> *Courage to Change*, p. 119

As a child I enjoyed helping my mother plant tulip bulbs every fall. She taught me to plant them in rows—neat and tidy. In my first home, I looked forward to my own tulips blossoming. One year my husband asked, "Why do you plant them in rows? Why not in clusters?" I noticed many of my neighbors planted flowers in clusters, a pattern I considered scattered.

Soon after an Al-Anon member shared how she did certain things her mother's way as if they were the only way. Suddenly it was clear why I did some things in certain ways. My mother had taught me.

Later while on vacation, I saw ducks in a pond, all in a row. There they were, the embodiment of a phrase my mother frequently used—"Wait, dear, until I get my ducks in a row." For the first time, I asked myself why I liked things so neat and orderly. In my alcoholic family, I was taught that if I did what I was told without question, I would be safer and happier. In my family, obedience meant following a strict, straight line.

I no longer care if my ducks are in a row. Sometimes I prefer they aren't. By not forcing my thoughts and feelings into a straight line, I can see all the possibilities. I can explore and be creative, innovative, and adventuresome. The sharings of fellow members, my sponsor, and our Conference Approved Literature expand my horizons to encompass unexplored avenues of perception and action.

Thought for the Day

I no longer need to have my flowers, thoughts, or family members in a row. They are free to be what and who they are—and so am I!

> "I want to remain teachable for the rest of my life, daily applying new ideas and letting life be a real adventure."
> *How Al-Anon Works for Families & Friends of Alcoholics*, p. 374

Making amends isn't about apologizing for every problem. It's about figuring out how a relationship or situation went wrong, determining the part I played in it, and doing what I can to make it right.

I knew my father belonged on my Eighth Step list, but I felt furious! Why should I make amends to him? He had raged and behaved violently as an adult child of an alcoholic. He beat, rejected, and then abandoned me. Why should I forgive the perpetrator of my abuse? Besides, he's dead now. What would be the point?

I applied a three-part approach. First, how had our relationship gone wrong? My father had been damaged, too. He hadn't asked to grow up in an alcoholic family any more than I had. Expecting him to be a nurturing person was unrealistic. Hating my father and continuing to suffer only perpetuated my problems. Second, what was my part? My father was long gone, so why was I still suffering? Eventually, I came to understand that I adopted some of his character defects as my own. Third, what could I do to remedy the situation and forgive my father? I needed to give myself what was not in his power to give—love, acceptance, wisdom, a safe childhood, and a healthy initiation into manhood.

It hasn't been easy. With the help of the program and my Higher Power, plus a relentless devotion to hope and the truth, I am forgiving my father each time I give myself something I need or want. In this way, I make amends and improve my life one day at a time.

Thought for the Day

How is making amends a way to treat myself better?

"What relief and acceptance I felt when I embraced and made amends to the person I had hurt the most—me."
Having Had a Spiritual Awakening . . ., p. 144

The concept of "God *as we understood Him*" was hard to grasp. My family believed there is only one way to view God. My parents used religion to keep me in line. I believed we went to the only true church. There was a list of do's and don'ts. I was afraid of God, viewing Him as a severe judge just waiting to punish me.

By the end of my first meeting, I was impressed with the acceptance I felt. There was no gossip or criticism. People were friendly even though they had differing opinions and beliefs. No one tried to change others by telling them what to think or how to feel. In Al-Anon I felt for the first time as if I could be myself. I could relax and let a Higher Power of my understanding evolve.

I realized the God of my parents had come in a very small box, not expansive enough for me. I fired that God and hired a new one. My new Higher Power is much bigger than the old one. He doesn't live in a box. He lives in me and in those around me. He loves me, cares for me, and accepts me just as I am—a work of art in progress. He is a God who wants the best for everyone. My Higher Power can turn tragedy into something positive, because out of my difficult childhood has come a God I no longer fear, but treasure.

Thought for the Day

Does my concept of God fit the new, recovering me?

> "In Al-Anon, we can come to understand the nature of a Power greater than ourselves in a personal, profound way and many of us have been amazed at the difference this understanding makes in our lives."
>
> *As We Understood . . .* , p. 71

My years in Al-Anon made me aware that I need to be careful about how I hear and interpret certain words. Consider "defects of character" and "shortcomings," which are found in Steps Six and Seven respectively. I came into Al-Anon believing I was responsible for bad things that happened and that I was "bad" or "defective." Years of meetings have led me to think otherwise. I now view my problem areas as survival skills that served me well while I was growing up. Now they work against me, preventing me from living a serene life. Today I have Al-Anon and its tools to thrive, not just survive.

I can also run into problems with the words "searching and fearless" in Step Four. To cope with the blaming and criticism in my home, I became a perfectionist. It's all too easy for me to interpret "searching and fearless" as "perfect." Then I end up frozen with fear, thinking I have to take the perfect inventory, which by my somewhat still twisted standards would mean inventorying every single, tiny word and action I have ever committed during my lifetime. I could drive myself insane! It helped when a member reminded me that when a grocer takes an inventory, he or she inventories what stock is on the shelves *today*, not what was on the shelves yesterday or the day before. That idea makes my inventory seem much more manageable. All I need to do is consider the things about myself that are bothering me and getting in the way of my growth, just for today.

Thought for the Day

Paying attention to how I listen, and how I interpret what I hear, can aid my recovery.

> "If I can get my mind off my own problems and really listen ... I'll learn a lot more today ..."
>
> *Alateen—a day at a time*, p. 227

"Wow!" That word expresses such wonder, excitement, surprise, and humility. It's a word I use often, yet I pay little attention to its meaning or power. For example, this morning when I awoke, the sun was shining brightly, the sky was a deep and cloudless blue, and the autumn trees radiated gold, bronze, and copper. Without thinking about it, my first reaction was to exclaim, "Wow!"

I was struck by the fact that I had nothing to do with creating such a beautiful morning. That meant I probably had no effect on the rainy or snowy mornings, either. In fact, weather was one of the many things completely out of my control. This perception relieved me of responsibility for the weather, sunny or cloudy, and reminded me of the many things in life over which I have no control. I can only let go and let them be. I felt grateful for this reminder, and I began to count my other blessings as well. My job was simply to enjoy the morning and be grateful for the experience of beauty. The day was off to a great start.

Now I take more notice of the "wow" moments in my life. I acknowledge my feelings, such as the gratitude, joy, and humility, that come with appreciating something I didn't affect or create. For each person or event that crosses my path today, I thank my Higher Power. I accept that I don't have to work hard for this day's delights because they are a gift from my Higher Power. All I need to do is pay attention and enjoy my honest emotions as the day progresses.

Thought for the Day

I take time to enjoy the beauty that surrounds me.

"When I gather flowers, or marvel at nature's wonders, I do not lose face when I concede that I am not in control."

Courage to Change, p. 283

When I was a child and asked my mother for permission to do something, she often said, "Ask your father." My father would say, "Ask your mother." My older sisters acted more like parents than my mother or father did, often assuming the duties left unattended. Responsibility and authority were all mixed up in my family. I never really knew who was in charge and I constantly felt confused.

How refreshing it was when I came to Al-Anon and found a group of people whose behavior didn't echo the confusion from my childhood. Different members of my home group signed up on a monthly basis to chair the meeting, put out the literature, provide refreshments, and perform other duties. Other members served as elected officers, such as group representative and treasurer. Each role and its responsibilities were clearly defined, and each trusted servant had the authority to carry out his or her job. If there were any problems, the group always had a specific person to consult, depending on the nature of the obligation. That way, conflicts were resolved in an organized, simplified manner. In other words, rarely was there any chaos. Imagine that!

I didn't realize it at the time, but my group was practicing Concept Ten: "Service responsibility is balanced by carefully defined service authority and double-headed management is avoided." Everyone knew who was answerable for what. No one tried to do anyone else's job, and all the work got done when it needed to be done. Clear, concise boundaries—and the right to work within them—made this possible.

Thought for the Day

If I made a list of the things I need to do—and want to do—today, how many entries would be my responsibility and how many would belong to others?

> "In practicing Concept Ten, we set clear goals and trust
> each other to accomplish them."
>
> *Paths to Recovery*, p. 311

I never realized how much my self-esteem disappeared while I was growing up with alcoholism. As a carefree child I possessed self-worth, but it slowly became buried and dormant as I dealt with this family disease.

When I came to Al-Anon, it took all aspects of the program to rebuild my sense of worthiness. At meetings I had the right to pass if I wanted, yet I gradually found my voice to speak my mind and heart. I asked someone to be my sponsor and then called her for help. I found a God of my understanding and learned that I had choices and could make good decisions on my own. Little by little, all of these things helped me rediscover my self-esteem.

To keep what I had received, it was suggested that I give it away. Therefore I continued to fortify my self-respect through service. I started by setting up chairs and making coffee. Eventually I chaired meetings, became a sponsor, and served as secretary, alternate group representative, and group representative. As I retained my self-worth by doing service work, I learned the Steps and Traditions through action.

The results of my hard work have been a sense of autonomy, self-esteem, and gratitude. Those qualities keep me open to the gifts God offers me through my relationships with others. They give me strength and courage to maintain the relationships already in my life. They also help me to be open to new connections, which used to frighten me. Thank you, Al-Anon, for offering me the loving support and guidance through which I have regained the self-esteem I lost so many years ago.

Thought for the Day

I will take time each day to nurture my new-found self-esteem.

"Today, when faced with choices, I will opt for the path that enhances my self-esteem."

Courage to Change, p. 118

One evening at my home meeting, a woman shared how she argues a lot with the alcoholic. I wasn't listening too attentively, but then she mentioned the slogan "How Important Is It?" Her words struck me hard and called me to attention. I decided to experiment with that slogan, applying it to my own situation.

The first time I tried it, it was a real eye-opener. My alcoholic husband had arrived home late, and I was ready to begin the drill, asking every conceivable question I knew I should *not* ask. To keep myself from doing so, I said the Serenity Prayer over and over and then asked myself, "How important is it?" A feeling of relief flowed into me as I answered myself, "It's not important enough for me to become the police!"

My husband knows me well and was prepared to walk into the house and be barraged with queries. I could see the muscles tighten in his neck as he stepped in and waited. All I said was, "Hello." He relaxed visibly, and we passed the rest of the evening together with serenity and even a little fun.

Since that evening, I've applied this slogan to many of my affairs. I've learned that if an issue isn't going to be important in 30 days, then it's probably not worth troubling myself with now. Today there aren't many things happening in my life with such lasting effect that I have to make an issue of them.

Thought for the Day

How easily do I give away my serenity?

> "The perspective we gain when we apply this slogan makes it possible to set aside petty worries, minor irritations, and baseless judgments so that we might celebrate the extraordinary richness and wonder that life offers."
>
> *How Al-Anon Works for Families & Friends of Alcoholics*, p. 72

Before I came into Al-Anon, I took disparaging comments to heart. I believed them and found myself wondering what was wrong with me. Even as I became older, I carried inside the person who grew up with alcoholic parents and endured the abuse that accompanied the disease. A large part of my recovery has been to rediscover and nurture the part of me that grew up with active alcoholism. I had to learn how to love this aspect of myself unconditionally.

When I took Step Three and truly surrendered my will and my life to the care of my Higher Power, I felt enveloped in healing love. Through Step Eleven's prayer and meditation, I bathe myself in this love every day. By diligently working the Steps, I've finally learned how to love all of me—my strengths *and* my shortcomings. I feel a much stronger sense of self, which I now allow no one to diminish. Al-Anon has given me wonderful gifts—the self-respect and self-esteem needed to protect myself from unacceptable behavior.

Now when my son tells me he was teased at school, I pass on my recovery lessons to him as we talk about self-love. I teach him what I have learned in Al-Anon. I help him by suggesting simple ways he can detach. I explain how he can let it begin with him by not retaliating. I help him understand that sometimes he also does things that hurt others and that he can feel better about himself by making amends. Not only has Al-Anon helped heal my past, it's helping me give my son a healthier future.

Thought for the Day

When I awaken to the gift I truly am, and wisely use detachment, no one's words or actions can hurt me.

"...The most important person to gain love and respect from is myself."

Courage to Be Me, p. 137

I asked my sponsor to meet with me before the Al-Anon adult child meeting to talk about taking my Second Step: "Came to believe that a Power greater than ourselves could restore us to sanity." She suggested we take a leisurely walk before the meeting and she listened patiently while I talked. I told her I thought I had the Power-greater-than-me part down, and the sanity or insanity part made sense, too. To me sanity meant being centered, feeling comfortable with myself. What escaped me about Step Two was "believing," not the abstract idea of believing, but the nuts-and-bolts "doing" that creates the basis for how I live my life. I asked how to transform the idea of believing into concrete action.

I can't remember what my sponsor said in reply to my frustration and confusion because a profound spiritual awakening overtook me. The moment will be forever frozen in time. The moon shone brightly over almost-bare autumn branches that swayed slightly overhead, sketching lines across the moonlight. The feeling that filled me that night was like the sun shining into my very being, bringing with it a burst of consciousness and clarity. The answer to my dilemma arose from somewhere deep inside me. It was trust. Trusting, then acting on that trust, was how I could turn my belief into something tangible.

I had never fully trusted anyone or anything—other than ideas—during my childhood. On that night, however, I *knew* my God was no longer just an idea. God became a great trust within me that will provide me daily, through the Al-Anon program, with all the guidance, comfort, and support I need to act faithfully on my beliefs.

Thought for the Day

Step Two invites me to develop my trust.

> "I don't need to understand the Power greater than myself, only to trust it."

As We Understood . . ., p. 159

I grew up in a family where scorn, criticism, and teasing were everyday modes of communication. To cope, I developed the ability to hide my pain and confusion behind sarcasm and ridicule.

Making myself feel bigger and better by making fun of others never filled the emptiness I felt inside. Until I could trust myself and others enough to ask for help, I was stuck in a spiritual hole with no hope of getting out. I eventually grew tired of my sarcastic behavior, and I worked with my sponsor to explore the pain behind my harsh words and attitudes.

With the support of God and my friends in Al-Anon, I am now working the Steps on this particular problem. I have accepted that I am powerless over changing my behavior alone. I now believe that a Power greater than myself can restore me to a more loving way of communicating if I'm willing to learn. Finally, I have reached the point where I am ready to have this defect removed from me. With humility and self-forgiveness, I ask my Higher Power to do so.

Sometimes I still find myself picking at the faults of others. Old habits are hard to break. Now, however, with the help of the program, I can see more clearly when I'm falling back into this spiritually destructive pattern. I know I'm not perfect and I still have miles to travel down the path my Higher Power has carved out for me. Al-Anon gives me awareness and trust that I can break these old patterns one day at a time.

Thought for the Day

Just for today I will release any need to judge or criticize others and begin to see them in the same way I might want them to see me.

"I cannot hurt others without hurting myself."

One Day at a Time in Al-Anon, p. 20

Often I am too defiant to hear my family members' feelings directly from them, but if I listen carefully, I can hear their voices at my meetings. I hear my mom when members share about the anguish of being a wife and mother in an alcoholic home. Then I realize how strong my mom was and how hard she tried. I become less judgmental when I realize how little I know about the difficulties inherent in loving an alcoholic husband. Recently I told my mom that if I could pick a new mother, I would ask God to give me her again.

I hear my father at least once a week in open AA meetings. Through hearing these sober members share about the person behind the bottle, I finally love my daddy. He continues to drink and does not call himself an alcoholic anymore. He says it was just a phase, and I don't argue. I've decided I'm not going to miss out on learning to love and forgive him just because he isn't living the way I want.

Thought for the Day

Listening to others' stories—other mothers, other fathers, and other children—can give me a compassionate perspective on my own struggles and those of my entire family.

> "Hearing AA members helps us to understand the alcoholic. Listening to Al-Anon speakers gives us an idea of the nonalcoholic's feelings. And, we can share with them what it feels like to be children of alcoholics. Keeping the lines of communication open helps us understand each other."
>
> *Alateen—a day at a time*, p. 169

A part of Al-Anon not often discussed, but essential to the program's survival, is our business meetings. Personally I like them. I rarely had a say in the daily functioning of my alcoholic home, even when the decisions affected me. Now I know I have a voice in my Al-Anon family. I feel sad when some members hasten for the door before the business meetings begin, believing this process has nothing to do with recovery.

To me recovery is intertwined with service, and the business of Al-Anon is about service performed by the entire group. The Traditions keep us focused on the *business of service*. For example, part of Tradition Five helps us focus on Al-Anon's reason for being—helping families and friends of alcoholics. We do this by opening and setting up the meeting room, providing Conference Approved Literature, paying rent, and participating in and supporting the various service arms of the fellowship.

Someone needs to take responsibility for the service functions of our worldwide fellowship, and that "someone" is each of us, the individual groups. Because we are fully self-supporting, as Tradition Seven states, no one else provides funds for the business we carry out to keep the fellowship available to others who still need help.

Al-Anon didn't just happen. There were and are many people behind the scenes making sure it survives. A group that pays attention to its affairs in all areas is a healthy group. To do my part, all it takes is a little willingness to attend the business meetings and to keep an open mind .

Thought for the Day

Attending a business meeting might be my stepping-stone into service and a deeper level of recovery.

> "Service helps me stretch my boundaries. Taking risks helps me grow, and Al-Anon is a safe place to do just that: take a risk and grow."
>
> *When I Got Busy, I Got Better*, p. 18

When I first came to Al-Anon, I wanted the "priceless gift of serenity," but I was convinced it couldn't exist. There were just too many balls to juggle, too many people's lives tied to mine. I couldn't possibly keep everything in place to make everyone happy.

Al-Anon taught me that I was right to think I can't control all of those outside forces. The program also taught me that manipulating people and events to my liking is not the path to serenity. Serenity is a matter of inner stability. If I keep the focus on myself and let my Higher Power take care of the rest, everything seems to work out for the best. Things outside of myself still seem disordered at times, and people still act in ways I believe are destructive and harmful. However, Al-Anon gives me the tools to keep myself on course, so I can maintain my serenity no matter what winds are blowing or which waves are washing over me.

I stay on my Higher Power's course for me by reading Al-Anon literature daily, attending meetings weekly, talking with my sponsor regularly, and taking personal inventories frequently. These internal inspections remind me of my destination—serenity and a spiritual awakening—and allow me to adjust my path as needed. As I keep the focus on myself and my responsibilities, I feel serenity growing inside. It's a wonderful feeling to take care of myself lovingly and no longer to fear the turbulence that sometimes still swirls around me.

Thought for the Day

Staying focused on my journey of recovery, plus turning the outside world over to God, equals serenity.

> "Recognizing that the world answers to its own Higher Power is inviting serenity's peace to embrace me."
>
> *Alateen Talks Back on Serenity*, p. 12

I've been struggling very hard to heal from the frightening effects of growing up in an alcoholic home. I often felt scared during my early years. Things got broken, adults fell down from drinking too much, and the dog sat in a corner and shook. To cope, I didn't move and kept quiet. I shut down. I didn't get involved. I didn't really live.

Now that I'm an adult, I want to get better and live a full, happy life. After all, I deserve it. Al-Anon provides me with a multitude of ways to become the person I want to be. For me right now, the most encompassing tools include the slogan "Live and Let Live," especially the first part; Concept Four, which teaches me that "participation is the key to harmony"; and performing acts of Al-Anon service, no matter how small.

I'm coming to realize that my longed-for healing takes place *in* the living. I don't get well first and then start to mend. To become a whole person, I need to live now, take part, and become involved with others. Sometimes I can do this just a little at a time. Until I can do more, I'm nurturing a willingness in me to become more open-minded to my life and the people in it.

Healing is a process that will continue the rest of my life. I know how unhealthy I've been, yet I also know that my recovery has begun. My participation in everyday, ordinary life is a small but firm step away from the pain of isolation and toward a life of loving involvement.

Thought for the Day

Life is for living. Today I will involve myself in the joy of living.

> "Participation also responds to our spiritual needs. All of us deeply desire to belong."

Al-Anon/Alateen Service Manual, p. 159

November 5

Our Suggested Al-Anon/Alateen Closing states, ". . . though you may not like all of us, you'll love us in a very special way—the same way we already love you." When I first came to Al-Anon, I found this statement too incredible to believe. If they really knew me, I thought, they wouldn't say that. How could anyone possibly like or love me? I certainly didn't.

Nevertheless, they kept on saying it at every meeting. As I began to really respect these people, I wondered if they could be so far off in their opinion of me. Maybe there was something lovable about me after all, although I didn't know. That's when members of my group encouraged me to know myself better through Al-Anon's Fourth Step.

At first all I saw were my defects. My fellow members encouraged me to seek out my assets as well. They even went so far as to suggest that I embrace my defects and my assets and celebrate them all as part of who I am. They assured me that with the help of the Steps that follow, I could let my Higher Power decide which ones I needed to keep.

I heard many members say their group loved them until they loved themselves. This was my experience as well. The more my group showed love and respect for me, the more I was able to love myself. Then I could begin to help love others into self-love. What a wonderful way of passing it on.

Thought for the Day

It's heartwarming to know I can lean on other members' self-love until I develop a measure of my own.

> "For the first time in my life, I'm starting to really care about other people, mainly because I feel like a worthwhile person. I believe the saying that you can't love someone until you first care about yourself."
>
> Alateen—Hope for Children of Alcoholics, p. 81

When I first heard of not accepting unacceptable behavior, I felt confused. The Al-Anon program forthrightly states I'm powerless over others—so how can I regulate them? Some members refer to limiting unacceptable behavior as setting boundaries. Boundaries, however, aren't rules I can enforce on others. They are standards of conduct I set for my own benefit.

In my program, boundaries are a civilizing ingredient in social interaction, a matter of self-respect and respect for others. Setting limits requires some degree of communication skills because others cannot read my mind nor I theirs. Others need to know how I feel and I need to lovingly communicate my feelings. Likewise, it is important that I listen to and respect their feelings.

I can't expect others to share my values. Sometimes I make choices in my own best interest that others don't understand. If my boundary is not respected, I remember the Serenity Prayer, communicate my limit, and in quietness and serenity do what is needed to take care of myself. I don't have to end the relationship. However, I do have to recognize my responsibility to honor myself as a child of God who is worthy of respect.

I am more mindful of my boundaries when I'm around those I do not trust. With those I do trust, I can be more flexible. If I allow my boundaries to be violated repeatedly, I am a volunteer rather than a victim. It's my responsibility to stick with people who are affirming and trustworthy and to limit my exposure to those who are not.

Thought for the Day

I demonstrate dignity and respect for myself and for others when I honor my values as well as theirs.

> "Today I have the option to set limits, to draw a line that I will not allow to be crossed."

How Al-Anon Works for Families & Friends of Alcoholics, p. 251

I had a habit of doing the same thing over and over again and expecting different results. After discussing this matter with a friend, I was given an exercise to practice.

When someone says something to me and I have a strong reaction—wanting to cry, wanting to rage, or thinking I am inferior—I stop and visualize two doors. One is marked "Same old, same old" or "My will." The other is marked "New and different" or "God's will." On seeing these two doors, I imagine opening mine and viewing what I would normally say or do in this situation. Then I close my door and open God's.

By the time I have done all of this, I've given myself several moments between the initial comment and my impulsive reaction. This gives me time to practice the slogan "Think" and to choose a healthier response. I've not had a single regret-filled incident since I began to practice this self-restraint. Ironically, most times what's behind God's door is absolutely nothing. What a message! Could this possibly mean that other people's behavior belongs to them and I don't have to make it mine by reacting to it?

Thought for the Day

Practicing detachment before I react allows me to maintain self-esteem by choosing my response.

> "We need to recognize our own reactions. Then we can decide whether we want to continue reacting in the same old ways, or if maybe we want to try something new."
>
> *Courage to Be Me*, p. 123

Why am I so attracted to alcoholics? I dwelled on that question for more than five years. Then while listening to an adult child speaker at Al-Anon's First International Convention, I had an unexpected spiritual awakening. It occurred to me that my maternal grandfather had a problem with alcohol. He was a loner filled with anger and resentment. He made nasty home-made wines and drank too much.

I realized that my mother learned many behaviors characteristic of living with an alcoholic and that I learned them from her. We both acquired the unhealthy aspects of martyrdom, managing, manipulating, and mothering—four qualities that go so well with alcoholism. The four Ms now made total sense and so did my attraction to alcoholics.

With the help of program literature, the Steps, a sponsor, and time, I began to learn the healthy aspects of the four Ms. Today I manage my own life, not the lives of others. I avoid martyrdom because it holds few assets for me. I have learned to manipulate a crochet hook rather than my husband. Most important, I nurture others but leave the mothering to their mothers.

Thought for the Day

What qualities of mine might cause me to be attracted to alcoholics?

> "Our only concern should be our own conduct, our own improvement, our own lives."
>
> *Alcoholism, the Family Disease,* p. 20

I grew up affected by someone else's drinking. I seldom knew what was good for me, yet I knew what was best for others and didn't hesitate to tell them. I didn't know what I enjoyed doing for fun, but I could tell you what activities the alcoholic enjoyed. I feared other people's anger and would do anything to avoid it, yet I was oblivious to my own. Whatever was wrong with my life on any given day, I always knew it was someone else's fault.

Then I came to Al-Anon and began to work the Steps. Step Four helped me set aside what others had done to me so I could see my own wrongs. My Fourth Step "spoiled" my resentments. It's not that I no longer have them. Rather, I can no longer harbor resentment and remain ignorant of my part in creating it.

I truly began to change by working through the rest of the Steps, asking God to remove my shortcomings, making amends, continuing to take personal inventory, and asking my Higher Power to direct my thoughts and actions. These changes gave birth to a new person, the person God intended me to be. My entire life transformed as a result of taking responsibility for myself, becoming willing to change, and taking the action I needed to recover. Now I know what I enjoy doing for fun. I've ceased blaming others, and I have a message of hope to carry to other individuals. I continue to work these precious Steps to see myself change and to become closer to God and those I love.

Thought for Day

If I were to draw "before" and "after" pictures related to my Al-Anon experience, what would they look like?

"Looking back and remembering what I was like . . . makes me realize how grateful I am to the program."

Alateen—a day at a time, p. 366

When I began my recovery, writing seemed like the most natural way to explore myself. It was a way of staying aware of my feelings by telling God and myself the truth about me. Now, each morning before my son wakes up, I spend my Step Eleven time writing a "Dear God" letter. As it turns out, I'm actually writing my life story. Through this writing I've come to terms with the reality that my father molested me when I was a youth. To cope with the trauma of that injury, as well as the emotional neglect and physical abuse I endured while growing up, I buried most of my childhood memories. This included the joyful as well as the painful ones. Writing allows me to recover the whole spectrum of my remembrances in a gentle manner, when I'm ready to receive them.

As I continue to explore myself through writing, especially in the Fourth, Eighth, and Tenth Steps, I give myself the gift of knowing myself better. I also give myself the opportunity to share my writings with a trusted Al-Anon sponsor or friend. My life matters. It's important to honor and remember my experiences. Then I release them to God, who will use them to help others as I share my experience, strength, and hope.

Thought for the Day

There's a reason why several of the Steps ask me to put my thoughts, feelings, and memories down on paper. Today I'll consider how I could use writing, or some other concrete form of expression, to discover myself.

> "... I set aside some time to get to know about myself, including a lot of the good things that I know about the kind of person I am."

> *Courage to Be Me*, p. 129

While working my Al-Anon program for many years as an adult child of an alcoholic, I have had many spiritual awakenings. Usually they are tiny awarenesses. Perhaps I see someone's annoying behavior, including my own, in a more compassionate light. Maybe I respond differently to an ongoing challenge in my life.

Once I did have a dramatic spiritual awakening, however. I was in great despair due to a profound loss and I was praying intently to know God's will. One night during this winter of the heart, my Higher Power took me on a journey through my life. I'm a very visual person and my Higher Power knows this. In a seamless stream of images that I felt as well as saw, She showed me all the difficult times I had been through—the losses, hardships, and abuses. At the same time, She let me know deep in my heart that I had never been in mortal danger, although I had felt like I was many times. I saw and felt in my heart the great love, compassion, and protection with which my Higher Power carries me through every moment of my life. In seeing how She had cared so thoroughly for me in the past, I knew without doubt and with deep humility She would continue to do so in the future.

The memory of that intense experience has faded somewhat, but the truth of it has permeated my life. Even during times of heavy fear and doubt, a part of me knows that these are just feelings and that my Higher Power is steadfastly watching over me as always.

Thought for the Day

"I needn't fear the challenges of the future, because I know that today, with the guidance of my Higher Power and with the strength and knowledge I have gained from Al-Anon, I am capable of facing anything life brings me."

Courage to Change, p. 332

Serenity? What's that? For years I was like a weather vane that spun around according to the air currents that other people generated. My husband criticized me, and I lost my serenity. My boss became upset, and I lost my serenity. Before Al-Anon, I attributed these mood swings to nervousness, lack of self-assurance, and whoever else occupied the room at the time. Serenity always seemed beyond my control. I was convinced I needed quietness to feel serene, so I retreated into my room and napped frequently.

Today I don't need to withdraw to quiet places nearly as often. I don't need to run away from life. Sometimes I can even stand in the middle of a frenzied atmosphere and let it swirl around me, while I remain unaffected. I can tell myself to hush when my mind enters the muddy waters of "what if." I can sit still in the present moment and feel grateful for the sound of rain falling on the roof and for the purring cat curled up next to me. In my gratitude I experience serenity that I never knew before.

Where does this serenity come from? It comes from trusting that everything in my life is exactly as it should be. I feel it when I apply a slogan rather than panic about something. It comes when I choose to care for myself rather than to fix someone else. It surrounds me when I seek God's will in prayer and meditation. It envelops me whenever I walk into an Al-Anon meeting, see the familiar faces of those who accompany me on my journey, and know, once again, I am not alone.

Thought for the Day

I am powerless over many things, but my serenity is not one of them.

> "Today I know that sanity and serenity are the gifts I have received for my efforts and my faith."

Courage to Change, p. 248

I came to Al-Anon to find solutions for my boyfriend's drinking. Members shared new ideas with me, such as "One Day at a Time", "Live and Let Live", "Easy Does It", "First Things First", "How Important Is It?", "Listen and Learn", "Think," and "Keep an Open Mind."

The first two slogans were easy to recall but hard to apply, especially "One Day at a Time." It took almost all my energy to stay in the present and not wander into yesterday or tomorrow. I also thought "Live and Let Live" would be simple. I believed I was good at letting others live their own lives. However, after attending meetings for a while, I began to understand that I was in Al-Anon because I interfered in my boyfriend's life by protecting him from the consequences of his actions.

I did better with "Easy Does It", "First Things First," and "How Important Is It?" These slogans went hand-in-hand for me. I found if I slowed down and prioritized my activities, I could accomplish what I needed to do for myself. When I practiced "Listen and Learn", "Think," and "Keep an Open Mind," I actually closed my mouth for a while and listened to other members. I thought carefully about what had been said and opened my mind wide enough to consider the positive results I might yield if I did something different.

Today the slogans offer me healthier ways to reflect. Along with the other Al-Anon tools, the slogans allow me the option of being serene and happy whether the alcoholic is drinking or not.

Thought for the Day

Do I believe my problems stem from the alcoholic's drinking? Perhaps the real problem is my thinking.

"I find the slogans a great help in taking a searching and fearless moral inventory of *myself*."

One Day at a Time in Al-Anon, p. 295

My sponsee and I were discussing how angry she was at having grown up in an alcoholic family. She asked me how I overcame my anger so I could have a loving, adult relationship with my mom.

To explain, I took her on a mini-journey through the Twelve Steps. First, I admitted I was powerless over my childhood. The survival skills that I developed made my adult life unmanageable. Second, I came to believe that only my Higher Power could show me how a healthy adult behaves. Third, I made a decision to notice the people and situations my Higher Power put in my life to illustrate healthy behavior. Fourth, I inventoried my attitudes and actions that hindered me from having a better relationship with my mom. Fifth, I admitted to God, to myself, and to my sponsor that my anger from the past prevented me from accepting the love my mom was able to offer today.

Sixth and Seventh, I became ready to have my defects removed, and I humbly asked my Higher Power to do so. The next Step was easy because I already knew my mom belonged on my Eighth Step list, and I wanted to make amends. However, the Ninth Step presented a challenge. Wouldn't I injure her by dredging up the past? Instead, I decided to change my behavior by accepting her love and loving her in return. Tenth, I examined my behavior every day to see if my actions stemmed from old patterns. Eleventh, I asked God to make me a more loving person, which I believe is His will for me. Twelfth, I began carrying this message of healing by sharing my experience with others and showing how I broke out of old cycles by living the Steps one day at a time.

Thought for the Day

"The Twelve Steps provide ways to live a new and different life. They help me to know myself."

Living Today in Alateen, p. 281

November 15

When I heard "Let Go and Let God" for the first time, it didn't make sense to me. Let go of what? And let God do what? The little I did understand was the futility of my efforts to try to control other people, places, and things. Al-Anon told me I could turn my attention to monitoring myself and my reactions.

I let go of other people and I began to feel some relief. I let go of what others said or didn't say, and what they did or didn't do. I let go of my expectations. I no longer felt a need to be a people-pleaser. As I let go, I found I lived more harmoniously with myself and with others. I began to take more responsibility for myself. I figured if I could accept myself, I could accept other people, too.

I let go of outcomes. It was okay if things didn't go the way I envisioned. Sometimes the results were better than I anticipated. It was no longer important that others read from the script that my expectations had written.

As I let go, I learned I could let God. "Letting God" doesn't mean I abdicate my responsibilities. In fact, I become more accountable for myself. "Letting God" indicates that I accept my imperfections and grow toward the person I dream I can be. "Letting go and letting God" means I can enjoy being responsible for what is rightfully mine and leave the rest to God.

Thought for the Day

"Let go" comes before "let God" for a reason. I can't expect God to do anything if I am still holding onto my problem.

"When we put this slogan to work, we get out of the way."
How Al-Anon Works for Families & Friends of Alcoholics, p. 76

I recently went on holiday in another country and was vividly reminded that my Higher Power works on other continents as well as in my hometown.

Before I left, I went through a period of mild anxiety. This was the first time I would be traveling alone since I had become handicapped many years earlier. I felt apprehensive about traveling by myself to another land where I wouldn't know anyone. So I attended extra meetings, discussed my fears, and practiced "Let Go and Let God."

At the vacation resort, the tile floors presented me with a challenge because I walk with the help of two arm-crutches. Everything went fairly well until two days into my trip when I slipped on the tile in my room and fell quite hard. I was alone at the time and felt vulnerable with no one there to help me.

After a few minutes of crying to my Higher Power that I wanted to go home, I went into "Al-Anon mode." I recited the Serenity Prayer, scooted myself over to the sink to pull myself up, and called the resort's management office. Within five minutes, a nurse was at my door. She helped me calm down and then made a doctor's appointment for me. She even accompanied me to the doctor and waited while I was treated. After that she called me each day, even on her day off, to make sure I was feeling better.

Thanks to the Al-Anon tools and to my Higher Power's care, I was able to continue my vacation joyfully, free of physical pain, and full of gratitude for the warmth of a stranger who soon became my friend.

Thought for the Day

The Higher Power and the Al-Anon tools: Never leave home without them!

> "This wonderful adventure called life in Al-Anon is always taking me to new places . . ."

> The Forum, August 1998, p. 4

When I feel called to service, I pray for knowledge of God's will for me to make sure it's not just me wanting to manipulate, control, or avoid something going on in my life. I have a finely honed sense of responsibility. It's a constant challenge for me to view my choices through the lenses of health and balance.

I'd wanted to be involved in Alateen for some time, but I didn't know how to go about it. I also wanted to heal the wounds I'd accumulated from growing up around alcoholism. Could these two things be related? Would getting involved with the teens be a wise choice for me?

As the God of my understanding would have it, a local Alateen institutions group needed a sponsor. I agreed to take on the role. Never could I have foretold then that I would receive far more from a group of hurting teens than they would ever get from me. As I listened to them tell their stories, buried feelings from my childhood surfaced—guilt, rage, shame, and abandonment—and slowly I started to heal.

At first the teens were skeptical of me. The more I shared my experience, strength, and hope in relating to them, the more they learned to trust me. Then our relationship began to work. As I availed myself of the Al-Anon tools and my Higher Power's help to heal my painful feelings from the past, it became easier to offer an honest and hopeful environment where these young people could blossom. I learned that I always get more than I give.

Thought for the Day

Recovery often means letting others touch my mind and heart as much, or even more, than I touch theirs.

> "When I begin feeling down, as I still sometimes do even though my life is stable now, I am lifted up by these Alateens."

A Guide to Alateen Sponsorship, p. 7

When I was eleven years old, my father was hospitalized. In an effort to protect me, I was told the *other* person in my father's room was very sick, not my father. Eventually I discovered what really happened. My father had suffered a heart attack. I felt devastated that I had not been told the truth. That event taught me that when disaster struck, I was supposed to deny the truth, stuff my feelings, and act as if nothing unusual had happened.

Al-Anon is an honest, sharing program. Looking at the part honesty and sharing played in my life opened me to certain realizations. When I'm uncommunicative or dishonest in my interactions, I set myself apart and feel rejected. Conversely, open, truthful communication nurtures feelings of trust and encourages me to participate fully in life.

However, as I begin to change my old habits, fear of rejection sometimes tempts me to respond in old ways. When this happens, I step back to really hear what I say. Then I can find a more appropriate, honest response. By being more open and honest I can be a part of all that is around me. This allows me to discover the truth in Al-Anon's Fourth Concept of Service, "Participation is the key to harmony."

Sharing my feelings openly and honestly may involve facing painful truths. Nonetheless, it is much less harmful than being dishonest or withdrawn. When I respect others enough to allow them to deal with the facts of a situation according to their own needs, I am allowing them to participate in life's experiences, too.

Thought for the Day

Participating fully in life requires being as open and honest as I can with myself and others.

> "If I persist in remaining apart . . . I upset my own harmony.
> I also deny the fellowship a gift that I can offer only by
> participating.
>
> *The Forum,* April 1998, p. 30

November 19

Several years ago I attended a workshop where the topic was the story of Lois W., one of Al-Anon's cofounders. I sat letting my thoughts ramble on about the inappropriate responses I sometimes have to situations. As usual I justified them by reminding myself that I learned these responses while growing up in an alcoholic environment. I was off in my own little world until I heard the words "smug" and "self-righteous." The presenter described how these character defects covered Lois's world in darkness where no light could show through. Just then I became aware that it didn't matter if I had alcoholic parents! I also had a program to improve myself, to recover.

Finally I realized that I am not unique. I'm not the only person who struggles with the effects of alcoholism. Yes, I may have learned some of my character defects and my negative responses to life from my parents, but they're *my* defects now. My parents cannot do the recovering for me. It's up to me! No more blaming. It's time to get on with my life.

I reached a turning point when I realized who was hurting when I blamed my past instead of correcting my present.

Thought for the Day

Every defect I learned while growing up with alcoholism, I can unlearn. That's where Al-Anon comes in!

> "Smugness is the very worst sin of all, I believe. No shaft of light can pierce the armor of self-righteousness."
>
> *The Al-Anon Family Groups—Classic Edition*, p. 58

Sometimes an alarm clock can be so welcome. Other times it is nothing but a disturbance. When I have a special visit planned and must catch an early plane, I'm thankful the alarm went off and I heard it. On other days when I'd rather not go to work, that same alarm is an unwelcome intrusion. It disturbs me when I would prefer to stay comfortable in bed.

Truth, like an alarm clock, can be comforting or disturbing. Sometimes I feel grateful to hear someone speak a comforting truth. On the other hand, there have been times when I felt intimidated to be honest. What about those times when I heard truths about myself that left me feeling angry, embarrassed, or upset?

When given the occasion to hear or speak an uncomfortable reality, I have choices. I can hear it and grow, I can share it and grow, or I can ignore it in favor of maintaining my comfort zone. The truth merely provides me with an opportunity for growth. The rest is up to me.

Thought for the Day

How do I respond when the bell of truth rings? Do I face the discomfort so I may embrace the growth?

"With the Twelve Steps, I've learned to face the truth, the whole truth . . ."

From Survival to Recovery, p. 260

Step Five, "Admitted to God, to ourselves and to another human being the exact nature of our wrongs," suggests a specific order for actions. It also gives me a guideline for prioritizing the relationships in my life.

First, I need to develop a relationship with the God of my understanding. This will be the source of my happiness and future recovery in Al-Anon. Without such a relationship, I will not have the strength, guidance, or wisdom I need to live and learn the Steps, Traditions, Concepts of Service, and slogans. My Higher Power will give me courage to develop the attitudes and behaviors that bring about solid recovery. Steps One through Three help me build this important relationship.

Next, I learn to become at peace with myself. I wake up with myself every morning and go to sleep with myself every night. I spend 24 hours a day with that one person, so it is important that I'm at least tolerable if not downright enjoyable company. I can't be that person when I'm overly controlled by guilt, fear, and resentment and negligibly aware of my gifts and talents. Steps Four through Seven help me get to know and accept myself.

Lastly, I start acting responsibly toward others. The best way to heal that guilt and resentment I've been lugging around is to take a good, hard look at the people I've harmed and do my best to make amends. I can even go one step further by carrying a message of hope instead of hurt as I may have done in the past. Steps Eight through Twelve help me clean up my past and plant seeds of benevolence in the future.

Thought for the Day

In what order of importance are my relationships today?

"The Steps are a guide to total good living."

One Day at a Time in Al-Anon, p. 141

Special celebrations were always hard while I was growing up in my alcoholic family. The atmosphere always seemed sad because Dad used to get depressed before holidays. Now that I'm grown, holidays are still hard and Dad still gets depressed. The difference is I don't live at home anymore, and now I'm a member of Al-Anon.

In Al-Anon I learned I have choices. I can let go of the parts of my life that are not under my control and I can take charge of the parts that are. Even in the midst of the sadness I felt while growing up, I knew life had to be more fun than what I experienced. So, with the help of the program and the people in it, I decided to act on that knowledge. I reclaimed the holidays for myself in ways both small and large. I bought pairs of earrings that symbolized each celebration, and I even bought matching socks! I never liked writing and mailing holiday cards, so I stopped.

The most wonderful holiday tradition I have started is spending time with my friends and spiritual family in recovery. We celebrate many holidays together, and we always have a great time. This way, if I do decide to spend some holiday time with my family and accept the challenges of that choice, I also celebrate with people I trust to accept me as I am. I may not have enjoyed many holidays while growing up, but I can start enjoying them now.

Thought for the Day

My friends in the program help me heal my childhood by creating happier memories today.

> "I knew deep down inside that God had not created me to feel sad, but I needed to learn how to get out from under that feeling."

The Forum, May 1998, p. 8

My parents argued again the other day. My alcoholic father decided to end his relationship with my brother for not giving him a birthday card. My mother wanted to continue the relationship with her son, and all came to a head when Dad took Mom to the hospital for a simple eye operation. Along the way he announced he was divorcing her for talking to my brother. He saw her communication with her son as a betrayal.

When I went to visit Mom in the hospital, I found her crying. I felt so sorry for her. In Al-Anon I have learned alcoholism is a disease that affects everyone in the family. I had already forgiven my mother for neglecting me during her preoccupation with my father's drinking. I had been making daily Step Nine amends to my mom by treating her better, but I had never made formal, person-to-person amends. Now was my opportunity.

I took her hand in mine. I kissed her tears away, the way I wanted her to do for me when I was a child. I told her all my good character traits that I finally realized had come from her. I shared with her how grateful I was that she was my mother and how much I loved her.

I held her, and we cried together in joy and love. We talked about the disease of alcoholism, my father's alcoholic thinking, and how we both thought it was easier for him to think of divorcing her than it was to lose her through surgery. As I left she said she felt better. I felt close to my mother for the first time.

Thought for the Day

"... If I have worked the Eighth Step and become truly willing to make amends, I believe the opportunities will arise when I am ready."

Courage to Change, p. 163

If I want what you have, I need to become willing to do what you have done. For me this is the central tenet of Al-Anon's practice of sponsorship. While growing up in an alcoholic environment, I had become afraid of people and mistrustful of intimacy. Initially I resisted many of the program's suggestions. It took me a long time to get a sponsor, but eventually, because I wanted what one particular person had, I asked her what she had done to achieve it. She became my sponsor. My recovery accelerated as I became willing to ask for another member's help.

Today I am blessed to have a sponsor and to be a sponsor for others. I am one link in a great chain of people helping people. Having once felt incredibly alone and isolated, I'm now connected once again with humanity. The roles of sponsor and sponsee have taught me so much about normal, loving human relationships. I have learned how to practice unconditional love and emotional detachment, how to set healthy boundaries, how to care for people without taking care of them, and how to let others get close to me without losing myself.

Thought for the Day

Sponsorship works when people love themselves enough to ask for help and when others love themselves enough to say yes.

> "The most important thing is to be willing to reach out
> and ask for the help we need, human to human."
> *How Al-Anon Works for Families & Friends of Alcoholics*, p. 37

About two years ago, my parents divorced. At that time I made it clear I was not going to do any mediating. I did fairly well staying physically out of their problems, but mentally I was a mess. My mother couldn't hear me when I said no. It got to the point that having no contact with either of them seemed to be the best choice for maintaining my sanity.

In principle this was a great idea, except that both my parents and I are actively involved in Al-Anon service. My father is a dual member, and my mother recently became a group representative. My husband and I were with my father at a program conference when my mother walked into the Al-Anon meeting. I panicked. What should I do if a conflict arose between them after the meeting? If it did, how could I keep from being pulled into it?

My husband noticed my reaction and gently reminded me of my tendency to obsess and project. His comment, together with my Al-Anon training, reminded me that the best way to handle the situation was to practice "Let Go and Let God" and do nothing. Later, after writing a little and talking with my sponsor, I was able to let both of them go and enjoy the rest of the conference.

Thought for the Day

Al-Anon teaches me to avoid the "have to" syndrome. When I feel like I just absolutely have to do something about a situation that is not a true crisis, it's best to sit still, do nothing, and wait for my Higher Power's guidance.

> "When I think of letting go I remind myself that there is a natural order to life—a chain of events that a Higher Power has in mind. When I let go of a situation, I allow life to unfold according to that plan."
>
> *Courage to Change*, p. 203

One thing is certain about my childhood. I learned first-hand the instability and chaos that rules a drinking home. I learned to trust no one, to stay silent at all costs, to stuff my feelings, never to stand up for myself, to take on more responsibility than I could handle, to love conditionally, and to tell white lies to cover up my home life. No wonder as an adult I perceived that close interpersonal relationships were like constantly moving targets. Usually I was the one who was moving because I lacked the skills to develop and maintain healthy adult relationships.

Thanks to Al-Anon I have learned that it's safe to trust again. First, I began to trust my Higher Power who loves me unconditionally—no matter what I say, do, or feel. I learned to trust the fellowship where many have experienced the same childhood traumas that I did. I'm also learning to trust the people in my life—my husband, friends, siblings, and even my parents. In spite of my unhealthy childhood, I forgive both of my parents.

Although it took me four decades to recognize my disease and find my way to Al-Anon, I have been strengthened and blessed by the miracles that have taken place in my life through this program. I owe this fellowship and God a huge debt of gratitude and love.

Thought for the Day

Trust is one of the first things to go in an alcoholic situation, but I can regain it through Al-Anon.

> "If I'm willing to give others a second chance and trust them a little more each day, . . . faith in people may start to come back."
>
> *Alateen—a day at a time,* p. 110

I used to think Tradition Seven, "Every group ought to be fully self-supporting, declining outside contributions," was limited to the financial matters of the group, such as paying rent and providing supplies. It was just a sentence that accompanied the passing of the basket at meetings. Lately I've become more aware of the significance and value of being self-supporting.

Practicing the Seventh Tradition in a broader sense means I give more than money to my group. I give my time and talent in the form of service, which rewards me with increased self-esteem and a greater sense of confidence. I also give my informed opinion during group conscience decisions, which reinforces my sense of worthiness. Contributing to my meetings on various levels also helps me make amends to myself for the times I was not self-supporting in other areas of my life, whether they were physical, emotional, or spiritual. I see a difference in my group and in myself as I contribute more and more. I receive a clear demonstration that I am a valuable part of the meeting and that my input really does matter.

Service is a win-win situation. As I contribute to my meetings, I make a direct investment in the groups that encourage, support, and maintain my well-being. The stronger my meetings become, the more my recovery grows.

Thought for the Day

When I contribute my part to keep my meetings self-supporting, I contribute to my own recovery.

> "To think of Tradition Seven as a protection for my spiritual growth is humbling and freeing."
>
> *Paths to Recovery*, p. 198

My parents didn't know I was angry with them, because I was the "good" kid. I felt angry about the drinking and the constant chaos, but I never said anything. I swallowed my resentment, thinking either my needs would go away or my parents would change. Of course, neither happened.

In Al-Anon I learned about alcoholism as a family disease and the role I played. My destructive childhood experiences were not due solely to my parents' alcoholism. I played a part in it, too, and I lugged my childhood grudges into adulthood. I healed much of my pain through Al-Anon's Fourth and Fifth Steps by pouring out my frustration and rage to my sponsor. All I really needed was to be heard. Then I could let go of some ugly feelings.

To make amends to my parents in Step Nine, I decided to practice being a better daughter. For example, instead of expecting them to phone me, I started to call them regularly. At first the conversations were awkward. Mom would answer the phone, greet me, and quickly pass the phone to Dad. I knew my parents hadn't been able to provide consistency for me because no one had given it to them. I "Let It Begin with Me" by calling them with the same reliability I yearned for as a child. Now when I call home, Mom seems more comfortable talking with me. We enjoy much longer conversations before she hands the phone to Dad. Sometimes she even asks for the phone back so we can talk more!

Thought for the Day

When I take my parents' inventory, I hold grudges and sink deeper into my disease. When I take my inventory and make amends, I grow, learn, and love more deeply.

"Let me remember that the reason for making amends is to free my own mind of uneasiness . . ."

Al-Anon Is for Adult Children of Alcoholics, p. 16

I was practically consumed with frustration and anger toward my mother when I first discovered Al-Anon. Although my father was the one who drank, screamed with rage, hit, and eventually abandoned me, I blamed my mother for not protecting me and for refusing to admit how harrowing my life had been.

In Al-Anon and through the love and patience of my sponsor, I found acceptance and understanding of my feelings. I was introduced to the idea of "Live and Let Live." Gradually I put aside my resentments by accepting my powerlessness over both the disease and my mother's reaction to it. As I continued my recovery, I discovered compassion for her and ended my struggle to force her to break her denial.

Today I can put the past where it belongs and focus on taking care of myself. I needn't wait for someone to do it for me. I am no longer a victim of my emotions or of circumstances beyond my control. Instead, I am free to enjoy what I have received through this fellowship—serenity, courage, wisdom, and love.

Thought for the Day

Acceptance is a form of living and letting live that frees all concerned to follow their Higher Power's will.

"Acceptance is a challenging but rewarding spiritual discipline."

From Survival to Recovery, p. 95

While listening to others share at Al-Anon meetings, I became aware that I hold myself to unrealistically high standards. I expect myself to be less fallible than everyone else. I acquired this character defect as a child in my attempts to control my alcoholic father by pleasing or appeasing him. It might have served a purpose then, no matter how illusionary it was, but it doesn't work for me now. Such perfectionism perpetuates dissatisfaction and low self-esteem.

What makes me think I'm different from everyone else? It's one thing to strive to do my best, but it's quite another to punish myself if results fall short of my high expectations. I am human, after all. It is in our very nature to have faults and limitations.

In my misguided quest for excellence, I often act as if my personal slogan were "If it's worth doing, it's worth making a major project out of it." As a result I usually don't have enough time to finish many projects. Rather, they languish in various stages of flawless incompletion. I need to remind myself continually to practice "Keep it Simple," and I'm getting better at it. Recently for the first time in my life, I heard myself say, "That's good enough."

The Seventh Step says, "I humbly asked Him to remove our shortcomings." To do so requires me to acknowledge my humanity, including my perfectionism. To be humble is to accept my place in the universe. It's unrealistic to expect perfection from an imperfect being in an imperfect world. The only perfection I can hope to attain is to be perfectly imperfect.

Thought for the Day

A mistake a day keeps my perfectionism at bay. Today I will endeavor to enjoy my humanness.

> "My sponsor's gentle reminder of 'Progress Not Perfection' encourages me to give myself credit."
> *How Al-Anon Works for Families & Friends of Alcoholics,* p. 323

I've struggled long and hard in Al-Anon to understand the idea of detachment with love. At first, it sounded like an oxymoron. Detachment was the opposite of love, I thought. It seemed like abandoning the people I loved because of their alcoholism. Was I supposed to just stop caring?

In Al-Anon I began to see that my way of caring often meant reacting and manipulating. I'd do something nice for someone because I wanted to be liked. I'd get so caught up in someone else's problems that I didn't have time or energy to seek solutions for my own difficulties. Sometimes I wanted to attach myself and feed off someone mentally, emotionally, and spiritually. Then I wouldn't have to deal with the scariness of being a separate person who took risks. Despite these intellectual glimmerings about my motives, I felt frustrated that I didn't know how to translate them into positive behavior. I simply decided my problem was that I loved too much. I began to regard any act of helpfulness or kindness on my part as a slip.

After I told my sponsor about my new insight, he explained the goal was *detachment*, not *amputation*! To detach isn't to stop caring about others; it means I care equally as much for myself. It means I love myself enough to stay out of others' insanity. It means putting enough emotional distance between myself and another to see each of us as a separate individual. Being helpful and kind feels wonderful. It's only when I do this with the belief that I can fix, change, or control the other person that I need to question my motives.

Thought for the Day

Sometimes what I call "love" is really just control.

> "Simply put, detachment means to separate ourselves emotionally and spiritually from other people."
> *How Al-Anon Works for Families & Friends of Alcoholics*, p. 84

Making decisions has always been hard for me. I've tried many of the conventional tools, such as listing the pros and cons of different alternatives and comparing those alternatives with my goals. The customary methods didn't work for me because I was setting goals that others wanted me to achieve. Although their goals might have been right for them, they were not always right for me.

It took me a long time to see this character defect of mine, but I finally did. My decisions were based on what others wanted so I could make them love and accept me. It was a matter of control. This was true while I was growing up with alcoholism, too. In my limited, childish mind, I thought if I said and did everything my parents wished, I would finally earn their love and attention.

When I first came to Al-Anon, I didn't have any idea who I was or what I wanted. My sponsor and other members walked me gently through my Fourth Step by explaining it as a way for me to get to know myself so I could make healthy choices. They showed me how to seek God's will in the planning and execution of every decision. It was suggested that if I were having trouble making a decision, I might want to ask myself if I was really seeking to please myself, my Higher Power, or another person.

Thought for the Day

Making decisions based on God's will for me is far more rewarding in the long run than making them based on other people.

"With the help of a Higher Power, decision-making can be one of life's great adventures."

Courage to Change, p. 53

I found it relatively easy to *make a decision* to turn over my will and my life to God. However, I didn't have any idea how to actually *do it*. I tried to turn myself over more times than a cook turns flapjacks at a pancake breakfast, but I just couldn't seem to let go completely. Finally I found two techniques that work for me—a God box and a basketball net.

A wise Al-Anon member suggested the idea of a God box. I tested it when I felt perplexed about some calculations on my income tax form. On a small piece of paper, I wrote, "The income tax forms are in Your hands until tomorrow." I folded up the paper, put it in a box, and let go of it. It was that simple, and it actually worked! I was able to forget what I was obsessing about and get on with my day.

I also use another letting-go method I call the "basketball technique." This technique helps me let go of work when I come home with my head full of unfinished business. There's a basketball hoop in our driveway. Before going into the house, I play one-on-one with my Higher Power. With each shot at the basket, I imagine the ball is one of my work projects. The hoop symbolizes my Higher Power. If the shot is good, then I've turned that issue over. If I miss, I keep shooting. Finally, the last thing I let go of is the ball. After I take this time for myself, I can go comfortably into the house and enjoy being a husband and a father.

Thought for the Day

If I supply the willingness, my Higher Power will supply the way.

"There are as many ways to approach turning our will and our lives over as there are definitions of God."

Paths to Recovery, p. 29

I came into Al-Anon many years ago filled with resentment toward my husband for leaving me to raise our son alone. There I met people just like me who helped me find a sponsor, learn to accept, to detach, and to work the Steps. I learned that alcoholism is a disease associated with certain behaviors. I slowly realized my husband's leaving was not a result of anything I had done or failed to do.

I keep coming back to Al-Anon, and not one thing has changed regarding the situation that brought me here in the first place. The father of my boy still drinks and still chooses not to have a relationship with his son. That boy is now 21 years old and is starting to experiment with alcohol. His drinking is beginning to affect his life, a clue that he may be traveling down his father's path.

What has changed, though, is me. Now it takes me only one day instead of years to get to a meeting. My sponsor's help is only a phone call away. I find experience, strength, and hope in the program literature. I no longer respond to my son's struggle by denying or enabling. The most significant benefit of Al-Anon is that we still have a loving relationship no matter where he is with his problem or where I am with my program.

Thought for the Day

Can I maintain my program while a loved one continues drinking?

> "Without Al-Anon, I might never have tapped into that grace and the ability to love myself and other people exactly where we are at this minute in time."

From Survival to Recovery, pp. 196-197

When my children were little, they didn't like cooked carrots. However, they loved to eat carrots raw, so I always kept some around for snacks. I don't care for those big, thick, pale carrots that seem to taste like wood. I prefer the slender, sweet, bright ones. So when I shopped for carrots for the kids, I carefully chose the skinniest, brightest ones I could find.

I didn't realize it at the time, but as I searched through those piles of carrots, my young son had been sitting in the kiddy seat of the shopping cart, coming to his own conclusions. Recently as a teenager, he expressed resentment that I always bought him scrawny carrots. Scrawny carrots? I had so lovingly selected them for him! I had been doing what I thought was best, and he was resenting it because he wanted, or thought he wanted, something different.

Once at an Al-Anon meeting, I heard sharings on the topic of spiritual gifts that come disguised as something one doesn't particularly like. This idea was in the back of my mind as I listened to my son. Suddenly I found new insight and understanding. Was I resenting God's "scrawny carrots?" Were the challenges and losses in my life actually gifts God had chosen carefully for me so that I might grow spiritually? I knew it to be so, and I felt simultaneously humbled and overwhelmed with gratitude for the nature of my Higher Power's love for me.

Thought for the Day

Mine is a disease of distorted perception. Higher Power, please help me appreciate the "scrawny carrots" of my life as the gifts they really are.

> "... I am constantly making choices about how I perceive
> my world. With the help of Al-Anon and my friends in the
> fellowship, I can make those choices more consciously and
> more actively than ever before."
>
> *Courage to Change*, p. 243

Sometimes when I'm in the midst of making a decision I really struggle with knowing my Higher Power's will for me. Occasionally I look outside myself for a sign. I'd rather see a neon light or something else just as obvious, but it doesn't often happen that way. Usually the messages are more subtle, like going to a meeting that I don't usually attend and hearing a speaker I've never heard before say exactly what I need to hear.

I need to remember to look inside for signs as well. How do I feel deep inside about a proposed course of action? Is my stomach churning with discomfort, or do I feel calm, quiet, and solid? Do I feel knotted up with tension, or light, relaxed, and expansive?

For me the dilemma comes from wanting to make the "right" decision. If I'm not careful, I can get stuck at a crossroad of choices. I try to remember that as long as I make decisions in the context of seeking my Higher Power's will, whatever I do will be the right thing. "Do" is the operative word here. I once heard, "Without God, man cannot; without man, God will not." If I don't take some sort of action, my Higher Power doesn't have anything to work with. Because decision-making is a self-correcting process, I can use any mistakes I make along the way to eventually guide me in the right direction. Even if I "decide" myself into a corner, I'm not alone. My Higher Power is with me everywhere I go.

Thought for the Day

Sometimes the choices I make are not as important as the fact that I make them.

> "In contact with my Higher Power my ability to make choices works."
>
> Having Had a Spiritual Awakening . . ., p. 68

The little family of deer living in our nearby woods was absent for weeks. I thought perhaps our garden's usual offerings had been too meager to draw them for a nibble. However, while sipping tea at the kitchen table on the morning of my birthday, I suddenly spied the deer grazing leisurely in the yard. They had appeared silently, gently, when I least expected it.

The deer's soft, dark eyes were a wonder. Their cautious movements showed me they had mustered enough courage to find nourishment in our sparse winter landscape. I wanted to reach out and stroke their downy heads, and touch their gray and tan fur. Instead, I sat quietly and watched while this tender birthday gift from my Higher Power filled me with delight, reminding me once again of how much I am loved.

Serenity is the sure knowledge of my Higher Power's unconditional love for me. It is an acceptance of myself that flows from God's approving embrace. Today I know I am worthy. I was created both to give and receive joy. I am unique and special in my ordinary humanness.

Thought for the Day

Today I will remember to rest in the beauty of God's care and concern for me. When I do, the priceless gift of serenity is mine to open and enjoy.

> "Once we have begun to experience serenity, we realize that Al-Anon is not just a program where sick people get well, but a way of living that is rewarding in itself."
>
> From Survival to Recovery, pp. 150-151

Tradition Five states Al-Anon's purpose, to help families of alcoholics, and describes how we can best carry that out. On a personal level, this Tradition helps me transform the character defect of resentment into the principle of compassion. Specifically, I become compassionate toward myself by working the Steps and healing from the devastating effects of alcoholism. In being compassionate to myself, I release the resentments that eat at my heart and soul, and keep me from my spiritual awakening.

As I release my resentments, I can extend compassion to the alcoholics in my life. I can love myself enough to love them, too, even though I hate the disease that hurts us both.

I become so full of love and compassion that I can't keep it bottled up inside. I need to share it with others. My compassion becomes the healing light of my Higher Power shining through me to welcome and comfort other friends and family members of alcoholics.

What are some ways in which I can extend compassion to myself, my alcoholic loved ones, or my group? If I am being hard on myself, I can practice "Progress Not Perfection." Reading about the disease aspect of alcoholism can help me to better understand the alcoholics in my life. I welcome newcomers to Al-Anon, offering my phone number, a hug, or the willingness to listen and love unconditionally. By giving them my support and understanding, I complete the circle of compassion that was so freely given to me.

Thought for the Day

How can I show compassion for myself and those around me?

"Today I will practice compassion. First I will be kind and loving to myself, but I will not stop there. I will extend this compassion to others."

Courage to Change, p. 355

I fell into a depression while grieving my father's death. I knew it was natural to mourn. However, I had not resolved certain emotions I felt toward my father's alcoholic behavior, and this complicated my grieving. I decided to consult a professional who, after several sessions about my alcoholic upbringing, suggested it might be helpful to attend Al-Anon. I had become very comfortable with this professional, and the idea of sharing my thoughts and feelings with strangers felt scary. However, I knew I needed something beyond therapy, so I gave Al-Anon a chance.

In Al-Anon I grew to understand many things about this disease called alcoholism. I started to regard my father in a different light, and my memories of our interactions took on a different perspective. During his years of active drinking, fear clouded my perception of him. I never regarded him as other than a scary authoritative figure who was even scarier when he drank. Now I don't see him as just an alcoholic. I regard him as a whole person who had needs, feelings, desires, and faults.

Al-Anon has given me many tools, including the Steps and slogans, to work through old feelings and to make amends to my father, even though he is no longer alive. Through this program, I have been able to forgive him as well as myself. For a long time I was hard on myself, thinking I was a coward for not facing up to him. Now I understand, just like my dad, I did the best I could under the circumstances.

Thought for the Day

Al-Anon has helped me understand alcoholism's true nature as a disease, thus transforming my relationship with myself and the alcoholics in my life.

> "I see now that alcoholics have a disease: They are ill, not bad."

Courage to Change, p. 110

"Thanks for mentioning the 'F-word'," someone said to me after a meeting. "You know, F-U-N. I don't hear about that as often as I'd like."

I *had* been mentioning fun at great length, because I was the speaker that night. I shared about my recent attendance at a family wedding, which I enjoyed very much. The fun was in the details, of course. The fact that I could recognize and delight in those details came from practicing my program. I made many choices before the wedding. Most concerned the development of alternate plans and options should family tensions erupt. For example, my wife and I chose to drive separately so either one of us could leave the reception temporarily should the need arise. I also considered how I might respond if someone tried to draw me into a conflict. In addition, I put a few copies of *The Forum* in my car and slipped a "Just for Today" wallet card inside the pocket of my suit just in case I needed a quick sanity break.

As my Higher Power would have it, I didn't have to employ any of those tools. However, because I had anticipated my needs and prepared for them, I was able to travel lightly and with a sense of playfulness. I clearly set my sights on celebrating a joyous occasion. As a result of thinking ahead and making plans to take care of myself, I truly enjoyed a day I wanted to enjoy.

Thought for the Day

One of the many miracles of recovery is that I can take my fun with me wherever I go! All I need to do is make a plan without anticipating the outcome.

> "Today I know that part of my recovery is respecting my need and my right to let go and relax."

> *... In All Our Affairs*, p. 149

I whined a lot when I came into Al-Anon. I was raised in an alcoholic home, and it took me quite some time to grow up. Thank God for the Al-Anon members who were patient with me and let me work things out in my own time. It's a good thing there are no timetables in Al-Anon, or I would have been expelled long ago.

The major form my complaining took was to ask, "Why me?" Why was I afflicted with such mean, drunken parents that I had to learn to protect myself from them? Why did I get a father who couldn't hold down a job and provide for our family? Why couldn't I have my friends come over without suffering embarrassment?

Although Al-Anon didn't seem to fit my needs at first, mainly because I wanted sympathy, I'm glad I kept coming back. Week after week I heard the stories of others who had it much worse than I did. I'll never forget the night I drove home after a meeting when my inner question changed. Instead of the same lament of "Why me?" this new question "Why *not* me?" popped into my head. Why did I think I was so special that I should have escaped the trials of life when no one else was exempt? I thought of how much worse my life could have been and actually felt grateful for my past. In that moment, I moved into greater acceptance. Now, instead of spinning the wheels of blame, I use my energy to learn all that I can in Al-Anon.

Thought for the Day

Healing starts when I stop asking, "Why me?"

"I therefore resolve to stop blaming the alcoholic for what is beyond his or her control—including the compulsion to drink. Instead, I'll direct my efforts where they can do some good: I will commit myself to my own recovery."

Courage to Change, p. 128

My partner, who is an alcoholic, often complained of feeling invisible around me. She said all I saw when I looked at her was the alcoholism. For years I had no idea what she was talking about. Now, after beginning my own recovery in Al-Anon, I understand what she meant.

Al-Anon has helped me understand that I wasn't aware of others because I wasn't really aware of myself. I couldn't acknowledge the alcoholics in my life as individuals, because I couldn't acknowledge my own disease. It's hard to see through the blinding hood of denial.

Working through the first four Steps gave me a "mirror" in which to view my real self. When I took the Fifth Step, "Admitted to God, to ourselves, and to another human being the exact nature of our wrongs," with my sponsor, it was like having someone I trust say, "I see you, too!" When I learned to love the person I found— myself—I started to perceive and love myriad qualities in the people around me.

In addition to making it difficult to see myself, my denial had veiled my vision of my partner, making it even harder to see her. The more I strived to accept alcoholism as a disease and to keep my focus on myself, the more my loved one came into focus as a person. Now instead of regarding her as a case of alcoholism with a human name, I consider her to be a wonderful child of God who just happens to have a disease.

Thought for the Day

Yes, some people I love are alcoholics, but they are a great deal more than their disease.

> "By listening, we can learn to distinguish the person from the disease, to have compassion for their efforts and their pain, and to recognize that they, too, are powerless over alcohol."

How Al-Anon Works for Families & Friends of Alcoholics, p. 34

I first came into Al-Anon because of my 16-year-old daughter's drinking. I felt insane and knew I needed help. My daughter attended AA meetings for more than three years, after which she decided her problems and her drinking were not due to alcoholism but to a difficult adolescence. I wondered whether I could stay in Al-Anon given my daughter's conclusion. As far as I knew, there were no other alcoholics in my immediate family. Once again, as I had so many times in my life, I thought I didn't belong.

I am so grateful for the Third Tradition, which tells me, "The only requirement for membership is that there be a problem of alcoholism in a relative or friend." The only qualification for me to be a member of Al-Anon is my own internal barometer. Do I feel I belong? Do I identify with others who have been affected by alcoholism? Does someone's drinking disturb me, even if that person doesn't believe he or she is an alcoholic?

Despite my misgivings, I decided to continue attending Al-Anon meetings, and the answers to my questions came in due time. In meeting after meeting, I heard others share thoughts and feelings with which I could identify. The stories and circumstances weren't always the same, but the feelings usually were. Now I know that although my daughter still maintains she doesn't have a drinking problem, I belong in Al-Anon because I feel affected by her drinking. More than that, I belong because I want to recover.

Thought for the Day

My membership in Al-Anon is about my feelings, not someone else's beliefs.

"It is up to each of us to decide whether we belong."

Paths to Recovery, pp. 155-156

When I feel my serenity being crowded out by fear and anxiety, I break down the Serenity Prayer in a clear and precise way that cuts through the deluge of my shortcomings. First, I broaden my acceptance to include *everything* exactly as it is, not only the things I cannot change. I look at my entire life through the lens of gratitude, trusting that everything is unfolding exactly as it should. As my sponsor reminds me, God's planning and timing are perfect. I ask my Higher Power to help me accept things exactly as they are and to see the opportunities in my circumstances.

Asking God for "courage to change the things I can" is dangerous for me at times. If I'm not careful, I overwhelm myself with all the various things I *could* change and I become paralyzed by inaction. It helps to pray for knowledge of exactly what God wants me to change at any given moment. I think of the "things I can change" as the things God *wants* me to change.

Asking for "wisdom to know the difference" can provoke my perfectionism. I yearn to know exactly what God wants me to change. I don't want to make any mistakes. To regain perspective, I remind myself that everything is already in God's hands and that decision-making is a self-correcting process. Wisdom is something I sense in my gut. If I change something and still don't feel right, I go through the process again until God's will becomes clear to me.

Thought for the Day

How deeply and broadly do I apply the Serenity Prayer to my life?

> "...I ask God for direction and wait, placing the problem in His hands. I ask for clarity in what I must do. He gives me clear direction."
>
> *Having Had a Spiritual Awakening ...*, p. 40

Newcomers often ask how it's possible to detach from the alcoholic with love rather than trying to change him or her. My answer is to concentrate on taking loving care of myself. Then I can detach from almost any obsession about other people, places, or things.

Changing myself is such a big job that it keeps me fully occupied. If it were easy, I could do it today and then proceed tomorrow with trying to change the alcoholic and the world. Yet by the end of the day, I haven't gotten that much further with my own self-improvement, let alone the improvement of anyone else. As for tomorrow, if my life in Al-Anon thus far is a reliable guide, I'll still have my hands full just working to change myself.

I don't let myself get discouraged. Perfection never really has worried me because I know it's unattainable. Instead, I'm thrilled with the small, daily changes I can make in my attitudes and actions. I see sufficient progress to push on, like a tortoise. Sometimes I detect my growth when I retake my Fourth Step and compare it with the results of the last time I took it. I also listen to my Higher Power. God often speaks to me through others who tell me how much I've changed and grown.

Thought for the Day

Changing myself is a permanent, full-time position that only I can fill.

> "I have to use a 'hands-off policy' with the alcoholic and concentrate on improving myself."
>
> *Alateen—a day at a time*, p. 252

I had a job in my alcoholic family, and I learned it very well. The job was to keep silent about what was happening in my home and how I felt about it. I became an adolescent with no coping skills. Gradually so much pain and anger built up inside me that I had to find some way to relieve it. My alcoholic parents' reservoir of coping skills was virtually nonexistent, so they had no way to recognize what I was going through, let alone help me through it. Left to my own devices, I escaped through food. Only later, when I started coming to Al-Anon, did I realize that my use of food was very similar in motive and pattern to my parents' use of alcohol.

First Al-Anon taught me through the Step Four process that it was all right for me to identify my buried emotions and to allow myself to feel them. Step Five encouraged me to share the results of this emotional inventory with another trusted person, and I chose my sponsor. These Steps helped me clear pain from my heart and fill that space with something healthy. Today instead of eating when I feel anxiety or some other uncomfortable emotion, I choose to use an Al-Anon tool. I call my sponsor or another Al-Anon friend. Sometimes I read from Al-Anon literature to calm my soul. Occasionally I sign up to volunteer as a monthly chairperson, or pick a few names and numbers from my phone list to offer words of hope to a hurting newcomer. I can't always control my pain, but I can choose what I do to heal it.

Thought for the Day

What coping behaviors do I use to soothe my pain? Are they really helping me?

> "I've learned a lot … about coping with my feelings and making my life better."
>
> *Living Today in Alateen*, p. 133

Looking back to my childhood, I don't remember any secrets. I just remember not talking about certain subjects—such as sex, money, and religion. My family also had trouble communicating about love, fear, insecurity, and anger.

Years later my husband, three children, and I didn't share at all. We didn't even argue. We thought we were respecting each other by swallowing our thoughts and feelings about potentially hot topics. Actually, we were all emotionally frozen.

I am grateful Al-Anon has helped me talk about almost any issue. Going to meetings and having time to share has been powerful for my recovery. I even told my 12-year-old daughter about a mistake I made and the amends I had planned to correct it. She looked so surprised, as if I had given her permission to be human, too.

Today my immediate family talks about all sorts of topics. We work hard at being honest with each other, and we are closer because of it.

Thought for the Day

Thanks to my healthy sharing and listening experiences in Al-Anon, I can risk being my true self with family members and allow family members to risk being themselves with me.

"I will dare to be myself."

Courage to Change, p. 24

One benefit of Al-Anon I rarely hear mentioned is the wide variety of people we meet. We are blessed to hear so many speak from their hearts, which reminds us that we are not so different after all. Not only do we learn tolerance for dissimilar folks, we learn to seek their wisdom because they offer us valuable perspectives we might not consider on our own.

I never realized the true value of this benefit until I went on a vacation alone in a different country. The resort where I stayed attracted people from all over the world. Dinner was served European-style, which meant solo travelers like me ate with whoever was sitting there at the time. At tables reminiscent of my Al-Anon meetings back home, I encountered strangers who eventually became friends.

At times I felt nervous about starting conversations, but I reminded myself of the practice I had already gained at Al-Anon meetings. I "Let It Begin with Me" many times, asking people about their homelands and occupations. Often this was enough to spark great conversations. I learned much from a great many people and brought comfort to one particular person. I even met a gentleman who, although he did not declare membership, knew about Al-Anon and its purpose.

If I hadn't had so many conversations with so many "strangers" around the Al-Anon circles, I might not have felt so comfortable or made so many new friends in this faraway land.

Thought for the Day

Al-Anon meetings help me become open to people who are different from me.

> "What I love about Al-Anon meetings is that I am getting close to people who normally I would not be able to know so well ... Walls are disappearing, and love and community are growing and expanding."
>
> *Al-Anon Is for Gays and Lesbians,* p.4

I was given few choices as a child growing up in an alcoholic family. I was told what to believe and how to believe. If I deviated even slightly from the chosen path, I was reproached and corrected. What I ate, what music I listened to, who my friends were, what clothes I wore, what I watched on television, and what church I attended depended on my parents' control. They wanted to show the world a "perfect family." Needless to say, I didn't develop any individuality. I was too busy caretaking and obsessing about the rules to find out who I was inside.

When Al-Anon asked me to focus on myself, I didn't understand what that meant. I had no idea what were my likes, dislikes, needs, or desires. When I listened to others share, I thought they were a little strange. How could it fix the alcoholic for them to talk about themselves?

Slowly I became aware that Al-Anon was for me, not the alcoholic. I learned that I already had inside myself all the answers I would ever need to all the questions I would ever have. The key to finding them, however, was to go inside and become acquainted with myself. Through my Fourth Step I got to know my own thoughts, feelings, and talents. What I found wasn't too pretty, but I stayed with the program and trusted the Steps. As I cleaned away the debris of shame and guilt in Steps Five through Nine, my inner knowledge and wisdom—the voice of my Higher Power—became clearer. I found a peace I never knew was possible.

Thought for the Day

I like the me I am discovering.

> "With the program to guide me, I can be myself and become something better than I ever thought possible."
>
> *Alateen—a day at a time*, p. 114

Detaching with love was a behavior I assumed would never be part of my recovery, even though I knew my resentment over having an alcoholic parent was destroying me. In spite of the negative effects of my bitterness, I couldn't imagine living without it. Without resentment, who would I be?

When I finally became tired of hurting, Al-Anon offered me tools to incorporate into my life. Listening to others share in meetings, reading Al-Anon literature, becoming involved in service, and attending Al-Anon workshops and conventions lent me a new perspective. This outlook gave me the opportunity to become a different and better person, one who enjoyed the serenity of acceptance. Simply put, I slowly came to the realization that my alcoholic parent had been incapable of meeting my particular expectations. In his own way and to the extent of his abilities, he had provided me with love, life's necessities, and support in all my endeavors. Finally, instead of seeing a completely empty glass, I saw that my glass was partially full. I realized that my growing up years could have been so much worse than they were.

My father's recent death showed me that, at some point, I began loving him with detachment. A sense of release washed over me as I realized I had let go of the bitterness and resentment I once thought was permanent. In their place I have a new-found sense of freedom from resentments and hope for the future.

Thought for the Day

What role do my expectations as a child play in my difficulties as an adult?

> "Relationships distorted by alcoholism and its effect on the drinker and on us are not healed overnight. It is not wise to expect too much too quickly."
>
> *This Is Al-Anon*, p. 9

Tradition Eight suggests that Al-Anon Twelfth Step work remain forever nonprofessional. This implies that there is no professional class of Al-Anons. We are all equals—experts only in sharing our personal experience, strength, and hope. Remaining anonymous about my economic class, social status, or current employment helps me maintain that sense of equality. I shudder to think how much wisdom I denied myself in the past because I judged others as having nothing to share before I even listened to what they said.

Tradition Twelve speaks of equality from a different angle. Suggesting anonymity is the spiritual foundation of Al-Anon's principles, Tradition Twelve affirms that individual differences are unimportant within the program. We set aside any desire for personal distinction and meld willingly into the group. Freed of worldly constraints, our principles, as practiced in the meetings, provide a secure environment where we can heal and grow spiritually as equals. Just as Tradition Eight says there are no "greater thans," Tradition Twelve proclaims there are no "lesser thans," either. We listen to what is being said rather than to who is saying it.

If I'm not looking eye-level at my fellow members, it's time for me to take a look at myself. Whether I find myself disregarding, minimizing, judging, or on the other hand fawning and worshiping, I'm not an equal anymore. No matter who we are and no matter how much or how little time we have in the program, each of us is important to our fellowship and to each other. Traditions Eight and Twelve help remind me not to put barriers between myself and other members. Anonymity breaks down barriers.

Thought for the Day

Each Al-Anon member is my teacher.

> "Anonymity unifies our fellowship by removing individual status so we can listen to the message rather than the messenger."

Paths to Recovery, p. 237

I turned my back on religion many years before my first Al-Anon meeting, so when the meeting ended with a closing prayer, I wondered how I could pray without feeling false. I closed my eyes and bowed my head, but I didn't say the prayer. I feared someone would tap me on the shoulder and tell me to say the prayer. The prayer ended, and no one chastised me. Instead, I was given literature and encouraged to return.

Although I didn't know it when I first walked through Al-Anon's doors, the words "must" and "should" nearly ruined my relationship with my daughter and with my spouse. I had no awareness of the role that "iron rules" played in my life. My chattering mental voice applied these rules to myself, and in turn I applied them to everyone else.

Life was not comfortable because I was constantly on guard. Al-Anon helped me see that right and wrong were not the issues. The important issues were maintaining my serenity, making contact with my Higher Power, and keeping my mouth shut about other people's business.

I used to think of myself as a responsible, disciplined adult. Yet the love and support of my fellow Al-Anon members showed me that my rigidity was a wall that hid my fear. Acceptance of my self-doubts enabled me to start turning away from the "musts" and "shoulds." Now I am gentler with myself and others. Years after my first meeting, I stand gratefully in the circle and *choose* to say the closing prayer.

Thought for the Day

There are no "shoulds" in Al-Anon. The program only *suggests* I practice the Steps, Traditions, Concepts of Service, and slogans to the best of my ability.

> "In addition to offering healing for a hurt spirit, the fellowship offers empathy and choice."
>
> *As We Understood . . .*, p. 29

During the past two years, I had to work with a senior-level administrator and alternately felt intimidated or furious at functions we attended together. I took personally everything he said or did not say. I believed he constantly attacked or minimized my beliefs and feelings. Obviously, I had a major problem because I had to be in his company every day.

By placing principles above personalities, as suggested in Tradition Twelve, I learned not to react to everything this man said and did. After a year of really paying attention, one day at a time, to my feelings, attitudes, and behaviors when I was around him, I began to feel better. I shared about my struggle at meetings and with my sponsor. I began to let go of caring what this coworker thought of me. I stopped trying to make him into a person I could like and started accepting him for the person he was.

I would not want this person as a friend, but I do need to work with him as a professional. I don't like him, and the Twelfth Tradition has taught me that this is my right. However, in order to practice the Al-Anon program, I treat him with the same courtesy and respect I would like him to give me, regardless of whether or not he gives it. I let it begin with me and act rather than react.

My workday is much more calm today. At times my coworker's behavior still irritates me, but I can let go of my annoyance much more quickly. My level of acceptance profoundly impacts my serenity.

Thought for the Day

Placing principles above personalities frees me from reacting and restores my self-respect.

> "When we commit ourselves to . . . placing principles above personalities, we choose a path of personal integrity . . ."
> *How Al-Anon Works for Families & Friends of Alcoholics*, p. 123

The Twelve Steps are the backbone of the Al-Anon program. I find the Second Step, "Came to believe that a Power greater than ourselves could restore us to sanity," to be particularly meaningful. In any situation, particularly when I'm with my family, I need only turn to my Higher Power for help. For instance, while visiting my family on a holiday, I started to feel uncomfortable about the behavior and comments going on around me. I felt an overwhelming urge to "fight or take flight." Fortunately I had enough recovery to choose the latter. I went into another room, where I knew I would not be disturbed, so I could be alone for a few minutes. I prayed for serenity and guidance as well as for the ability to keep the focus on myself and the moment. I returned to the gathering refreshed and centered.

Later in the day I visited my brother. I made it a point to get to his home a little earlier than everyone else. I asked my sister-in-law, who is also in recovery, if I could use her room for a few minutes to pray and meditate. This made all the difference in the world, and I was able to enjoy the rest of the day with renewed serenity.

Thought for the Day

Being with my family for all or part of a day can be a stressful undertaking. Fortunately I don't have to be there alone. Conscious contact with my Higher Power is only a prayer away.

> "I had started working the Second and Third Steps, not out of faith or belief, but because it worked for other people and maybe 'It' would work for me. And I believe 'It' did."
>
> As We Understood. . . , pp. 239-240

Serenity is . . .

. . . a way of life absorbed slowly and practiced one day at a time . . . perspective . . . becoming aware of and accepting my many characteristics and not judging what's "bad" or "good" but what's useful to keep and what to release . . . a spiritual journey without a destination . . . the space between the impulse and the action . . . accepting what is . . . honoring my feelings without aiming them at someone else or letting them run my life . . . a gift I choose to give to myself . . . knowing that what works for someone else may not necessarily work for me . . . knowing that what works for me may change from moment to moment . . . understanding I may be powerless, but I'm not helpless . . .

. . . realizing my Higher Power does for me what I cannot do for myself . . . minding my own business. . . the comfort of knowing I can hold my own hand . . . balance and relief from black-and-white thinking . . . understanding that reacting to life and responding to life are not the same thing . . . deliberate realignment with my Higher Power. . . feeling at peace with my past. .-. a matter of internal stability. . . becoming a complete being with my body and mind in one place at the same time . . . becoming one with my Higher Power.

Thought for the Day

Serenity opens my mind to new ideas.

"God grant me the serenity

To accept the things I cannot change,

Courage to change the things I can,

And wisdom to know the difference."

Serenity Prayer

As a child I grew up waiting for my alcoholic parents to show me the love I needed. When I left home, I transferred this expectation to my alcoholic boyfriend. I lived for his love and waited for him to change his behavior, which I felt was hurting me. As long as I clung to my hope that he would love me the way I wanted to be loved, I remained a prisoner of alcoholism.

After coming to Al-Anon for a while, it dawned on me how much of my life had been spent waiting for others to change so I could be happy. I had wasted so much time trying to change the things I couldn't control. When I finally accepted I couldn't regulate my boyfriend's drinking, I was set free. I also realized my powerlessness over family members.

I felt some regret along with these spiritual awakenings, but Al-Anon kept me busy learning about alcoholism as a disease and moving forward with the Steps. I wondered why I should try to fight alcoholism, so I decided to admit that alcoholism is more powerful than I. Now I am free to discover the person inside me who is spirited, fun, loving, and loveable. Today I am learning to give myself the unconditional love and acceptance I always wanted from people who didn't have it to give.

Thought for the Day

What can I change so I can be happy? Is this realistic?

> "The only person who can love me the way I want to be loved is me."

Courage to Change, p. 107

Concept Eight states, "The Board of Trustees delegates full authority for routine management of the Al-Anon Headquarters to its executive committees." In my family I was the "executive committee," meaning much of the routine household management fell to me. No one consciously delegated it to me; it seemed to be mine by default.

My mother was an alcoholic. For the most part, she acted like one of the walking dead, while Dad was gone most of the time. In addition to his full-time job, my father spent another 40 hours every week doing church charity work. As a result, I assumed many of the household responsibilities. I made sure my brothers and I ate, dressed, got to school, and did our homework. It wasn't long before taking on others' responsibilities became a habit for me, a habit I carried into my adult life.

When I finally came to Al-Anon, I noticed people doing things differently. For example, when someone offered to be our group's anniversary chairperson, she passed around sign-up lists and people volunteered for setup, refreshments, and cleanup. Everyone shared responsibility for the arrangements and worked together. When I went to district meetings, I observed the district representative delegating responsibilities to the various group representatives. Concept Eight tells me this goes on at the World Service Office, too.

Now that I know I have options, I'm not so quick to pick up on others' responsibilities. When I do have a task that seems overwhelming, I ask for help. Amazingly the work gets done even when I'm not the one doing it.

Thought for the Day

Is there something going on in my life that I could ask for help with today?

"...Concept Eight is about letting go and trusting others."

Paths to Recovery, p. 299

One of the most beneficial things I have learned from my Al-Anon experience is to be consistent in my thoughts, words, and actions. In my alcoholic home, I learned to mask uncomfortable situations with words and actions I thought would promote harmony. I have since learned that agreeing with others simply to keep peace causes me to be resentful. As difficult as it may be, today I won't automatically concur with the thoughts and opinions of others. If I have a different point of view, I express it, then let go of the other's reaction. I practice "Live and Let Live" and "Let Go and Let God."

To be consistent, I need to know what I believe. The Al-Anon program, especially through the Steps, helps me to gain clarity for myself. Such clear understanding helps me be consistent in what I think, say, and do and sustains my serenity. Consistency helps me to practice "Keep It Simple" and saves me from the need to second-guess myself. It helps me to identify boundaries. Consistency helps me to remain true to myself.

Thought for the Day

Al-Anon offers me the skills I need to define and express my beliefs without diminishing the integrity of others.

"... Unity really starts within me. I think of it as a feeling of 'getting things together' inside my own head."

Alateen—a day at a time, p. 217

I've always had poor balance—unsteady on ladders, unhappy hiking downhill, unable to put my socks on while standing. Some time ago I watched a karate black-belt competition. Much of the fighter's attention was focused on how his foot was planted on the ground. Only partial attention went to the other, airborne foot. I decided to undertake developing some of the same partnership with gravity, to learn to center myself over my planted foot. In time I became much better at putting on my socks.

Recently while picking my way across wet rocks beside a favorite stream, I felt a strong connection with the earth. My balance was sure, my choice of foothold certain and carefree. I could turn my attention to the scampering squirrels and grazing deer. I realized that in the same way I am learning to walk within the inexorable pull of gravity, I am also learning to center myself in God's will. By using the many tools of Al-Anon, I am releasing my need to control, and I am learning to find my balance despite the strong, often unexpected winds of change and desire.

Thought for the Day

Little by little, one day at a time, by accepting the things I cannot change and changing the things I can, I will become more centered in God's gift of serenity.

"Al-Anon helps me to find some balance."

Courage to Change, p. 54

I like how Step Three begins. It states, "Made a decision . . .," This means I have an active choice to turn my will and my life over to a Higher Power. No one is going to force me. No one is going to make me do *anything*. My recovery is my choice. What I choose to do with my will and my life is my decision, and today I choose to turn it over to the God of my understanding.

What a relief it is to finally make that decision and to realize that I don't have to do or fix everything. I have begun to learn what is and isn't my responsibility. I feel lighter knowing that my Higher Power is with me 24 hours a day to help me with my life and its challenges. From the smallest decision to the largest, I pray, "God, what would you have me say and do today?"

This process of turning my will and life over to God sounds so simple, yet it certainly didn't happen at my first meeting! Actually, it didn't happen for a long time. I had to build a foundation for my Step Three decision, first by diligently working Steps One and Two. Taking Step Three was a natural outgrowth of that groundwork.

Along the lines of "Progress Not Perfection," my relationship with my Higher Power evolves day-to-day, one day at a time. What a gift I have been given! Turning my will and my life over to a Power greater than myself provides me with a bottomless well of love, peace, and serenity, if I choose to drink from it.

Thought for the Day

Choices are important parts of Al-Anon recovery. What do I plan to do with mine today?

"The first phrase of Step Three, 'Made a decision,' shows us that we have choices."

Paths to Recovery, p. 28

December 31

At my first Al-Anon meeting, I felt like a parched person drinking cold, refreshing water. With gratitude I took in the words of the Suggested Welcome and Closing. Every time I went to a meeting I'd close my eyes and let those precious words refresh me.

Years later I realized I was listening to Al-Anon's words of hope—hope I could claim as my own, if I was willing to work the Steps. When I felt boxed in by despair, you assured me that no situation is really hopeless and I could find contentment, and even happiness, despite my mother's drinking. When I felt worn out from replaying awful scenarios in my mind, you told me I could put my problems in their true perspective and they would lose their power to dominate. When I felt alone, you reminded me I wasn't. You pointed out my choices when all I knew were rules and appearances. I didn't have to agree to belong. I could take what I liked and leave the rest.

You even claimed that you already loved me in a special way, even though I hated myself, and that I would learn to love you, too. You offered me sponsorship, hugs, and phone numbers even when I hadn't "earned" them. I didn't know what a loving interchange was, and you took the time to show me.

Thanks, Al-Anon, for the persistent repetition of these hope-filled words and actions. Gradually they came true for me. Now when I share them with others, I have the joy of seeing them come alive again.

Thought for the Day

When I count my blessings, I remember to count Al-Anon's gift of hope.

> "If you try to keep an open mind, you will find help. You will come to realize that there is no situation too difficult to be bettered and no unhappiness too great to be lessened."
>
> Suggested Al-Anon/Alateen Closing

Study of these Steps is essential to progress in the Al-Anon program. The principles they embody are universal, applicable to everyone, whatever his personal creed. In Al-Anon, we strive for an ever-deeper understanding of these Steps, and pray for the wisdom to apply them to our lives.

1. We admitted we were powerless over alcohol–that our lives had become unmanageable.

2. Came to believe that a Power greater than ourselves could restore us to sanity.

3. Made a decision to turn our will and our lives over to the care of God *as we understood Him.*

4. Made a searching and fearless moral inventory of ourselves.

5. Admitted to God, to ourselves, and to another human being the exact nature of our wrongs.

6. Were entirely ready to have God remove all these defects of character.

7. Humbly asked Him to remove our shortcomings.

8. Made a list of all persons we had harmed, and became willing to make amends to them all.

9. Made direct amends to such people wherever possible, except when to do so would injure them or others.

10. Continued to take personal inventory and when we were wrong promptly admitted it.

11. Sought through prayer and meditation to improve our conscious contact with God *as we understood Him,* praying only for knowledge of His will for us and the power to carry that out.

12. Having had a spiritual awakening as the result of these steps, we tried to carry this message to others, and to practice these principles in all our affairs.

These guidelines are the means of promoting harmony and growth in Al-Anon groups and in the worldwide fellowship of Al-Anon as a whole. Our group experience suggests that our unity depends upon our adherence to these Traditions:

1. Our common welfare should come first; personal progress for the greatest number depends upon unity.

2. For our group purpose there is but one authority—a loving God as He may express Himself in our group conscience. Our leaders are but trusted servants—they do not govern.

3. The relatives of alcoholics, when gathered together for mutual aid, may call themselves an Al-Anon Family Group, provided that, as a group, they have no other affiliation. The only requirement for membership is that there be a problem of alcoholism in a relative or friend.

4. Each group should be autonomous, except in matters affecting another group or Al-Anon or AA as a whole.

5. Each Al-Anon Family Group has but one purpose: to help families of alcoholics. We do this by practicing the Twelve Steps of AA *ourselves*, by encouraging and understanding our alcoholic relatives, and by welcoming and giving comfort to families of alcoholics.

6. Our Family Groups ought never endorse, finance or lend our name to any outside enterprise, lest problems of money, property and prestige divert us from our primary spiritual aim. Although a separate entity, we should always co-operate with Alcoholics Anonymous.

7. Every group ought to be fully self-supporting, declining outside contributions.

8. Al-Anon Twelfth Step work should remain forever non-professional, but our service centers may employ special workers.

9. Our groups, as such, ought never be organized; but we may create service boards or committees directly responsible to those they serve.

10. The Al-Anon Family Groups have no opinion on outside issues; hence our name ought never be drawn into public controversy.

11. Our public relations policy is based on attraction rather than promotion; we need always maintain personal anonymity at the level of press, radio, films, and TV. We need guard with special care the anonymity of all AA members.

12. Anonymity is the spiritual foundation of all our Traditions, ever reminding us to place principles above personalities.

The Twelve Steps and Traditions are guides for personal growth and group unity. The Twelve Concepts are guides for service. They show how Twelfth Step work can be done on a broad scale and how members of a World Service Office can relate to each other and to the groups, through a World Service Conference, to spread Al-Anon's message worldwide.

1. The ultimate responsibility and authority for Al-Anon world services belongs to the Al-Anon groups.

2. The Al-Anon Family Groups have delegated complete administrative and operational authority to their Conference and its service arms.

3. The right of decision makes effective leadership possible.

4. Participation is the key to harmony.

5. The rights of appeal and petition protect minorities and insure that they be heard.

6. The Conference acknowledges the primary administrative responsibility of the Trustees.

7. The Trustees have legal rights while the rights of the Conference are traditional.

8. The Board of Trustees delegates full authority for routine management of Al-Anon Headquarters to its executive committees.

9. Good personal leadership at all service levels is a necessity. In the field of world service the Board of Trustees assumes the primary leadership.

10. Service responsibility is balanced by carefully defined service authority and double-headed management is avoided.

11. The World Service Office is composed of selected committees, executives and staff members.

12. The spiritual foundation for Al-Anon's world services is contained in the General Warranties of the Conference, Article 12 of the Charter.

GENERAL WARRANTIES OF THE CONFERENCE

In all proceedings the World Service Conference of Al-Anon shall observe the spirit of the Traditions:

1. that only sufficient operating funds, including an ample reserve, be its prudent financial principle;

2. that no Conference member shall be placed in unqualified authority over other members;

3. that all decisions be reached by discussion vote and whenever possible by unanimity;

4. that no Conference action ever be personally punitive or an incitement to public controversy;

5. that though the Conference serves Al-Anon it shall never perform any act of government; and that like the fellowship of Al-Anon Family Groups which it serves, it shall always remain democratic in thought and action.